STONES RIVER
—*Bloody Winter in Tennessee*

STONES RIVER
—*Bloody Winter in Tennessee*

James Lee McDonough

The University of Tennessee Press / Knoxville

Library of Congress Cataloging in Publication Data

McDonough, James L   1934–
   Stones River — bloody winter in Tennessee.

   Bibliography: p.
   Includes index.
   1. Murfreesboro, Tenn., Battle of, 1862–1863.
I. Title.
E474.77.M32   973.7'33   80-11580
ISBN 0-87049-301-9

FOR *Nancy, David, Sharon, and Carla*

CONTENTS

ILLUSTRATIONS

PREFACE

I was born, raised, and have lived most of my life within thirty miles of Stones River. Nevertheless, I had visited many of the famous battlefields of the Civil War before I ever tramped around the lines at Murfreesboro. Like most Americans, and even Tennesseans, I had not realized what a big, bloody struggle took place among the cedars and along the banks of the west fork of Stones River. I was surprised when I learned that the casualty figures were approximately the same as Shiloh, Tennessee's most celebrated battle, and far higher than the state's other better-known engagements at Fort Donelson, Chattanooga, and Nashville. Also, the ratio of losses at Stones River was greater than in the more famous eastern battles at Fredericksburg and Chancellorsville, which were fought close to the same time. By any Civil War standard, Stones River was a monumental, sanguinary, and dramatic story. In the interest of a proper perspective on the Civil War, the battle deserves more attention than it has received.

The two large armies that clashed on December 31, 1862, were fighting for control of Middle Tennessee's railroads and rich farms. Still more significant, the engagement was the first big battle in the Union campaign to split the southeastern Confederacy, driving along the line of the railroad from Nashville through Chattanooga to Atlanta, the campaign that finally ended with Major General William T. Sherman's march to the sea and capture of Savannah in December 1864. The Union victory (the armies had fought to a tactical draw but the Confederates retreated) helped to offset the disasters suffered at the battle of Fredericksburg in Virginia earlier in December and at Chickasaw Bayou in Mississippi on December 29, and gave the United States ambassador to Great Britain, Charles Francis Adams, more evidence that the United States could win the war, evidence he could well use in his effort to discourage the British from intervening on behalf of the Confederacy. This was highly important because in the late fall of 1862 and early 1863 the possibility of British recognition of the Confederacy, which would have almost certainly been followed by French recognition as well, seemed very real.

Psychologically, the defeat at Stones River was particularly detrimental to the Southern cause. The army that fought at Murfreesboro was the same that had been driven back at Shiloh and from Kentucky. When it was again forced to retreat—and from Middle Tennessee and the vicinity of the state capital, the recovery of which many had cherished—a feeling of despair weighed upon the western Confederacy. There had been too many defeats. Was it possible, Southerners wondered, ever to reverse the tide of war? And the battle served to confirm the opinion of large numbers of Confederates that General Braxton Bragg could not successfully command an army. The battle left the army torn by dissension in the high command.

The engagement at Stones River involves a number of perplexing questions, such as the strategic wisdom of detaching one division from the Rebel army at Murfreesboro, on the eve of battle, and sending it to Mississippi. What difference, if any, did this make in the outcome of a closely contested fight? Why, on the first day of battle, were Confederate troops led into the struggle against the Union center and left in piecemeal fashion? After driving the Union right wing for almost three miles, why could the Rebels not complete the triumph? Could Major General William S. Rosecrans have launched a counterattack on the first day of battle? Did the Union artillery play the decisive role in breaking Major General John C. Breckinridge's assault on the final day of battle? Was personal tension between Bragg and Breckinridge a significant factor in the events of the last day of the engagement? These are some of the most troublesome questions associated with the battle, questions for which I have tried to provide answers or clues to answers.

This book is based upon extensive research in the *War of the Rebellion: A Compilation of the Official Records of the Union and Confederate Armies*. I have also freely employed letters, diaries, and memoirs of soldiers on both sides whose writings add the "you are there" touch without which the book would be far less readable. Convinced from my own observations and experiences that often truth is indeed stranger and more fascinating than fiction, I have accepted at face value these accounts of men in the ranks, unless there seemed to be a good reason for doubting their record. The perusal of many secondary works has strengthened my overall understanding of the period and the events leading up to the battle. While I have profitably employed some of the best secondary works, the narrative and description of the battle itself, from first to last, is founded upon the *Official Records*. I would like to acknowledge that the National Park Service report on Breckinridge's January 2 assault, prepared by Edwin C. Bearss, was particularly helpful on that aspect of the engagement.

Because my purpose was to write a history of the battle at Stones River, and not an account of western campaigning in the late summer, fall, and winter of 1862–63, I have not attempted an indepth, detailed account of the preceding Kentucky campaign, the battle at Perryville, the fighting in north Mississippi, or the cavalry operations. Another book could be devoted to such a campaign history. What I have done, I hope, is to establish a setting for understanding why and how the engagement developed at Murfreesboro, and to describe that battle in detail.

Until now there has been no modern, documented history of the battle. Alexander F. Stevenson's *The Battle of Stone's River* was published almost a hundred years ago. Gates P. Thruston's *Personal Recollections of the Battle in the Rear at Stone's River, Tennessee*, a twenty-one-page booklet, dates from 1906. The last book about the battle, published in 1914, was by Wilson J. Vance, who stated a surprising thesis, conveyed in the title, *Stone's River: The Turning Point of the Civil War*. Only eleven pages were devoted to the first day of the fight and four pages to the last day.

As one of the major battles of the Civil War, Stones River merits more recognition than it has been accorded. I hope this book makes a contribution toward that end.

Acknowledgments

Several people deserve special recognition for their generous assistance while I was researching and writing this volume. Mr. Phil J. Hohlweck, Milwaukee, Wisconsin, was particularly helpful, undoubtedly serving "beyond the call of duty" in contributing to Civil War historical scholarship when, on a trip to Atlanta, he packed up about thirty pertinent regimental histories from his extensive collection and brought them to Nashville for my use. Dr. Robert Womack, living in the battlefield area of Murfreesboro, Tennessee, and an expert on the Stones River battle, pointed out several sources on Confederate soldiers that provided color for the book. Mr. Walter K. Hoover, Smyrna, Tennessee, allowed me to work several days in his personal library, filled with Civil War lore. Mr. Rudolph Sanders, Nashville, Tennessee, spent a day on the battlefield taking pictures which have certainly enhanced the attractiveness of the book.

I am grateful to David Lipscomb College for a Faculty Fellowship Grant that provided financial support during one summer while I pursued this project on a full-time basis. Also, I am very appreciative of the Justin Potter Professorship that alleviated much of the economic burden of researching *Stones River*. The efficient staff of the Crisman Memorial Library of David Lipscomb College deserves credit for locating several resources. The National Park Service has been very helpful upon various occasions. Finally, I would especially like to thank three fine secretaries who were pleasant to work with and have contributed significantly to the completion of this book: Suzanne Hurst, Teresa Jackson, and Beth McGready.

January 1980   JAMES LEE MCDONOUGH
Nashville, Tennessee

STONES RIVER
—Bloody Winter in Tennessee

1

A Bit of Pluck and Bluff

The town was silent in the warm July morning. Its name was Murfreesboro,[1] in honor of Colonel Hardy Murfree, a soldier of the American Revolution who had once owned some of the village's land. For several decades after the Indians were driven out, the town had sat undisturbed in the center of Tennessee, about thirty miles southeast of Nashville. Perhaps its only distinctions were that it had hosted the state General Assembly for a few years and once entertained visiting dignitaries Andrew Jackson and Martin Van Buren. Increasingly, since the railroad from Nashville to Chattanooga had been constructed, Murfreesboro had been a place that people passed through on their way to somewhere else.[2]

It was the railroad that now gave the town military importance and largely explained why a community of close to four thousand inhabitants was in the fifth month of Union occupation. Everywhere in Murfreesboro there were blue-uniformed soldiers. The Federal garrison at the town was the largest and most important along the railroad, consisting of two regiments of infantry, a cavalry detachment, and a four-gun battery. There were nearly half as many soldiers in Murfreesboro as there were citizens.[3]

On this Sunday morning, in the jail at the courthouse square,

[1]At the time of the Civil War the name of the town was spelled with three more letters, Murfreesborough. For the sake of simplicity the modern spelling of Murfreesboro will be used throughout this book.

[2]C.C. Henderson, *The Story of Murfreesboro* (Murfreesboro, Tenn., 1929), 5, 6, 10, 11, 3, 41, 52, 53.

[3]Robert S. Henry, *"First With the Most" Forrest* (Indianapolis, 1944), 86. Robert Wo-

luck seemed about to run out for nineteen-year-old William Richardson, a Confederate soldier from Athens, Alabama. Severely wounded and captured at the Battle of Shiloh, he had survived and escaped from an Indiana prison camp. Having made his way back to Tennessee, he was captured again near Murfreesboro, in company with a man named James Paul. Evidence was found upon Paul proving that he was a Confederate spy and both men had been condemned to hang at sunrise. A minister, the Reverend D.T. Hensley, spent the early part of the night attempting to comfort them, after which they talked with each other about their agonizing fate, finally falling asleep just before dawn.[4]

Unknown to Richardson, or anyone else in the sleeping town, help was near. Moving in on Murfreesboro from the east, as rapidly as the dim pre-dawn light permitted, was a Rebel cavalry column, fourteen hundred strong, led by Brigadier General Nathan Bedford Forrest. The troopers, riding from the village of Woodbury since one o'clock in the morning, gained the outskirts of Murfreesboro before sunrise, where they surprised and captured a group of Federal sentinels who were given no chance to sound an alarm. From these prisoners Forrest learned the disposition of the Union soldiers in the town, realizing at once that his enemy was not properly concentrated.[5]

Having been apprised at Woodbury of a large number of Confederate sympathizers held in the Murfreesboro jail, some of whom were condemned to death, the Confederate commander determined to make the most of his opportunity. Possibly, as he formed his cavalry for the attack, Forrest may have thought that this day was especially significant. Sunday, July 13, 1862, was his forty-first birthday.

The Union garrison, about equal in number to that which Forrest was bringing against it, was under a new commander, Brigadier General Thomas T. Crittenden. A thirty-year-old graduate of Centre College, Danville, Kentucky, Crittenden had studied

---

mack, "Stone's River National Military Park," *Tennessee Historical Quarterly*, Dec. 1962, p. 303.

[4]*Confederate Veteran*, 40 vols. (Nashville, 1893–1932), XIX, 378. John A. Wyeth, *Life of General Nathan Bedford Forrest* (Dayton, Ohio, 1975), 90.

[5]Henry, *"First With the Most,"* 86.

law under his uncle, Senator John J. Crittenden of Kentucky, and then set up a lucrative practice in Lexington, Missouri, from where he entered the Union service soon after the Civil War began. Crittenden had just taken over the Murfreesboro post on the morning of the twelfth. He recognized that the camps of his several units needed to be concentrated, but he was in no great rush to accomplish the work. After all, Crittenden was advised, no Rebel force had been closer than Chattanooga since the Union had occupied Murfreesboro. The new commander did order that the cavalry patrols, which went out every day on the turnpikes radiating from the town, should be doubled in number, but nobody informed him that the patrols came in each night, leaving open all five roads.[6]

Thus the Union force remained vulnerable. The Third Minnesota Infantry and a Kentucky battery were camped about a mile and a half northwest of the town, while on the eastern edge of the village lay the Ninth Michigan Infantry and a detachment of the Seventh Pennsylvania Cavalry. One company of the Michigan regiment was serving as a provost guard and held the center of Murfreesboro, including the courthouse and the jail.

At 4:30 in the morning, with no one in the Union camps awake except a few cooks chopping wood for the breakfast fires, Forrest's cavalry struck. Divided into three columns, one segment charged into the camp of the Michigan infantry and the Pennsylvania cavalry, while the other Rebel units pounded into Murfreesboro, part of the troopers surrounding and storming the jail and the others sweeping through the town to attack the Minnesota regiment on the west. Instantly, Murfreesboro was in an uproar. "We sprang from our beds and rushed to the windows to see the streets full of gray-coated, dusty cavalrymen," wrote a lady of Murfreesboro, "while . . . the glad cry of 'our boys have come' rang from one end of the town to the other. . . . That day . . . was the happiest day experienced by the citizens of Murfreesboro during the war."[7]

Probably no one was more elated than Richardson and Paul,

[6] *War of the Rebellion: A Compilation of the Official Records of the Union and Confederate Armies*, 129 vols. (Washington, D.C., 1880–1901), Serial 1, vol. XXII, 749–97. Hereafter cited as *OR*; all references are to Serial 1, vol. XX, pt. 1, unless otherwise noted. Allen Johnson and Dumas Malone, eds., *Dictionary of American Biography*, 21 vols. (New York, 1928–1937), IV, 550.

[7] Henry, *"First With the Most,"* 87, 88.

still in the jail awaiting their execution. "I was lying asleep in the cell," recalled Richardson, "when I was awakened by Paul's tugging at my arm." Then, hearing a sound which he described as "like an approaching storm," Richardson climbed up on a box and, looking through the small grating of the prison window, saw the Rebel cavalry charging into the town. Now there was a chance; maybe they would be saved before it was too late.[8]

Suddenly several of the Union soldiers in the prison yard, seeing they were about to be overwhelmed by the Rebels, burst into the jail. Hurrying to the passageway in front of the condemned men's cell, the Yankees attempted to shoot Richardson and Paul. Terrified, the two saved themselves only by scrambling forward to crouch in the corner of the cell by the door, where the Federals could not bring their guns to bear upon them. Fortunately for the prisoners, no one among the would-be executioners possessed a key to the cell. The Union soldiers then made a rapid exit from the jail, but not before one of them set fire to the building. The fire was blazing when the Confederates finally battered in the jail's metal door, pried open the cell door with an iron bar, and saved the men who, only a short time earlier, had supposed that their doom was sealed.[9]

The day may have been bringing happiness to some, but for others, of course, the hours of fighting meant terror and tragedy. One such person was Mollie Nelson, a little girl struck in the face by a stray bullet. She wore the ugly scar of battle for the rest of her life.[10]

Meanwhile, the Rebel attack had not developed according to plan. The greater part of one regiment, instead of turning off to charge the enemy on the east side of the town as ordered, became confused and rushed on into Murfreesboro. And in spite of being roused from their Sunday morning sleep, the Federals were fighting with courage and determination. The Union forces west of the town, forewarned by the noise of battle coming from Murfreesboro, had advanced to a little rise of ground about a mile from the square where they were drawn up with a section of artillery on

[8]*Confederate Veteran*, XIX, 378.
[9]Wyeth, *Life of Forrest*, 91. *Confederate Veteran*, XX, 373.
[10]Bromfield L. Ridley, *Battles and Sketches of the Army of Tennessee* (Mexico, Mo., 1906), 111.

Riding into Murfreesboro on his forty-first birthday, Confederate cavalry commander Nathan B. Forrest, a fierce fighter and rugged leader, surprised and routed the Yankee garrison, freeing the Rebel prisoners held in the jail at the center of town.

each flank. Here they were making a good fight. The Confederates, both east and west of the town, were stymied. Then Forrest
asserted his genius for battle.

The vigorous six-foot, one-inch cavalryman was born in Bedford County, about twenty-five miles from Murfreesboro, and
grew up with little educational opportunity because of family responsibilities. He became wealthy through land purchases and later as a slave dealer in Memphis. Forrest entered the Confederate
army as a private, equipping a mounted battalion at his own expense. He soon demonstrated outstanding leadership qualities and
a native military ability which raised him to the rank of brigadier
general. A tough, aggressive fighter, Forrest seemed to be getting
even tougher as the war progressed.

Riding west of the town with a band of troopers, he swept
around the Union flank and charged into the enemy camp, driving off and capturing the guards, destroying tents and baggage,
and spreading panic. A few Confederate officers tried to persuade
Forrest to be satisfied and ride away before Federal reinforcements from Nashville might arrive. Furious and determined, the
general replied abruptly: "I did not come here to make half a job
of it; I mean to have them all." Leaving only seven companies to
hold the Federals in check on the west, he next thundered back
through the town and, with additional troops shifted from the
other fights, brought the weight of his command against the be-
leaguered enemy east of Murfreesboro.[11] With his men in position, Forrest sent in a demand for surrender, the first of a type he
was to use more than once.

The message was simple and direct: "Colonel: I must demand
an unconditional surrender of your force as prisoners of war or I
will have every man put to the sword. You are aware of the over-
powering force I have at my command, and this demand is made
to prevent the effusion of blood. I am, Colonel, very respectfully,
your obedient servant, N.B. Forrest, Brigadier General of Cavalry,
C.S. Army."[12]

At twelve o'clock the Federals east of Murfreesboro surren-

---

[11]Henry, *"First With the Most,"* 88. Charles F. Bryan, Jr. "'I Mean to Have them All':
Forrest's Murfreesboro Raid," *Civil War Times Illustrated* (Jan. 1974), 31.

[12]*OR*, XXII, 805.

dered. Now free to concentrate on the enemy forces west of the town, Forrest's cavalry pounded in that direction again, and once more he sent in a note demanding immediate surrender to "save the effusion of blood." The Minnesota colonel, Henry C. Lester, requested a conference with the Ninth Michigan's Colonel William Duffield, who by that time was a prisoner of Forrest's command. So that Lester could be assured that the rest of the Union garrison had surrendered, the interview was arranged. Forrest also planned for Lester to see something else as he walked through the town to the house where Duffield was held — glimpses of Rebel soldiers marching through the streets. Actually, although Colonel Lester did not know the fact, he was seeing the same Confederate column being maneuvered back and forth, again and again. Lester too surrendered.[13]

The total of Federal prisoners was about twelve hundred officers and men, and the value of captured property was probably a quarter of a million dollars. By six o'clock the day's work was done and the last of Forrest's command, which was relatively unscathed, had departed from Murfreesboro by the same road on which it had come. This was Forrest's first independent operation as a brigade commander and added illustriously to his reputation, already established at Sacramento, Kentucky, Fort Donelson, and Shiloh, as a daring cavalry leader. Also, this was the first great foray made by any Confederate commander in the western theater within the Union lines.

By the time Forrest was back in McMinnville, local Yankee garrisons in Middle Tennessee were being called in for the protection of Nashville against his force, estimated by some Union commanders to be as high as seven thousand men. Even larger bodies of troops were soon ordered back into Middle Tennessee from Major General Don Carlos Buell's army, which was strung out along the Memphis & Charleston Railroad. Forrest's remarkable achievement in capturing Murfreesboro was afterward summarized by Field Marshal Viscount Garnet Wolseley, commander-in-chief of the British army, as "a rare mixture of military skill and what is known by our American cousins as 'bluff'."[14]

[13]Henry, *"First With the Most,"* 89.
[14]Wyeth, *Life of Forrest,* 83.

In Murfreesboro itself the proud citizens were soon referring to the events of July 13, 1862, as "the Battle of Murfreesboro." Indeed it was a dashing and dramatic affair, but when real battles and their casualties are considered, it was no more than a mere prelude, hardly to be compared with the bloody struggle that would come at Murfreesboro, on the banks of the Stones River,[15] about six months later. It is a striking fact, however, that like the clash on July 13, the big battle at Murfreesboro, punctuated by the largest number of total casualties of any Tennessee battle,[16] would also begin early in the morning with the Rebels launching a devastating surprise attack against the Yankees.

---

[15]The river is properly "Stone's," named after an early hunter, Uriah Stone, but has frequently been spelled "Stones," which has generally been accepted as the proper designation for the name of the battle. See Stanley J. Folmsbee, Robert E. Corlew, Enoch L. Mitchell, *Tennessee, A Short History* (Knoxville, 1969), 5, 335. Also Womack, "Stone's River," 308.

[16]Thomas L. Livermore, *Numbers and Losses in the Civil War in America: 1861–1865* (rpt. New York, 1969), 79, 80, 97. Casualties at Shiloh and Stones River were very near the same figure and these two battles saw much heavier casualties than any other engagements in Tennessee. Livermore places total casualties at Stones River as 24,645 compared to Shiloh's 23,741. The major difference in these figures is in the number of Confederates missing: 2,500 at Stones River contrasted with 959 at Shiloh. On the Union side the number killed at Shiloh (1,754) is slightly higher than at Stones River (1,677), and significantly higher on the Confederate side, 1,723 compared to 1,294.

2

Advance and Retreat

December had come to Middle Tennessee. Gone were the delicious fall days with their gorgeous array of many-colored trees and warm sunshine, followed by cool, invigorating evenings. Maybe one or two more Indian summer days might bless the region, but it was clear that winter was rapidly approaching. The late fall weather grew progressively colder, more rainy and gloomy. On December 4 the first snow fell. Perhaps it all seemed fitting when one considered the bleak presence of tragedy in homes all across the land.

The war had become long and promised to become even longer. It was now more than halfway through its second year. Many people, North and South, especially those whose loved ones had been killed or wounded, were stripped of romantic illusions they once held about the glory of war, the cause for which they fought, and the expectation of a brief struggle. Furious battles at Manassas (Bull Run), Shiloh, the killing and maiming of the Seven Days, and the bloodiest single day of the war at Antietam, were monumental struggles shocking people into a realization that the conflict would not be won by either side until there had been immense sacrifice by both sides. Americans were hardening to the realities of war and learning an unwelcome lesson of how quickly emotionalized issues can entangle people in unforeseen and uncontrollable events.

One of the harshest realities was that Americans were killing each other at a rate which would eventually total approximately

11

622,000 people — more than were killed in all the rest of America's wars put together until Viet Nam. About 260,000 would be Southerners. With a much smaller manpower pool than the North, the South's percentage of loss was far greater than the North's. The South was being devastated. When the bloodletting was finally over in 1865, one-half of the Southern white male population between the ages of eighteen and thirty was either killed or so severely wounded as to be classified as crippled. By the end of 1862, the awful scale of the war was clearly evident and deeply disturbing to thoughtful, sensitive people. But they, of course, were a small minority.

Months before, the Confederacy's manpower problem had been clearly dramatized when, in April 1862, the Richmond government enacted a draft law. Conscripting all able-bodied white males between the ages of eighteen and thirty-five for the duration of the war, the legislation was the first such measure since the state drafts to meet militia quotas in the Revolutionary War. When the maximum age was raised to forty-five in September, and with the act's exemptions for newspaper editors, pharmacists, ministers, teachers, and particularly the despised "twenty-nigger law" that exempted anyone who owned at least twenty slaves, the draft was increasingly unpopular.[1]

Even Confederates whose credentials as Southern patriots were beyond question viewed the conscription law as a blight that infested the new nation. The draft fueled the flames of discontent and class-consciousness that were manifested by the cry, "a rich man's war, but a poor man's fight." Or, as one small farmer expressed it, the war was a slaveholder's plot, and "all they want is to git you . . . to go fight for their infurnal negroes. . . ."[2]

The common people of the South became less willing to die for the planter aristocracy. Resistance was widespread in areas where the poor abounded — the isolated regions of Arkansas, Florida, Mississippi, and the hill and mountain country from Virginia to northern Alabama. Opposed to secession in the first place, many

[1]William B. Hesseltine and David L. Smiley, *The South in American History* (Englewood Cliffs, N.J., 1960), 305.

[2]David Lindsey, *Americans in Conflict: The Civil War and Reconstruction* (Boston, 1974), 128, 129.

found no reason to risk their lives in a planters' war, and sometimes these conscripts returned home to work their farms — with
the approval of their relatives and neighbors.[3]

Also, the states'-rights men proclaimed that a blow had been
struck at constitutional liberty by the passage of the conscription
law. Never popular in any part of the South, the basic effect of the
draft, where it did work, was to stimulate volunteering, done to
avoid the odious stamp of being a conscript. Ultimately, the draft
produced some three hundred thousand volunteers. Probably
more effective than the draft at recruiting soldiers, however, were
Confederate women, who often stigmatized and ostracized those
able-bodied men who did not fight. Nannie Haskins, a young
woman in Clarksville, Tennessee, showed her disgust for Southerners who would not join the Confederacy, referring to them as
"fireside rangers." She wrote of attending a party at which there
were no other type of young men. "I had almost as soon see Yankees," she claimed; "the only difference is, I have a 'little' more re-
spect for the latter." When a former beau named Joe Elliot visited
her, Nannie remarked that he had "taken the 'non-combatants'
oath — I think it is a shame."[4]

Besides manpower, the war was also costly in money and materials that the Confederacy did not have. While the Northern economy was stimulated by the war, the Southern economy was being
paralyzed. The war destroyed the economic function of the cotton
planters and all those — suppliers of plantation essentials, trans-
porters of the crops, and financiers — who were associated with the
business. When plantations turned to producing food there were
neither adequate facilities for transporting it nor, far more important, a large enough public with buying power to provide a commercial market.

That will-o'-the-wisp of Southern hope, King Cotton diplomacy, had been torpedoed by numerous factors: large cotton surpluses stockpiled in Britain, Richmond's decision to withhold the

[3]Robert Cruden, *The War that Never Ended: The American Civil War* (Englewood
Cliffs, N.J., 1973), 165.

[4]Lindsey, *Americans,* 127. Emory M. Thomas, *The American War and Peace: 1860–
1877* (Englewood Cliffs, N.J., 1973), 131. Betsy Swint Underwood, "War Seen Through a
Teen-ager's Eyes," *Tennessee Historical Quarterly,* June 1961, p. 181.

staple early when it could have been shipped before the Union blockade became effective, the British need for United States wheat, a lucrative Northern market for British war supplies, and invading Union armies confiscating the crop. King Cotton diplomacy was rapidly slipping beneath the waves of a vast sea of Confederate "might have beens."[5]

While the normal Southern economy languished and then worsened as the wealthiest and largest of Southern cities, the strategic mart of ocean and river commerce, New Orleans, fell to Union forces in April 1862, the Confederacy's meager industrial capacity was being swamped by insatiable war demands. Obtaining military equipment, munitions, and supplies posed an ultimately insurmountable hurdle for the Confederacy. At the beginning, the Tredgar Iron Works in Richmond was the only Southern factory capable of turning out heavy artillery guns, and its capacity was limited. The Confederacy developed other munitions plants but the output was never sufficient. As early as winter 1862, the South had suffered a major disaster when the heart of Middle Tennessee, with its growing industrial complex and great war potential, fell to Union invaders. Tennessee was the Confederacy's largest producer of such essential war materials as pig iron and bar, sheet, and railroad iron.

Considering the industrial difficulties, the South did amazingly well. At the outset of the war, privately owned arms had come down from the walls and out of the drawers in substantial numbers. Imports from Europe perhaps added more than 300,000 rifled-muskets and revolvers in the war's first two years — before the Union blockade stifled virtually everything except Wilmington, Charleston, Mobile, and the Texas coast. The Confederate States contributed another 270,000 weapons, and captures from the Yankees numbered in the tens of thousands.[6]

But as the war lengthened, supplies of everything in the South, from clothing and shoes to horses and food, became scarce. When the Confederates gave up Pensacola in the spring of 1862, they took up the railroad iron on the line back toward Montgomery

---

[5]David M. Potter, *Division and the Stresses of Reunion: 1845–1876* (Glenview, Ill., 1973), 118–20.
[6]Lindsey, *Americans*, 127.

and used it to lay a new line to the port of Mobile, which they still held. This was a practice that continued throughout the war — robbing a line which could be spared for a while, and laying track on a line which was of higher priority. And it occurred with all kinds of iron articles from iron rails to horseshoes and nails. Dead horses and mules were stripped of their shoes, and sick or wounded animals were sometimes killed for them. There was no way that the newly built, government-operated factories could keep pace with the enormous demands of the Confederate army.[7]

In Nashville, under rigidly enforced martial law, backed by the bayonets of the Union occupying army, a determined resistance movement was helping the Confederates secure supplies in every possible manner. A Federal observer described the city as "the great center to which thronged all the . . . smugglers, spies and secret plotters of treason, whom a love of treachery or gain had drawn to the rebel cause. . . . Lines of communication were kept open to every part of the South, and the rebel army supplied with valuable goods and still more valuable information. Their shrewdness and secrecy seemed to defy every effort at detection. . . . The Government was victimized," so the Union writer claimed, "at every turn. Horses and mules, stolen from neighboring farms and stables, were hawked about the streets for purchasers, at prices ranging from ten to fifty dollars per head. Arms were pilfered and sold for a trifle. Boots, shoes, uniforms, camp-equipage, ammunition and supplies of every kind, serviceable to the rebel army, were daily sent beyond our lines in every possible way. . . ."[8]

The lack of medicine was a serious problem in the South. Some medical supplies came from abroad, shipped on blockade runners. Another source was smuggling from the North, although smugglers often failed to get through. The Washington *Evening Star* of October 31, 1862, reported the arrest, about twelve miles out from Centerville, Virginia, of three women and a man. "They had passes allowing them to go beyond our lines with family supplies," the *Star* reported, "but they were also carrying large supplies of morphine, quinine, etc." The youngest woman, according

[7]Robert S. Henry, *The Story of the Confederacy* (Indianapolis, 1931), 333.
[8]John Fitch, *Annals of the Army of the Cumberland* (Philadelphia, 1864), 457, 349-50.

to the paper, "wore a double-decked bustle, loaded with near 300 ounces of quinine. . . . Her bustle, exhibited in the War Department yesterday, created universal merriment." In Nashville, it was reported that one woman was getting down from her carriage when "two pairs of heavy cavalry boots fell from their 'delicate hiding place,' while a pocket, 'spacious as a market basket,' was found crammed with quinine."[9]

Women smuggling drugs to Confederate troops were a particular source of difficulty for the head of the Federal army's secret service in Nashville, an unsavory character named William Truesdail. The forty-eight-year-old chief of police, who preferred to be addressed by the self-conferred title of "Colonel," was described by Military Governor Andrew Johnson as a "pet" of Major General William S. Rosecrans and a man "wholly incompetent, if not corrupt, in the grossest sense of the term." Coming from Johnson, one of the most well-hated figures in Nashville's history, a man bitterly called "the King of Devils" by one young woman, the evaluation is noteworthy. Operating with Gestapo-like tactics, Truesdail bragged that his men had infiltrated every hotel, railroad car, steamer, and gained access to the "proudest and wealthiest . . . families. . . ." But the "colonel" so frequently came away a loser in his clashes with the Southern Ladies Aid Society, which was smuggling contraband quinine and other drugs to the Confederate troops, that he officially promulgated to his subordinates the cynical slogan: "Don't Trust Women!" The smuggling of drugs into the Confederacy might be slowed, but it was never stopped.[10]

Probably the most irritating and insoluble task facing the Confederate government was financing the war. In the face of an ever-tightening Federal blockade, export and import duties produced very little revenue. A direct tax on real estate, slaves, and other property, levied as early as August 1861, brought in a disappointingly small $17.5 million. By the end of 1862, Jefferson Davis' government, frightened of a states'-rights backlash, had still not

[9]William M. Lamers, *The Edge of Glory: A Biography of General William S. Rosecrans, U.S.A.* (New York, 1961), 191.

[10]Stanley F. Horn, "Nashville During the Civil War," *Tennessee Historical Quarterly*, March 1945, p. 16. Horn, "Dr. John Rolfe Hudson and the Confederate Underground in Nashville," *Tennessee Historical Quarterly*, March 1963, pp. 43, 44. Louise Davis, "Box Seat on the Civil War," *The Tennessean Magazine* (March and April 1979), 32.

resorted to an income tax. Nor had borrowing money been sufficient, with bond issues at home and the Erlanger loan in France,
which was backed by cotton, yielding $712 million. Consequently,
the Rebel government relied largely on paper money.

Running the printing presses on a massive scale, the Confederate treasury cranked out over $1.5 billion of paper notes by the
end of the war, promising that two years after Confederate inde-
pendence, the printed notes would be redeemed in bullion. Such
currency held up surprisingly well for more than a year, but by the
end of 1862 it was slipping noticeably in value. Measured against a
gold dollar, a Confederate paper dollar that stood at 90 cents in
1861 had declined to 29 cents in 1863. The downward trend was
well established by late 1862.[11]

Such suffering as inflation produced substantially weakened
Confederate morale. It would be early 1863 before the underground rumblings of discontent erupted into violent action with
mobs of poor women in Atlanta, Mobile, and even Richmond
raiding stores and helping themselves to food, shoes, clothing, and
other supplies. But by December 1862, there were many signs of
suffering and destitution. It was in this month that the governor of
Mississippi, John J. Pettus, said that the high prices were "putting
the means of living beyond the reach of many of our poor
citizens." The New Orleans *Delta* stated that flour was $55 a bar-
rel in Pass Christian and that children's shoes were selling for an
all-time high of $15 a pair. It was reported that half the popula-
tion of New Orleans was hungry, and the "rebel war clerk" in
Richmond, John B. Jones, would soon record in his now-famous
diary that "none but the opulent . . . can obtain a sufficiency of
food and raiment."[12]

Nashville, in the grip of the enemy occupying force, had been
suffering from lack of food as early as mid-1862. Rebel cavalry
raids had blocked traffic on the Louisville & Nashville Railroad by
destroying the tunnel near Gallatin, Tennessee, and, as the Cumberland River was at a low stage, food supplies began to run short

[11]Lindsey, *Americans*, 127, 128. Shelby Foote, *The Civil War: A Narrative*, 3 vols.
(New York, 1958–75), I, 790.

[12]Cruden, *War*, 162. The New Orleans *Delta*, quoted in the Nashville *Dispatch*, Nov.
30, 1862. Allan Nevins, *The War for the Union*, 4 vols. (New York, 1960), II, 291.

during the late summer and early fall months. Business was prostrated during the summer as prominent citizens were arrested and many of the ordinary activities of the city were almost completely halted. A local paper sarcastically remarked: "The health of Nashville is wonderful, considering the amount of filth that is to be found in our streets and alleys. When the sun shines . . . after a light fall of rain, it is absolutely nauseating to pass through even our most frequented thoroughfares."[13]

The coming of the cold weather may have relieved the stench, but the problems remained. The Nashville *Dispatch* on Sunday, December 7, 1862, reported that winter had arrived "in earnest" and exclaimed, "What of the Poor of our City?" Telling its readers to "look in the alleys, byways, and hovels in the suburbs," the paper stated that "you will see an amount of suffering you never dreamed existed in Nashville," where "business has been in stagnation and the working man can find nothing." John M. Palmer wrote his wife in the autumn of 1862 that Nashville had become intolerable, for "the war has undermined and demoralized the whole foundation of society in Tennessee."[14] And, of course, as the deprivation, suffering, and casualties mounted, vindictive passions seared people's hearts.

Leaders such as Howell Cobb and Robert Toombs of Georgia were calling for unrelenting warfare against an invader who came "with lust in his eye, poverty in his purse, and hell in his heart," while Parson William G. Brownlow was touring the North asserting that he would arm every devil in hell to defeat the South and would put down the rebellion if the task exterminated every man, woman, and child in the Confederacy.[15]

The war was coming home to the South. Gradually being strangled by blockade, dismembered by invasion, and sapped of resources, it was the only section of the United States ever really to know the devastation of war on its own soil.

Forever lost for some people, who experienced the most profound psychological trauma of their lives, were such expendables

[13]Horn, "Nashville," 13.
[14]Palmer to wife, Nov. 22, 1862, John M. Palmer Papers, Illinois State Historical Lib., Springfield.
[15]Nevins, *War,* II, 298.

as innocence, idealism, and romance. Sacrificed also, bloody and mutilated on the supposed glorious altar of war, were thousands killed, tens of thousands wounded. Since June 1, 1862, when Robert E. Lee had assumed command of the Confederate forces in front of Richmond, his army alone had suffered fifty thousand casualties.[16] Immense sums of money and property were gone too, as the Confederate economy, characterized by an ever-rising inflation rate, increasingly manifested the disturbing signs of inability to weather the wartime pressures. But in spite of it all, the late summer of 1862 had been a time of hope and a season of promise. That was when Confederate fortunes, regardless of the problems, seemed to be at high tide, as the Rebels advanced in both east and west in the one great, coordinated counteroffensive of the war.

It was a startling turnabout. Shortly before, in the spring, the Confederacy had been on the defensive everywhere. New Orleans was lost. The Rebel defeat at Shiloh enabled the Union army to hold its position on the line of the Mississippi, clearing the Federal path of conquest to Corinth with its vital east-west rail communications, while the fall of Island Number 10 opened the Mississippi River down to Fort Pillow. When the Rebels were soon forced to evacuate Corinth, Fort Pillow and Memphis had to be abandoned and all of West Tennessee and northern Mississippi slipped into Yankee hands. The great river itself became virtually a Federal waterway as the deepwater fleet under Flag Officer David G. Farragut steamed past the fortifications at Vicksburg in late June and rendezvoused with the gunboats of Flag Officer Charles Davis' western flotilla above the city on July 1. And west of the Mississippi, the Rebels had been driven out of Missouri. In Virginia, where all eyes seemed always to be focused, Major General George B. McClellan's powerful Union army, which outnumbered the Rebel defenders nearly two-to-one, was approaching the very gates of the Confederate capital at Richmond.[17]

But by late summer, except for the slow strangling of the Fed-

---

[16]Thomas L. Connelly, "Robert E. Lee and the Western Confederacy: A Criticism of Lee's Strategic Ability," *Civil War History,* June 1969, p. 118.

[17]James Lee McDonough, *Shiloh—in Hell before Night* (Knoxville, 1977), 218–21. Henry, *Story,* 151. E.B. Long and Barbara Long, *The Civil War Day by Day* (New York, 1971), 236.

eral blockade, about which the South could never do anything, the fortunes of the Confederacy had changed dramatically—so much in fact that the Rebels had gone on the offensive. Stonewall Jackson's strikingly successful campaign in the Shenandoah Valley had almost panicked Washington, the Lincoln administration fearing that a Rebel army would suddenly emerge from the valley and descend upon the nation's capital. Even more spectacular was the triumph of the Rebel army under Robert E. Lee. Taking command when the Confederate defenders were almost in the suburbs of Richmond and significantly outnumbered by his enemy, General Lee had driven the Federals away from Richmond in the Seven Days' Campaign and then defeated the relieving army, led out from Washington by blustery, untactful, and overconfident Major General John Pope, in the Second Battle of Manassas. By the first of September the war had been transferred from the vicinity of Richmond to the neighborhood of Washington, and Lee had determined to invade the North.

Desiring to retain the military initiative and swing the people of Maryland to the side of the Confederacy, Lee also hoped to strengthen the antiwar movement in the North. Possibly he would draw off Federal troops from areas where they were menacing the Southern nation, relieve Virginia from the ravages of war during the harvest season, and enhance the prospects of foreign recognition of the Confederacy. There was much to be gained as Lee marched across the Potomac and into enemy territory, leading fifty thousand battle-hardened veterans.[18]

It was not only in the east that the Union was in trouble. The western theater had seen a similar reversal of fortune since the triumphant spring days. The powerful Union army at Corinth under the bookish Major General Henry W. Halleck, numbering well over one hundred thousand soldiers, had been split up, part of it sent to Memphis and West Tennessee, part of it eastward to occupy Chattanooga, and still other troops were sent to other duties. Halleck was then called to Washington, but he had stayed in the West long enough to surrender the initiative and bring the war in

---

[18]Mark M. Boatner III, *The Civil War Dictionary* (New York, 1959), 17. Hereafter cited as *CWD*.

the West to stagnation. Quickly the Rebels took advantage of their opportunity.

Federal Major General Don Carlos Buell, moving cautiously eastward to occupy Chattanooga — immobilized two days by fear of an attack by a non-existent Rebel army and further delayed by a foul-up in supply arrangements — never reached the strategic city at the foot of Lookout Mountain. The Rebels got there first. The main Confederate army in the West, soon to be known for the rest of the war as the Army of Tennessee,[19] marched into Chattanooga under its new commander, Major General Braxton Bragg, an 1837 West Point graduate. P.G.T. Beauregard's ill health, failure at Shiloh (the defeat he insisted on calling a "victory"), and inability to get along with President Davis had finally led to his removal from command. Now the forty-five-year-old Bragg, a somewhat quarrelsome, pessimistic martinet who had gained fame in the Mexican war as an artillery captain under Major General Zachary Taylor and enjoyed a close relationship with Davis, seemed to hold the fortunes of the western Confederacy in his hands.

Possibly there was not a more controversial high-ranking general in the Rebel army than Braxton Bragg. One may read the contrasting comments of ladies who knew little about generalship but nevertheless offered their opinions, such as Mrs. Mary B. Chestnut, who denounced Bragg as "a worthless general," or Mrs. Bettie B. Blackmore, who claimed that Bragg did "more with his men and means than any other general." Or one may set in opposition the evaluations of high-ranking military men like Lieutenant General Leonidas Polk who, after the Battle of Chickamauga, wrote to President Davis that Bragg had "let us down as usual and allowed the fruits of . . . victory to pass from him by the most criminal incapacity. . . ," while Brigadier General James R. Chalmers told Bragg: "I have seen no man in this war who looked, talked and acted on all occasions so much like my beau ideal of a General; you have shown yourself a great military chieftain. . . ."[20]

---

[19]Under Beauregard it had been known as the Army of Mississippi; Bragg called it the Army of Kentucky until after that fateful campaign, renaming it the Army of Tennessee, by which it was known at the Battle of Stones River and for the duration of the war.

[20]Grady McWhiney, "Braxton Bragg," *Civil War Times Illustrated*, April 1972, pp. 42, 6, 43.

(*Above*): West Point graduate and a hero of the Mexican War, General Braxton Bragg commanded the Army of Tennessee that gained the initial advantage at Murfreesboro with a strong attack on the Union right. When the Confederate assault was finally stopped and the Rebels retreated, criticism of Bragg reached a new height. (*Below*): This home, occupied by General Bragg for his headquarters, was located near the intersection of the Nashville Pike and the railroad. The site, today starkly marked by a pyramid of cannon balls on a square granite base, is nearly a mile and a quarter southeast of the visitor center.

When the gamut has been run from the derogatory to the laudatory evaluations, both of which become rather lengthy, the reasonable conclusion from the conflicting statements is that Bragg, from beginning to end, was just what he seemed in his first great battle at Shiloh, a puzzling mixture of competence and ineptness.

Probably his greatest military talent was logistical, not tactical. A tireless worker and a rigid disciplinarian, Bragg, according to his biographer, "actually enjoyed managing detailed affairs." Rather than leading a corps or an army in battle, he would have been more valuable behind the lines directing communications, organizing stragglers, and sending reinforcements and ammunition to critical points. Perhaps also he listened too much to his interfering wife, who seemed to have a ready answer for every question. For instance, believing that Tennessee troops were disloyal, she urged Bragg to place them where he could shoot them down if they ran. The Mississippi and Louisiana troops, she prognosticated, "will never fail you." The general's response about the Tennessee troops was: "I never realized the full correctness of your appreciation of them until now."[21]

Bragg possessed a lowering brow and a haggard, austere, no-nonsense look. He may not have deserved the description of the Georgia girl who wrote that if John C. Breckinridge was the handsomest man in the Confederate army, Bragg, who "looks like an old porcupine, might be called the ugliest,"[22] but certainly he was not good-looking. And a general's appearance is a factor, even if a minor one, in determining his ability to inspire confidence in the soldiers.

Hampered by ill health all his life, which was probably partly psychosomatic and seemed to become more pronounced when his responsibilities increased, Bragg was frequently despondent and frustrated. He was, as Grady McWhiney has observed, too ambitious to be satisfied with himself or others and represented "an unusual combination of potentially dangerous eccentricities and high ability."[23] For better or worse, Bragg would command the

[21]McWhiney, "Braxton Bragg at Shiloh," *Tennessee Historical Quarterly,* March 1962, pp. 20, 23, 22.

[22]McWhiney, "Braxton Bragg," *Civil War Times Illustrated,* 5.

[23]*Braxton Bragg and Confederate Defeat: Field Command* (New York, 1969), I, 20, 390.

Confederacy's main western army longer than any other general.

For a while Bragg's good qualities of organizational ability, energy, and a strong sense of duty came to the fore as he capably planned and began to execute a campaign to carry the war into Kentucky. Possibly he could drive all the way to the Ohio River, taking steps as he went to cut Buell's supply line, the Louisville & Nashville Railroad.

On August 28 Bragg began to move northward with an army of thirty thousand soldiers. Actually it was a double-pronged offensive. Earlier in the month, Major General Edmund Kirby Smith, a thirty-nine-year-old West Point Floridian, had led an army of twenty thousand men from Knoxville into central Kentucky. A former mathematics professor at the Point and Indian fighter on the frontier, Kirby Smith had been severely wounded at the Battle of First Manassas, after which he convalesced at Lynchburg. There he met and married a young lady who had made him a shirt on the joking promise that whoever made the garment would get the handsome colonel who went with it.[24]

The Floridian conducted a masterful campaign into Kentucky. Finding the Union garrison at Cumberland Gap too strong and too well fortified, Kirby Smith left one division to watch them and with the rest of his army pushed northward toward Richmond. There, on August 30, he met, routed, and scattered a Yankee army under Major General William "Bull" Nelson, the profane, gigantic former naval lieutenant who had done much to hold Kentucky in the Union—a man who had only a month to live before he was shot to death in an altercation with Brigadier General Jefferson C. Davis at the Galt House in Louisville.

The energetic Kirby Smith took about forty-five hundred prisoners at the Battle of Richmond and then moved on to Lexington, where he rested and waited for the advance of Bragg's army. The campaign for Kentucky was off to a good start.[25] If General Bragg could do his part, the two Rebel forces would join in the north-central part of the state, carry the war to the Ohio, gain recruits, and boost Confederate morale.

Until he arrived in southern Kentucky, Bragg too had handled

[24]Boatner, *CWD*, 770.
[25]*Ibid.*, 698. Henry, *Story*, 194.

his part of the campaign with admirable skill. Marching north along the Highland Rim west of the Cumberland Mountains, Bragg actually won a race with General Buell, whose army was retiring along the railroad line from Nashville to Louisville. The strategic point was Munfordville, where the railroad crossed Green River.

There a Union fort and a garrison of four thousand men defended the crossing. But the Rebel cavalry pounded into Munfordville ahead of Buell, Bragg hurried up his infantry from Glasgow, and in the afternoon of September 17 the Confederates received the surrender of the fort and garrison. Bragg had succeeded in placing his army between Buell and his base. The Rebels were astride the Union army's line of march, in excellent position either to fight or advance into Louisville, defended only by a small number of raw and untrained troops.[26]

Then it happened. That "fatal hesitancy at critical moments," as one writer described Bragg's behavior, that "loss of nerve," as others have suggested, that "lack of resolution," as still another student characterized it, had taken hold of the general. Whatever it was that always seemed to happen to Bragg at the decisive moment of a battle or campaign occurred at Munfordville. With the successful climax of the campaign within his grasp, Bragg muttered something about "the campaign must be won by marching, not by fighting" and inexplicably decided to abandon his commanding position and let Buell pass into Louisville, safety, and reinforcements, while he marched off to the east to join Kirby Smith.[27]

September 17 is a day that stands out dramatically and tragically in the history of the Confederacy. It was the day that Bragg had won the contest with Buell but apparently did not recognize the fact. It was also the date, in the east, that saw the bloodiest single day of the Civil War and, more significantly, ended any hope that Lee's invasion of the North could succeed.

It seemed almost as if fate were aligned against the Rebels. A copy of Lee's orders, lost by some Confederate officer (perhaps D.H. Hill), fell into the hands of General McClellan, who thus discovered that the Confederate army was split into several frag-

[26]Henry, *Story*, 195-96.
[27]Nevins, *War*, II, 275. Bruce Catton, *The American Heritage Short History of the Civil War* (New York, 1960), 96, 97.

ments. Even with all Lee's forces united, McClellan had nearly a two-to-one bulge on the Grayclads. If the Union commander had moved quickly and decisively, he could have destroyed the Army of Northern Virginia. But George McClellan was a careful man— too careful to be a successful commander.

After wasting time and allowing Lee to pull his army back together in front of the little town of Sharpsburg, McClellan should still have administered a smashing defeat if he had used his superior manpower efficiently. Instead, on September 17 McClellan sent his men against Lee's positions in piecemeal fashion, the action gradually moving along the lines from north to south. Even so, near the center the Yankees almost, but not quite, broke the Rebel army in half at the "Bloody Lane." Little more than a frazzled thread of a line maintained the Confederate center—and McClellan had two corps that were hardly engaged at all!

When the day was over the Rebels had maintained their lines, but over twenty-three thousand Rebels and Yankees were casualties and Lee's hope to win a major victory on Northern soil had come to a bloody end as more than ten thousand of his soldiers lay dead and wounded along the banks of Antietam Creek. In two days the Confederates were recrossing the Potomac, and the Union, although Lincoln was bitterly disappointed that his general had allowed the chance to smash the Rebels to slip away, had won a great strategic victory.[28]

Meanwhile in Kentucky, where the puzzling Bragg had strangely relinquished one of the outstanding opportunities of the war when he marched away from Munfordville, the Federal prospects were improving. With the road clear of Rebels, Buell rapidly marched into Louisville, where he showed remarkable zeal and ability in collecting fresh troops from Indiana and Ohio and reorganizing his army. Then on October 1, with three corps numbering about sixty thousand soldiers, he moved southeast in three columns, searching for the enemy.

Bragg's Rebels had tramped northeastward from Munfordville

---

[28]Catton, *Short History*, 95–97. Catton, *This Hallowed Ground* (New York, 1956), 199–207.

through Lincoln's birthplace at Hodgenville, on past Gethsemane Abbey, and into Bardstown, famous for its Old Kentucky Home. There Bragg left his army and rode with his staff to Lexington, conferred with Kirby Smith, and spent several days arranging for the inauguration of Richard Hawes as Confederate governor of Kentucky. At Frankfort, on October 4, the inauguration took place. The new governor cut short his address as Union guns lobbed shells into the outskirts of the town and the generals hurried away to their armies.

The subsequent maneuvering that culminated in the battle at Perryville was a very muddled affair. Neither Bragg nor Buell knew where the other's army was located. The Confederates were still widely separated, Bragg having failed to join forces with Kirby Smith, whose army was in the Frankfort-Lexington-Harrodsburg region. Thirty to sixty miles separated it from Bragg's command in the Bardstown sector.

Bragg got the mistaken idea that Buell, whose columns were also widely separated, was moving his main force toward Frank-fort and Kirby Smith. The Rebel commander thus ordered Major General Leonidas Polk to move north and strike the Federals in flank. Fortunately for the Confederates, the Rebel cavalry ascertained that the weight of the Union army was actually moving toward Bardstown and Polk decided to fall back to Harrodsburg while William J. Hardee's corps moved to Perryville, ten miles to the southwest.

By the evening of October 7, a large portion of Buell's Federals were occupying the high ground west of Perryville along a stream known as Doctor's Creek. In and around Perryville were about sixteen thousand Confederates under Hardee. The weather had been hot, water was scarce, and advance elements of the armies began to fight for the pools of water in the creek. On October 8 the two armies blundered into a peculiar battle which neither commander understood. In fact, Bragg was at Harrodsburg when the fight began and did not arrive at Perryville until mid-morning. Buell's headquarters was only a few miles away but he did not even learn of the battle until about four P.M. when it was nearly over, having reached its peak about two-thirty.

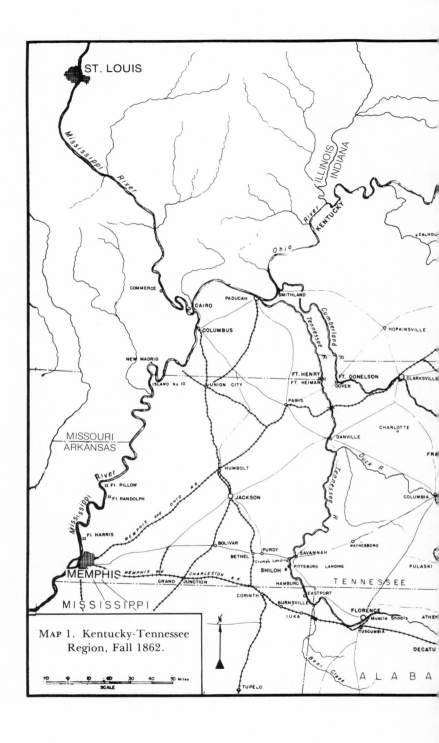

MAP 1. Kentucky-Tennessee Region, Fall 1862.

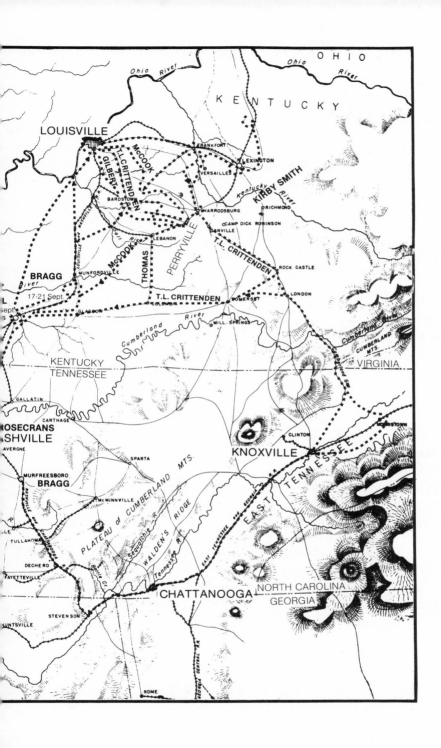

Both generals had a bad misconception of the other's strength. Buell supposed that he was facing Bragg's whole army, whereas it was only a small part, and Bragg thought he was confronting only a relatively small portion of Buell's force, when in actuality nearly forty thousand Federals were in his front.

The Rebels of Brigadier General B. Franklin Cheatham's division savagely attacked the left end of Buell's line and routed a considerable part of Brigadier General Alexander McDowell McCook's corps. Altogether the Confederate forces dealt out more than four thousand casualties while taking about thirty-four hundred in a bloody, vigorous, but inconclusive struggle. The Federals prepared to receive another attack the next day, but Bragg's information now rightly convinced him that most of Buell's army was in his front. The Rebel commander had allowed his army to be drawn into battle before he had concentrated his troops with those of Kirby Smith. Confronted by superior forces, he retreated to Harrodsburg, where all the Confederate troops were at last united.

Buell followed and the two armies lay across from each other at Harrodsburg, each waiting to see what the other would do. Neither commander did anything. Kirby Smith pleaded with Bragg to fight; the general promised that he would, but he did not.

The simple fact was that Bragg had had enough. Whatever possessed him a few weeks earlier at Munfordville now seized the general once more. The Kentuckians had not risen to support the Confederacy as he had expected. Bragg still had wagonloads of weapons that he had carried along to arm the new recruits who never came. His mind seemed obsessed, not with the possible results of victory, but with the dire consequences if he fought and lost. Also, there was disturbing news from north Mississippi that Earl Van Dorn and Sterling Price had failed to retake Corinth. Bragg knew, of course, that Lee had been driven back into Virginia and, it seemed, there were armed Unionists all over Kentucky. The great endeavor to claim Kentucky for the Confederacy was over. Bragg gave the order to withdraw.

Abandoning much of the spoils they had gathered and leaving behind hundreds of men who were too sick or badly wounded to be moved, the Confederates slowly and painfully struggled over the mountain roads, tramping toward Knoxville. It was a disillusioned and disheartened force, to have started out so well, that re-treated into Tennessee.[29]

Some Rebels in the ranks were vehement in their criticism of Bragg. W.E. Yeatman, Second Tennessee Infantry, lost several of his schoolmates and friends in the battle at Perryville. He called the order to fall back to Tennessee "cowardly" and reported that he nearly starved on the march to Knoxville. Another Confederate, John Gold of the Twenty-fourth Tennessee Infantry, also related that he thought he would starve on the trek back from Perryville. Still another soldier reported that "the retreat from Perryville was one of fearful suffering." More than two hundred men in his brigade were barefooted, he said. "We were ordered to draw ten days rations and march to Knoxville by way of Cumberland Gap," he continued. "We failed to draw the ten days rations, as we did not overtake any provision-wagons and those we guarded were loaded with ordinance. For ten days we had nothing to eat save what we could find on the march . . . through a mountainous and sparsely settled country . . . ravaged by both armies before our retreat. . . . "[30]

If the men in the ranks were angry — and some of them, as Allan Nevins has written, "would gladly have burned [Bragg] at the stake" — so were the generals.[31] John C. Breckinridge, Patrick R. Cleburne, William J. Hardee, and Leonidas Polk all criticized Bragg, not so much for what he had done as for what he had not done. They seemed to sense that a great opportunity had been frittered away. The most vocal of all was Kirby Smith, who wrote to the War Department bitterly complaining of Bragg's direction of the campaign and requesting a transfer, preferably to Mobile, but anywhere, if staying where he was would require further coop-eration with Bragg.

[29]Lowell H. Harrison, *The Civil War in Kentucky* (Lexington, 1975), 48–54. Henry, *Story*, 199. Catton, *Hallowed Ground*, 211–15. Boatner, *CWD*, 644. Foote, *Civil War*, I, 728–40. Thomas L. Connelly, *Army of the Heartland* (Baton Rouge, 1967), 243–70. Stanley F. Horn, *The Army of Tennessee: A Military History* (New York, 1941). Horn, "The Battle of Perryville," *Civil War Times Illustrated*, February 1966, pp. 4–11, 42–47.

[30]W.E. Yeatman memoirs, Confederate Collection, Tennessee State Library and Archives, Nashville. Hereafter cited as TSLA. John E. Gold narrative, Confederate Collection, TSLA. John B. Lindsley, ed., *The Military Annals of Confederate Tennessee* (Nashville, 1886), 535.

[31]*War*, II, 289.

When Bragg reached Knoxville he found a summons to Richmond waiting for him. Swamped by complaints of dissension in the ranks of the army, along with insistent demands that Bragg be removed from command, Jefferson Davis had decided that he must talk with his general face to face. "The President desires," wired the adjutant general, "that you will lose no time in coming here."[32] It was only the beginning of the problem that would never be resolved as long as Braxton Bragg commanded the Army of Tennessee.

[32]Foote, *Civil War,* I, 743.

3

A Time of Change

December 13, 1862, was a glorious day in the annals of the Confederate States of America. Firmly entrenched on Marye's Heights about one-half mile west of Fredericksburg, the Army of Northern Virginia, commanded by General Robert E. Lee, smashed a major Union assault and almost wrecked the Army of the Potomac. More than thirteen thousand casualties were inflicted. Simultaneously hope was destroyed in Washington that Major General Ambrose E. Burnside could be a successful army leader. Rebel losses were comparatively light, the Confederacy's Virginia front was stable, and a new spirit of optimism was in the air as the holiday season approached.

On the day of the Fredericksburg triumph Jefferson Davis, president of the Confederacy, was in Murfreesboro, Tennessee, accompanied by Custis Lee, General Lee's son. The presence of Davis in the little town thirty miles southeast of Nashville must have seemed highly unlikely to the casual observer.

The reason for Davis' visit to Murfreesboro was to talk with General Braxton Bragg and evaluate, first hand, the condition of his army.[1] In a sense, the story began months before, as far back as the Battle of Shiloh. Acting as a corps commander, and despite the advice of subordinate officers, Bragg had ordered charge after futile charge against the Union stronghold in the Hornets' Nest. The plot thickened when Bragg was chosen to lead what had now

[1]Horn, *Army*, 192.

become the Army of Tennessee and soon demonstrated more fully his already well-known and widely disliked trait as an officer who demanded strict, many said unreasonable, discipline. With the failure of the Kentucky campaign the climax had come.

The high hopes of the late summer offensive had faded, lost in the enigmatic muddling at Munfordville and the dismal, frustrating retreat following the battle of Perryville. The long trek back from Kentucky had been over for weeks but the recriminations and the placing of blame continued. Rebel soldiers, with good reason, did not feel that they had been whipped. The army, they thought, had been mishandled. Conferences that Davis held in Richmond with Bragg, Polk, and Kirby Smith had failed to resolve the problems. Reports of general poor morale among the soldiers and disaffection within Bragg's officer corps still trickled into the capital. Deeply disturbed about the Army of Tennessee and also troubled by the need to reinforce Lieutenant General John C. Pemberton's troops in Mississippi, Davis entrained for Murfreesboro where the army was gathered either to defend southeastern Tennessee or, it was hoped, to threaten the Union forces at Nashville.

While Davis had chosen to sustain Bragg in his command after the Kentucky campaign, the president had made a significant command change in the western theater. On November 24 General Joseph E. Johnston, sufficiently recovered from the severe wound received at the battle of Fair Oaks or Seven Pines, as it was also known, was placed in charge of a broad new theater. It stretched from the Appalachian Mountains to the Mississippi River, encompassing the departments of Bragg, Kirby Smith, and Pemberton. Johnston's basic assignment was to coordinate the efforts of Bragg and Pemberton for the defense of Tennessee and the Mississippi.

In theory, the concept of a theater commander to supervise military moves in such a vast area was good; in practice, there were major problems. For one, there was tension between Johnston and Davis. Early in the war the two had disagreed over the need to concentrate troops in Virginia; also, Johnston had expected to be named the ranking officer in the Confederacy but Davis had placed Samuel Cooper, Albert Sidney Johnston, and Lee ahead of him in the list of nominations sent to the Congress. Then in 1862, they clashed about strategic matters in Virginia and the defense of Richmond. In fact, before the war ever started Davis and Johnston had had problems. In 1860, as United States senator from Mississippi, Davis had opposed Johnston's appointment as quartermaster general of the army. Earlier, when secretary of war, Davis had turned down Johnston's application to be appointed colonel of a new regiment. Some people said, although it cannot be documented, that the problems between Davis and Johnston went all the way back to a bitterness created in their cadet days at West Point when they got into a fight. Even their wives became involved in a quarrel in 1861.[2]

Now Johnston felt that he had been appointed theater commander simply because only three available officers outranked Bragg. Lee was busy in Virginia, Beauregard's relationship with Davis was even worse than Johnston's, and therefore, Davis was left with Johnston as his only choice. Johnston also suspected that he had been given a nominal command with little power and heavy responsibilities to make him look bad.

From the very day of his appointment Johnston protested the impossibility of his assignment. A quick look at the map showed him that Bragg's and Pemberton's armies were separated by several hundred miles and both Major General U.S. Grant's army and the Tennessee River were between them. Any shuttling of troops between the two Confederate armies would necessitate a long trip, all the way south to Montgomery or Mobile, and, Johnston thought, would probably require a month. Johnston saw that Bragg's army was actually closer to Lee's forces in Virginia than it was to Pemberton's army in Mississippi.

First, Johnston argued that Lieutenant General T.H. Holmes' force in the trans-Mississippi region should be concentrated with Pemberton. President Davis contended that Holmes must stay west of the Mississippi to defend his own department and insisted that any Yankee threat to Bragg or Pemberton could be met by shifting reinforcements from one army to the other. Continuing to argue that it would be impossible to stop simultaneous Union movements against Bragg and Pemberton, Johnston wanted Davis

[2]Thomas L. Connelly, *Autumn of Glory: The Army of Tennessee, 1862–1865* (Baton Rouge, 1971), 34. Foote, *Civil War*, I, 790.

to tell him whether Middle Tennessee or Mississippi was considered more vital. Davis considered Middle Tennessee less important but argued that both Mississippi and Tennessee could be held. Johnston disagreed with the president both on which area was more vital, as well as on the question of holding both regions.

Further frustrated by Davis' decision to allow department heads to continue making their reports directly to Richmond, thus guaranteeing that Johnston could never feel sure of being completely informed, the general was soon disgusted and discouraged. Finally, he was suffering from a flareup of the wound at Seven Pines that had cost him his Virginia command. This was the situation when Davis made his journey from Richmond to Murfreesboro—a trip that resulted in exasperating Johnston still more.[3]

Davis' journey into Murfreesboro was a colorful affair as crowds gathered at wayside stations from Chattanooga to Murfreesboro to wave and pay tribute to the president as his train went by. The Murfreesboro *Daily Rebel Banner* hailed his arrival and reported that the president was staying at the residence of Lewis Maney.[4] Davis held a review of Hardee's and Polk's corps, which attracted much attention. James A. Hall, a soldier in the Confederate army, wrote his sister, Mary Louisa Hall in Montgomery, and said that the review was a real "Monkey Show." "We had to march two or three miles to the place where the review was to take place," Hall reported. "I knew Mars Jeff as soon as I saw him. He was dressed in a plain broad cloth suit, and, as the men said, you could not tell him from any other *old citizen*." Hall said it was difficult for some of the men to believe they had really seen Jefferson Davis. "Some of them," he continued, "hardly believe yet that he was the real Simon pure Jeff. They have been deceived so often by reports that Jeff Davis was in camp that they would not really believe it when he did come!"[5]

Not all Davis' time was spent with military regalia. For the better part of a day and a half the president conferred with Bragg

[3]*OR*, XX, pt. 2, 424. Connelly, *Autumn*, 34–38.
[4]Dec. 13, 1862.
[5]James A. Hall to sister, Dec. 14, 1862, Hall Papers, Alabama State Department of Archives and History, Montgomery.

and his subordinates. Ultimately he concluded that the army was in good condition and that the enemy in Nashville had only defensive purposes in mind. Then Davis, without consulting Johnston, made a strategic decision, possibly a fateful decision. Convinced that Pemberton's Mississippi army was in a more seriously threatened position than was Bragg's force, Davis detached Carter Stevenson's three-brigade division of seventy-five hundred officers and men and ordered it to Mississippi to reinforce Pemberton. Bragg protested that this would encourage the Union army at Nashville to attack him, but his words were to no avail. Davis told Bragg that if necessary he must fall back beyond the Tennessee River.[6]

While the president and the generals deliberated behind closed doors they were careful, of course, to keep up a front of optimism and confidence. The Murfreesboro *Daily Rebel Banner* reported that "at night Mr. Davis was serenaded, and in response to the compliments, he made a brief address. His words were cheering, thrilling and earnest. Generals Breckinridge, Bragg and Polk also made short speeches and were enthusiastically cheered."[7] Then it was time for Davis to leave Murfreesboro.

The decision to send Stevenson's division to Mississippi was taken better by Bragg than by Johnston. When Davis got back to Chattanooga and informed Johnston about the transfer of Stevenson's unit to reinforce Pemberton, Johnston became even more gloomy. Again he pleaded with the president to order Holmes across the Mississippi, which the adjutant and inspector general's office had earlier and mistakenly told him was being done, but Davis was unyielding. Johnston had had enough. On Christmas Day he requested Davis to transfer him to another command. The request was denied, as Davis contended he needed Johnston to transfer troops during emergencies and Johnston did accompany Davis on an inspection trip to Mississippi. But the effort to give the

[6]Connelly, *Autumn,* 38, 39. Archer Jones, *Confederate Strategy from Shiloh to Vicksburg* (Baton Rouge, 1961), 127. A somewhat misleading figure of 10,000 is often cited for Stevenson's division. This is because Col. Alexander Reynolds' brigade, then stationed in East Tennessee, also accompanied Stevenson's three brigades to Mississippi. This gives a figure of 10,000 but only 7,500 came from the troops in and around Murfreesboro.

[7]Dec. 15, 1862.

western Confederacy a theater commander was far from satisfactory as the New Year approached.[8]

In the Union camp at Nashville, meanwhile, there was also a major effort to bring about a change. The army had a new commander, the Lincoln administration having at last removed General Buell, a soldier never noted for being aggressive. The general's retreat from southern Tennessee all the way to the Ohio at Louisville had shaken both the White House and the War Department. In fact, he almost lost his command right then. Soon Buell fought the Battle of Perryville — and fought it badly, following up that struggle with a lackadaisical pursuit of Bragg's retreating army, a pursuit that Buell abandoned just when Lincoln and Secretary of War Edwin M. Stanton were thinking he might at last move into East Tennessee. Instead he broke off and headed for Nashville.

The general admitted that there would never be real security for Kentucky until East Tennessee was occupied. And he knew how dear to the heart of Lincoln was the control of that heavily Unionist part of the Volunteer State. Nevertheless, Buell was preoccupied with the supply problems of a campaign into East Tennessee, apparently preferred Nashville, and chose to continue to ignore the order, now a year old, to march his troops into East Tennessee.[9]

This time Lincoln would not be placated. Buell was removed and "Old Rosy," as the men called him, became the new commander of the Union forces concentrating on Nashville.

Forty-three-year-old Major General William Starke Rosecrans was nearly six feet tall, compact with little wasted flesh, a large red nose, and a somewhat impulsive, excitable personality. Graduated fifth in his class at West Point, the general was a heavy drinker and freely employed profanity, but he was also a devoted Roman Catholic who carried a crucifix on his watch chain and a rosary in his pocket and enjoyed religious discussions that might keep his staff up half the night. Tearing and chewing on a cigar, from which he seemed inseparable and derived immense satisfaction, he would sometimes defend his firm religious convictions to the point that his righteousness seemed to become self-righteousness.

[8]*OR*, XX, pt. 2, 435–38, 459–60. Connelly, *Autumn*, 41, 42.
[9]Catton, *Hallowed Ground*, 215. T. Harry Williams, *Lincoln and His Generals* (New York, 1952), 183–85.

(*Above*): Surprised by the Confederate attack on the morning of December 31, 1862, General William S. Rosecrans, popular new commander of the Army of the Cumberland, quickly recovered and doggedly held his line along the railroad and the Nashville Pike. (*Below*): General Rosecrans' Union headquarters, located about three-quarters of a mile northwest of the visitor center, is marked by a pyramid of cannon balls on a square granite base.

He also had, as his biography suggested, "the dubious good fortune to be both articulate and talkative."[10]

From religion, his conversation might be turned to display a vast theoretical knowledge of war. He often quoted authorities and cited maxims of war, comparing the problem at hand to similar cases in military history. Always he was energetic and apparently needed very little sleep. In battle he became restless, likely to talk so fast that he could hardly be understood. In fact, any time he was excited his speech was apt to grow hurried and difficult to comprehend.[11]

No one ever seemed to think he was the least bit afraid of a fight, and generally he was highly popular. James Garfield said once that he "loved every bone in [Rosecrans'] body." The general was, wrote Jacob Cox, "altogether an attractive and companionable man," and Whitelaw Reid concluded that "few officers have been more popular with their commands, or have inspired more confidence in the rank and file."[12]

Rumor alleged that Rosecrans favored Catholics and permitted religion to warp his judgment. Milo S. Hascall, for example, wrote that the general was "a great enthusiast in regard to the Catholic Church; seemed to want to think of nothing else, talk of nothing else, and in fact do nothing else, except to proselyte for it and attend upon its ministrations. . . . No occasion, however inappropriate," Hascall continued, "was ever lost sight of to advocate its cause; in fact, he was . . . a crank on that subject. . . ." Such charges were false, according to William D. Bickham of the Cincinnati *Commercial*, who lived at Rosecrans' headquarters for a year. "He never interferes," Bickham declared, "with the spiritual affairs of any subordinate," and this, it should be noted, seems to have been the general opinion of those who had opportunity to observe Rosecrans closely.[13]

There were factors other than his religion, however, that caused

---

[10]Boatner, *CWD*, 708. Foote, *Civil War*, II, 80. Lamers, *Rosecrans*, 6, 55.

[11]Catton, *Hallowed Ground*, 216, 234.

[12]Lamers, *Rosecrans*, 55.

[13]Milo S. Hascall, "Personal Recollections and Experiences Concerning the Battle of Stone River," *Military Order of the Loyal Legion of the United States, Illinois Commandery* (Goshen, Ind., 1889), 151, 152. Hereafter cited as *MOLLUS*. Lamers, *Rosecrans*, 188.

him more serious problems. The general, usually very kind to subordinates, had an unfortunate tendency to irritate his superiors.
Independent, outspoken, occasionally short of temper, and with
an uncompromising moral sense, he sometimes made enemies
needlessly and unwisely — enemies in high places.[14]

But with his successes against Robert E. Lee in western Virginia
during the first year of the war and most recently at Corinth, Mississippi, where his troops put up a terrific fight, turning back generals Earl Van Dorn and Sterling Price, Rosecrans had emerged as
the logical successor to Buell. His coming to command was greeted
by the soldiers with almost universal approval.

"We were glad to be delivered of Buell," wrote William Hartpence of the Fifty-first Indiana Infantry. Hartpence told about a
song concerning Rosecrans that was popular shortly before the
Battle of Stones River. A tall, raw-boned fellow calling himself
William E. Lock came to the army as a poet and singer of patriotic
songs, said Hartpence. Actually, he was a spy, later shot and
killed while running the picket line, but he told the Union soldiers
that he had a pass from Abraham Lincoln to travel through the
western army. Standing on a cracker box he would sing a patriotic
ballad in tribute to General Rosecrans, asking the soldiers to join
him in the chorus, which according to Hartpence, thousands
eagerly did, loudly bellowing out:

> "Old Rosy is the man, Old Rosy is the man;
> We'll show our deeds where'er he leads;
> Old Rosy is the man."[15]

Ira S. Owens of the Seventy-fourth Ohio Infantry was impressed
by Rosecrans. He remembered the general's reviewing the troops
and telling them: "Boys, when you drill, drill like thunder. It is
not the number of bullets you shoot, but the accuracy of the aim
that kills more men in battle." And in the Eighth Kansas Infantry,
Colonel John A. Martin concluded, "On the whole, the army re-
joiced to learn that Rosecrans had been assigned to command. To

---

[14]Lamers, *Rosecrans,* 6.
[15]William R. Hartpence, *History of the Fifty-First Indiana Veteran Volunteer Infantry*
(Cincinnati, 1894), 93–95.

those who served under him in Mississippi, his presence was peculiarly gratifying, and the enthusiasm with which they hailed his coming was unbounded. . . . The glory of his recent victories gave a fresher and greater charm to his name."[16]

There was no doubt about it; the presence of William S. Rosecrans as the new commander of the Union army assembled at Nashville inspired hope and confidence and held forth the promise of significant action against Bragg's Rebel forces gathered around Murfreesboro. But while outposts and patrols sparred and the Blue and Gray armies made ready for the battle that many thought would soon be upon them, one of the most momentous, far-reaching changes in American history was taking place.

It is strikingly evident when the newspapers from the time are examined. In the Murfreesboro *Daily Rebel Banner* of December 13, 1862, the word "Abolitionists," a term now used to describe the Federal army and all supporters of the Union, appears eight times in only three columns of print. What was true in Murfreesboro was true in many newspapers all over the Confederacy, the Union army having recently become the "Abolitionist" army to Southerners. The letters, diaries, and writings of Northern soldiers also reflect an increased awareness of the slavery issue. "But for slavery," wrote Mead Holmes, Jr., a Federal soldier at Nashville, "Middle Tennessee would be densely populated. This 'peculiar institution' curses whatever it touches. It is truly wonderful," he concluded, with pronouncd satisfaction, "to see the difference between free and slave territory." Holmes was sure that "the God of battles is on our side." Another Federal at Nashville said, "we were much encouraged by the recent emancipation proclamation of President Lincoln."[17]

Probably it was inevitable, as the war continued, that emancipation of the slaves would occur at some point. Of course, there had been pressure on Lincoln from the war's inception. The Abolitionists were a strong and vocal minority in the North; radicals within the Republican party who favored a decisive blow against

---

[16]Ira S. Owens, *Seventy-Fourth Ohio Infantry* (Yellow Springs, Ohio, 1872), 29. Lamers, *Rosecrans,* 185.

[17]Mead Holmes, Jr., *A Soldier of the Cumberland* (Boston, 1864), 126, 127. Hartpence, *Fifty-First Indiana,* 93.

slavery had to be considered if party unity were to be maintained; some military officers such as Major Generals John C. Frémont and David Hunter had tried to take independent action against slavery; and in maintaining the Peculiar Institution the United States was out of step with the mainstream of western civilization, a most important factor when evaluating the position that Great Britain might take in the American Civil War.

Possibly overriding all these considerations was the widely held belief in the North that slavery had somehow caused the great conflict. As the war became longer, costing immense sums of money and the lives of thousands and thousands of men, with no end to the struggle in sight, the sentiment to strike down the evil institution that had brought all this misery upon the land naturally became stronger. Whether or not slavery, in some sense, caused the Civil War (and while slavery may not have been the sole cause of the war it now seems clear that the coming of the war can not be adequately explained apart from slavery with all of its ramifications, especially racial, moral, and emotional) is actually beside the point. The decisive factor was that many Northern people *thought* slavery caused the war. Therefore, in increasing numbers, they demanded that to the aim of restoring the Union must be added the destruction of slavery.

For all these reasons, President Lincoln was convinced by the summer of 1862 that he must move against slavery. Waiting for a Union victory on the battlefield in order that his action would not be interpreted as a last-gasp measure to stave off defeat, the president chose the bloody, strategic victory at Antietam as the occasion to announce the preliminary Emancipation Proclamation on September 22, 1862.[18] The proclamation, which stated that only slaves in disloyal states were to be freed and urged the loyal states to adopt voluntary programs for emancipation, was to go into effect January 1, 1863.

There is no doubt that the great document put a new perspective on the war. Some historians have even contended that the battle at Antietam was the decisive struggle of the war because it not only turned back the Rebel invasion but also served to launch

---

[18]Lindsey, *Americans*, 134–37. Cruden, *War*, 133–38. Thomas, *War and Peace*, 107–10. Potter, *Division and Reunion*, 157–59.

emancipation of the slaves, virtually ending any chance that Great Britain might have extended recognition to the Confederacy and intervened decisively in the war.

Impressive though this argument may first appear, it is an over-simplification. The winds of change sweeping across the British Isles were not yet decisive. Certainly with the preliminary Emancipation Proclamation, the war assumed a moral dimension, but it took time for a massive tide of Union sentiment to arise in Britain. Not until after January 1, 1863, and the final proclamation did a really notable change begin to occur, with mass meetings held throughout the country among the working people who, led by John Bright, hailed Lincoln and condemned intervention and the building of war vessels for the Confederacy. But in the fall of 1862, even after Lincoln's September pronouncement on slavery, there were still influential figures in England who wanted to intervene on behalf of the Confederacy.

It was on October 7, 1862, that William E. Gladstone made his famous Newcastle speech giving many people, erroneously, the impression that the British government was about to act: "We may have our own opinions about slavery," he said in the course of his remarks. "We may be for or against the South; but there is no doubt that Jefferson Davis and other leaders . . . have made an army; they are making, it appears, a navy; and what is more than either, they have made a nation." The Gladstone pronouncement was dramatic and led to much speculation, but the voice of Great Britain's government was not behind the finance minister's statement. The issues were very complex and conflicting, and the question of how close the British ever came to intervention is highly debatable.

British industry had stockpiled large surpluses of raw cotton before the Civil War, enough by June 1861 that even if all supplies were cut off, Britain would not feel the pinch until the summer of 1862. By that time the British did experience a significant shortage. Between June and September, unemployment in textiles drove the number of destitute up from 490,000 to 1,108,000 and by December 1862 the number reached its maximum at 2 million. While this was obviously very serious and might possibly have led Britain to break the Union blockade in order to get out the Confederacy's cotton, other British industries were booming as a huge and lucrative market developd in America for war supplies for the Union armies. Also, the failure of British grain crops caused Britain to seek American wheat. And some cotton was beginning to seep into Britain again as Northern armies advanced into the South and captured cotton supplies at various points. Also to be considered, on the other hand, were British shipyards that profited from constructing commerce raiders and rams for the Confederacy, and British merchants who might profit from the Confederacy's destruction of United States merchant vessels.[19]

One final factor that could, apparently, irrevocably be counted upon was that traditional British policy never knowingly recognized a lost cause — even a cause with which the British sympathized. And, contrary to the arguments of some historians, it was not clear after Antietam that the Confederacy was a lost cause.

The one-sided Rebel triumph at Fredericksburg on December 13 was a tremendous boost to the Confederate cause, all the more after the Union papers, like the Washington *Evening Star* of November 19, 1862, had been exuding an arrogant optimism with headlines such as "Stonewall Jackson Left Out In The Cold," and "Burnside To Be In Richmond In Ten Days." If the Rebels, with the battle at Stones River, could have entered the New Year with back-to-back victories by two of their three major armies, which they almost did, it is certainly conceivable that Great Britain's policy toward the Confederacy might have been different.

Undoubtedly, the American ambassador, Charles Francis Adams, played up the battle at Murfreesboro as a great Union victory, using it effectively in his efforts to win points for the United States and to offset the Fredericksburg disaster. Might not a different outcome of the battle, coupled with Fredericksburg, have created an equally different effect on British thinking — an effect highly favorable for the Confederacy?

[19]Potter, *Division and Reunion*, 118, 119.

4

The Christmas Season

The age was one of romanticism, the twilight of the Old South with its chivalry, glory, and privilege — for the favored few. Their courtship and marriage seem unreal, the imaginative creation of a naïve, sentimental dreamer. Unbelievable as it may be to a skeptical mind of the late twentieth century, it actually occurred: the marriage of Mattie Ready and General John H. Morgan. She was seventeen, he was thirty-six, and the manner in which they met was most unusual. During the summer, while Union troops occupied Murfreesboro, Mattie Ready heard some Federal officers downgrading Morgan, then a colonel. The spirited young woman, said by some to be the best-looking girl in the area, came to Morgan's defense so quickly and staunchly that one of the Yankees asked her name. "It's Mattie Ready now," was her reply. "But by the grace of God one day I hope to call myself the wife of John Morgan."

The story soon made its way to the widower cavalryman, who, although he had never seen her, came to call on Mattie when the town was once again in Southern hands. Apparently the attraction was mutual and in a short time they became engaged. The wedding took place on December 14 and the occasion started a celebration that lasted until Christmas. Bishop General Leonidas Polk performed the ceremony, which was attended by all the Rebel brass in the area. The only one conspicuously absent was Brigadier General Nathan Bedford Forrest who, with twenty-five

46

hundred cavalry, was attempting to aid Pemberton's Confederates at Vicksburg by raiding Grant's communication line in West
Tennessee. Although some officers viewed Morgan's marriage
with misgiving, fearing it would hurt the efficiency of the Confederate raider, even these offered their sincere congratulations to
Morgan and his beautiful bride.

Foremost among the doubters was Morgan's adjutant general,
St. Leger Greenfell, renowned veteran of conflicts all over the
world while in the service of Great Britain. But even Greenfell felt
better when he saw the bishop in uniform and all the sabers and
spurs at the wedding. Such a spectacular military ceremony, concluded this war-lover, would never quench the fighting spirit of
any man. In fact, Greenfell was so completely reassured that he
joined in the festivities, singing "Moorish songs, with a French accent, to English airs, and was as mild and agreeable as if some one
was going to be killed."[1]

Morgan was the newest hero of the Confederacy, fresh from a
dazzling raid on the Yankee garrison at Hartsville, Tennessee.
Hitting hard and fast at daylight on Sunday, December 8, Morgan's Rebel cavalry had captured more than two thousand prisoners and thousands of dollars worth of supplies after an hour of
fighting. At Murfreesboro, soldiers and citizens alike had crowded
the icy, wind-swept streets to jeer the frost-bitten Federal prisoners as Morgan brought them in. General Bragg and President Davis
had welcomed Morgan with a brigadier general's commission.

With a glorious reputation, a promotion, and a lovely new wife,
Morgan stood at the Ready home receiving congratulations from
the most important generals in the Army of Tennessee. But lying
in the fields somewhere around Murfreesboro, perhaps unaware
even that a wedding was taking place, was a Rebel sergeant in Major General Patrick R. Cleburne's command named Andrew Campbell. By a strange twist of fate, Campbell would play a prominent
role in the eventual destiny of John H. Morgan, a more decisive
role than any of the friends who surrounded him at his wedding.

[1]Basil W. Duke, *Morgan's Cavalry* (New York, 1906). Mary B. Chestnut, *A Diary from Dixie,* ed. Ben Ames Williams (Boston, 1905), 310, 354. Mrs. L.D. Whitson, *Gilbert St. Maurice* (Louisville, 1875), 109, 110. Nashville *Tennessean,* Aug. 5, 1979.

Battles and Leaders of the Civil War

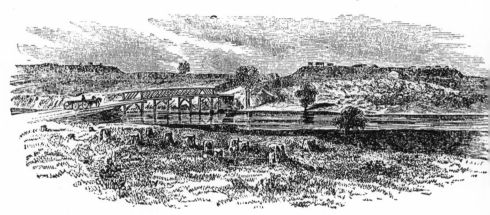

Pictorial Field Book of the Civil War

(*Above*): One of the most dashing figures of Confederate history, General John H. Morgan, after a storybook romance, had been married in Murfreesboro shortly before the battle. (*Below*): A simple bridge over the West Fork of Stones River conveys an idea of the stream's size. Varying from 50 to 100 feet in width and from a few inches to several feet in depth, the principal flood season for the meandering river is December through April. The water was higher than normal at the time of the battle.

In the early morning hours, almost two years later, Campbell would kill General Morgan.[2]

A week after the wedding the cavalry commander, inspired by his success at Hartsville and in celebration of the brigadier's commission (and perhaps to allay fears on the part of some that the marriage would impair his command efficiency), was off on another jaunt that would become famous as his "Christmas Raid." Acting upon the orders of General Bragg, Morgan headed for the Louisville & Nashville Railroad north of Bowling Green, especially the great trestles at Muldraugh's Hill, which were five hundred feet long and eighty feet tall.

With twenty-five hundred cavalrymen he crossed the Cumberland River and swept into Kentucky, passing through Glasgow, fording the Green River, and pounding on north of Munfordville. He laid siege to the Yankee garrison at Elizabethtown, which surrendered on December 27, opening the path to Muldraugh's Hill where the enemy garrison also surrendered. Soon Morgan had burned the trestles, after which he dashed east through Bardstown to Springfield, then turning south and riding triumphantly back into Tennessee. The raid, covering four hundred miles, was a success. Besides burning the trestles, Morgan destroyed four bridges, perhaps $2 million in Federal supplies, captured nearly two thousand Yankees, and tore up twenty miles of Rosecrans' supply line, the Louisville & Nashville Railroad. But Morgan's ride also took his command out of the Battle of Stones River.[3]

Morgan had left on the Christmas Raid, but the celebrating at Murfreesboro continued. The approach of Christmas brought with it a holiday atmosphere for the troops in Bragg's army. Many of the Rebels began the celebration early and did not sober up until much later. Another great battle was shaping up; perhaps it would be more bloody than any yet experienced. Living only for the present, believing their enjoyment was likely to be of short duration, many a Rebel soldier simply could not get enough alcoholic beverage. The story was told of a new recruit who was sent by his veteran comrades to invest a dollar in food and drink. When

[2]Robert Womack, "The River Ran Red with Men's Blood," *Accent,* magazine of the Murfreesboro *Daily News Journal,* Dec. 26, 1976, pp. 3, 4.
[3]Foote, *Civil War,* II, 84.

the young Rebel returned to camp with ten cents' worth of bread and ninety cents' worth of whiskey, he was severely reprimanded by those who thought it was ridiculous to have spent so much on bread.[4]

On Christmas Day the officers of the Twentieth Tennessee Infantry bought a barrel of whiskey for the men, that they might spend a merry Christmas. The result was not too merry. One soldier of the regiment reported: "We had many a drunken fight and knock-down before the day closed." Nobody was seriously hurt. When the men sobered up everybody was friendly and, perhaps, the soldiers had gotten in a little more preparation that would be helpful for combat.[5]

Certainly not all the soldiers appreciated a propensity for drinking. Captain Jim Womack was critical of his colonel, John Savage of the Sixteenth Tennessee Infantry. Womack thought Savage favored his drinking pals when it came to assigning camp duties, making those who did not drink do the work while those who did went out on the town. In fact, Jim thought the old colonel was "no good and not to be trusted."[6]

Some of the Rebels were literally camping in their own back yards and others were not a great distance from home. Officers found it virtually impossible to keep them from making unscheduled trips to visit their families. Usually such visits were short and no real harm was done—except when the wrong officer found out. Families from nearby counties also took advantage of the chance to visit the soldiers, and almost every day there were groups of relatives in and around the camp sites.

Gervis D. Grainger, Sixth Kentucky Infantry, wrote that "We lived like lords. . . . Many friends and parents visited the boys. . . . Numerous boxes were received, filled with the fat of the land from old Kentucky." One of the soldiers in the Twenty-eighth Tennessee Infantry, named Spencer Talley, was from nearby Lebanon,

[4]Womack, "River," 2.

[5]W.J. McMurray, *History of the Twentieth Tennessee Regiment of Volunteer Infantry, C.S.A.* (Nashville, 1904), 224.

[6]J.J. Womack, *The Civil War Diary of Captain J.J. Womack, Company E., Sixteenth Tennessee Volunteers* (McMinnville, Tenn., 1961), 79.

Tennessee. Arriving at home, he was pleasantly surprised to find that his mother had made him and his brother "a goodly supply of heavy jeans and wool socks that reached well near the knees. Many of our neighbors had clothing ready for their sons and we had a full load of good clothing and other things to bring back to the boys in camp." W.E. Yeatman, Second Tennessee Infantry, risking capture by the Union army, slipped west into Nashville to see his father and mother. In addition to the good food and clothing that he received, Yeatman said, "I remember that my mother decorated my felt hat with a lot of her old fashioned black Ostrich plumes, and the boys thought I was a General when I rejoined them." The feathers, however, proved to make a good target and Yeatman quickly realized he could not wear them in battle.[7]

Visits with the home folks did not constitute the only source of desirable goods. Confederate soldiers, seeing something they wanted, often declared open season on it regardless of who the owner was. The Forty-fifth Tennessee Infantry had been organized in the vicinity of Murfreesboro and most of the men were given furloughs to visit their homes. When the men returned to camp, bringing home-cooked pies, cakes, and other delicacies, the desires of some of their neighbors were greatly aroused. The soldiers in the Twentieth Tennessee Infantry soon devised a plan to appropriate some of the good things for themselves. According to one member of the Twentieth, a snowball fight was arranged between the two regiments, and "a charge was ordered and the boys of the Twentieth mixed up with the Forty Fifth in their own camp and the battle waxed warm; and while about three-fourths of the Twentieth were waging war in the heart of the Forty Fifth's camp, the other one-fourth was packing off into our camp whatever they could. When the fight was over the Forty Fifth did not have near as many good things as they did when it opened; they even lost a large per cent of their cooking utensils, and the best of their arms. I fared badly," the chronicler admitted, stating that "in the thickest of the fight two large soldiers caught me and I was thrown into a ditch; one of them held me while the other nearly smothered me

[7]Gervis D. Grainger, *Four Years With the Boys in Gray* (Franklin, Ky., 1902), 13. Womack, "River," 2. Yeatman memoirs, TSLA.

with snow, but I was doing my best to entertain them for I knew that some of our men were confiscating what they had."[8]

Frolicking, of course, was manifested in various ways. Lewis Peach of the Eighth Tennessee Infantry said that a man named Lige Hester applied to the colonel of the regiment to be appointed as a chaplain. The colonel told Hester that he would not appoint him unless a majority of the regiment expressed a preference for him. Soon Hester was conducting a canvass for votes, but Mack Luna, "a rollicking, jolly good soldier," as Peach described him, decided to give Hester some competition and also announced for the office of chaplain.

According to Peach, Luna

swore that he could preach as good a sermon as Lige Hester, and he appointed a time and place where the boys could have a sample of his sermons. He would mount a stump or woodpile, and the service would begin by his lining out a song, "Old Grimes," "Ryestraw," or some other doggerel familiar at that time. He would then announce as his text, "Whar de hen scratch, dar be bug also," or "Gnaw a file and flee to de wilderness, whar de lion roars and de whangdoodle moans." After his "sermon," he would say: "Now, if you don't believe I'm a better preacher than Lige Hester, vote for him, darn you!"

When the vote was taken Mack Luna was elected by a big majority, but the regiment's colonel told Luna to go back to his company and behave, or he would be sent to the guardhouse. Hester was seen no more and, for a while, nothing else was heard about a chaplain.[9]

Furloughs, drinking and frolicking helped to pass some of the dull hours, but much of the soldiers' time was spent in work, picket duty, and drill. Since most of the men supposed the army might remain at Murfreesboro thoughout the winter, they began building all sorts of huts and houses to protect themselves from the wintry blasts. And they could not forget the enemy thirty miles away at Nashville. An advance post was established at La Vergne, about halfway between Nashville and Murfreesboro, and from there a close check was kept on the Yankee army.

[8]McMurray, *Twentieth Tennessee*, 223, 224.
[9]*Confederate Veteran*, XXIII, 520.

Private Sam Watkins of the First Tennessee Infantry was sent to La Vergne as a picket. He had hardly assumed his duty when he discovered a cocked pistol pointing at his face and a Yankee behind it saying, "Drop that gun; you are my prisoner." Not wishing to spend the winter in a Northern prison, Watkins wrote that he made several proposals to his captor which he believed might work to the advantage of both. But the Yankee was in no mood to listen. After giving up on talking himself out of captivity, Watkins decided to try violence. Catching the Federal relaxed, Watkins jumped him. After a considerable hassle, the Yankee got away, leaving Watkins with his former captor's horse, which turned out to be crippled and of no value. There was one consolation — at least he was not a prisoner.[10]

Jim Womack also recounted being out at La Vergne, which he found cold and disagreeable. At dark his regiment halted in the woods; the men had no axes, the ground was covered with snow, and blankets were not plentiful. But the regiment, Womack reported, "chanced to halt near a small lot that, fortunately for us, had been fenced with cedar rails, and never did I see rails burn more freely in my life." The Christmas season was certainly not a pleasant one for Womack. His diary reveals that he was evidently depressed much of the time. The worst came on December 17, when he finally got an opportunity to ride to McMinnville to visit his sister Martha, who had been sick for several days, only to learn that she had died shortly before he arrived.[11]

There was, in fact, a great deal of sorrow — and bitterness — among the Rebels, regardless of the celebrating and the Christmas season. General Bragg, seemingly never one to be influenced by sentiment, chose this season to sentence three men to death before firing squads. While the Confederate commander celebrated the Christmas season with his wife in a palatial residence south of town, James A. Hall was writing his father in Montgomery, Alabama, about one of the executions. "A man in our Brigade was condemned to be shot for desertion," Hall said. "The whole brigade was turned out to witness. It was horrible. Owing to some

[10]Samuel R. Watkins, *"Co. Aytch," Maury Grays, First Tennessee Regiment* (Jackson, Tenn., 1952), 91, 92.
[11]Womack, *Diary*, 73, 74.

blunder, the squad fired three volleys into him before he was killed. It made a deep impression. I think any man who witnessed it would resolve never to die such a death."[12]

Members of the Twenty-fourth Tennessee threatened to leave the army en masse should the death sentence be carried out on one of their members. Frank H. Smith described the event: "The execution was to take place at four o'clock in the afternoon. The grave had been dug, the troops of the brigade and division were all in position on the conventional three sides of a hollow square. The wagon had driven up with the man seated on his coffin; the firing squad had taken position ten paces in front of the doomed victim, who had been blindfolded and placed at the grave, when an officer dashed up, his horse in a foam of sweat, with a reprieve. . . ." The story was that a man who could prove the innocence of the soldier, condemned on a charge of desertion, had ridden all night and well up in the day, nearly killing his horse in an effort to reach Murfreesboro in time. The sentence of the court martial was reversed and the soldier released.[13]

A member of the Sixth Kentucky, Asa Lewis, was not so fortunate. Lewis, an only son whose father's death had occurred only a few months earlier, had asked for permission to visit his mother, whose home had been burned by the Yankees. The permission was refused, but Lewis left Murfreesboro anyway. On the road to Kentucky the young man was captured, brought back to Murfreesboro, and warned not to try again. Lewis left for the second time and was again apprehended. That time he was sentenced to die before a firing squad.

Johnny Green, a fellow soldier who witnesssed the execution, wrote: "The whole division was formed in three sides of a square. Poor Lewis was brought from prison in a wagon riding on his coffin and a detail of twelve men was made to shoot him. . . . All was ready. He asked General Breckinridge for permission to say only a few words to the detail." Calmly he said, "Comrades I know you

[12]Hall to Father, Dec. 22, 1862, in the James A. Hall Papers, Walter K. Hoover Collection, Smyrna, Tenn.

[13]Frank H. Smith, "'The Duck River Rifles,' the Twenty Fourth Tennessee Infantry," in Jill K. Garrett and Marise P. Lightfoot, eds., *The Civil War in Maury County, Tennessee* (Columbia, Tenn., 1966), 86, 87.

are all grieved to do this work but don't be distressed; none of you will know who kills me for you know one of your guns has no ball in it. Each man may think his was the harmless gun. But I beg of you to aim to kill when the command 'fire' is given; it will be merciful to me. Good bye."

In a moment twelve guns flashed and the lifeless body of the Kentucky soldier, who according to one source had "displayed more than ordinary gallantry at Shiloh," lay upon the ground. "All was over and a gloom settled over the command," concluded Johnny Green. The resentment that the execution aroused among Kentucky soldiers was long-lasting. Bragg had increased the number of those within his army who hated him.[14]

Christmas at Murfreesboro thus turned out to be a great spectrum, running the gamut from joy, revelry, and delight to misery, despair, and gloom. The Second Tennessee Infantry's Robert Smith celebrated Christmas with his father and mother, even if he had only a twelve-hour pass and was compelled to journey all the way from Murfreesboro to Columbia and back again. Katherine Cumming had come from Augusta, Georgia, and was very happy to be enjoying Christmas dinner with her soldier husband. One Rebel reported that a good Christmas dinner was prepared, with a goose instead of a turkey, and a supply of liquor had been captured at Hartsville, in which some of the boys found their merry Christmas. James Hall wrote home that "We have tried hard to make a Christmas of it here. We have had foot races, wrestling and base playing. All the officers in our brigade . . . ran a foot race . . . and a rare time we had of it."[15]

Some, like Jim Womack, were in a more serious and somber mood. Said Womack, confiding to his diary, "Another Christmas is past and gone! How differently spent from that of '61! That I passed in Charleston and Fort Sumter, where I was delighted and pleased; this I have spent in my tent by the fire near Murfreesboro, attending to many of the daily duties of the soldier. May the

---

[14]A.D. Kirwan, ed., *Johnny Green of the Orphan Brigade: The Journal of a Confederate Soldier* (Lexington, 1956), 59–61.

[15]Robert Smith, "Confederate Diary," transcribed by Jill K. Garrett (Columbia, Tenn., 1975), 42. *Confederate Veteran*, XIII, 410. Kirwan, *Johnny Green*, 59. Hall to father, Dec. 25, 1862, Hall Papers, Hoover Collection.

coming Christmas in '63 find our now distracted and unhappy country reposing in the lap of . . . peace."[16]

The social highlight of Christmas at Murfreesboro was the gala ball at the town square, given on Christmas Eve by the First Louisiana and Sixth Kentucky regiments. The new courthouse, the same one stormed by Forrest's men the previous summer, was elaborately decorated. A witness wrote,

the decorations of the hall were magnificent, and constructed with much taste and ingenuity. And if "bright lamps" did not shine over "fair women and brave men," at least many candles did — behind each one a bayonet, which brightly reflected the light on the festive scene. . . . There were trees of evergreen with colored lanterns in them in the corners of the hall, and . . . flowers contributed by the Murfreesboro ladies, on the window-sills. There were two "B's" entwined in evergreen, on one side of the hall, representing Bragg and Breckinridge, while just below it hung a magnificent regimental flag, and also, in different parts of the hall, a good many splendid trophies from the different battle fields — Yankee flags, captured by General John Morgan.[17]

The gathering celebrities gave notice that this was to be no ordinary occasion. Only generals and colonels were allowed to go inside with their ladies, but such a ruling failed to stop some of the more enterprising captains. Spencer Talley's colonel, P.D. Cunningham, had no desire to attend the ball and generously offered to lend his uniform to the young captain, who definitely had his eye on the bright lights and merry-making in the courthouse. To Talley, the ball was "a most delightful time. We had the best band of musicians in the army and our table was loaded with the best things that Murfreesboro could afford." Reports of the ball reached the Union army in Nashville where it was said that the arrogant Rebels had spread the United States flag upon the floor, the drunken revelers doubly desecrating "Old Glory" by dancing upon it.[18]

While the Confederate soldiers around Murfreesboro drilled and worked, sometimes drinking and frolicking, often lonely and despondent, experiencing everything from the trauma of execu-

[16]Womack, *Diary,* 76.
[17]Whitson, *Maurice,* 112, 113.
[18]Womack, "River," 5.

tions to the exhilaration of weddings and Christmas, their Union counterparts in Nashville knew much the same emotions and led very similar lives. Many of the Yankees in Tennessee's capital city were doing their best to keep up with the Confederates in the Christmas celebration. Some, in fact, had long been "celebrating" any and every time there was an opportunity — and certainly Nashville provided more opportunity than Murfreesboro.

On the South bank of a large loop in the Cumberland River, Nashville, Tennessee, was the largest and most important city in the Confederacy west of the Appalachians, except for New Orleans. With a population of almost twenty thousand white people and about five thousand blacks, most of whom were slaves, the city's strategic geographic position explains its significance.

When the war began, the docks at Nashville regularly serviced more than one hundred steamboats annually, and railroads led north to Louisville, south to Decatur, Alabama, southeast to Chattanooga and Atlanta, and west to Johnsonville. There were numerous manufacturing establishments, wholesale business houses, printing offices, churches, and educational institutions. With free public schools opened in 1854, the earliest of any southern city, Nashvillians took pride in the title "Athens of the South." At the start of the war the city had five public high schools, numerous private grammar schools, and several institutions of higher learning.[19]

By December 1862, after nine full months of Yankee occupation, Nashville was changed. Its business activity was drastically curtailed and, as it was one of the biggest Union army bases in the west, soldiers outnumbered citizens by more than two-to-one. All the problems that accompany any army were present. There were so many prostitutes that an Ohio soldier declared the army's very existence was threatened. Interestingly, the Nashville census of 1860, unlike any before or since in the city, or apparently any other city, listed the number of women who were willing to call themselves prostitutes. The total was 207, a sizable number for a

[19]Edwin Huddleston, "Nashville: Its Personality and Progress," pamphlet in Nagy Collection on Nashville Public Schools, TSLA. MacMillan S. Watson, "Nashville During the Civil War" (M.A. thesis, Vanderbilt Univ., 1926), 2, 7. Henry McRaven, *Nashville: Athens of the South* (Chapel Hill, N.C., 1949), 93. John H. DeBerry, "Confederate Tennessee" (Ph.D. diss., Univ. of Kentucky, 1967), 212, 236.

city no larger than Nashville, with the largest brothels located along North Front Street. Considering Nashville's religious emphasis, this traffic must have been particularly distasteful to some of the population. But the number in 1860 was meager compared to the influx of "women of pleasure" after the enemy occupation of the city. The authorities finally took a provost guard, rounded up fifteen hundred of the women, and moved them by rail, under guard all the way to Louisville, with clear orders not to come any farther south.[20]

What the city of Louisville thought of this move was apparently not of major concern to the army authorities in Nashville. Most of the prostitutes may have been removed, but there seemed to be an endless supply of liquor, which sometimes seemed equally troublesome. The Nashville *Dispatch* frequently carried accounts of the problems caused by too much alcohol. Under the heading "Robberies and Outrages Perpetrated by Soldiers," the December 2, 1862, edition of the *Dispatch* printed the following account: "From the depot to Whiteside Street, on Market, the people were kept in a constant state of alarm all night by the breaking of fences, firing of pistols, and the most hideous noises. The common center and cause . . . is a whiskey shop on College Street, where the poison is dealt out to soldiers at all hours of the day and night. . . . We are also informed that there are other houses in the neighborhood where stolen property is sold and whiskey bought daily and almost hourly."

On Sunday, December 7, the *Dispatch* reported: "Yesterday was especially marked for the unusually large number of drunken men — mostly soldiers — seen in the principal thoroughfares of the city. All the liquor saloons were closed several months ago by order of the provost marshal, but it is painfully evident that there is but little difficulty of late in getting any quantity and at any time parties may desire. The evidence may be seen almost every hour . . . in boisterous men . . . , reeling through the streets."

Reports of the problem in Nashville even made their way into the Washington papers. On December 19, the Washington *Evening*

---

[20]Catton, *Hallowed Ground,* 251. David Kaser, "Nashville's Women of Pleasure in 1860," *Tennessee Historical Quarterly,* Dec. 1964, pp. 379-81.

Star, under the heading "The War in Tennessee," proclaimed that "General Rosecrans has dismissed a large number of officers for drunkenness and disobedience of orders."

Besides prostitutes and liquor, Nashville was also infested with brigands and "wandering guerrillas," as the *Dispatch* described them. The paper carried many accounts of violence perpetrated upon both citizens and soldiers. In addition, poor people, without adequate clothing and shelter, suffered increasingly from the worsening cold weather. Many people, of course, were out of work. In fact, even the well-to-do now found life very hard at times. One day in December, when fuel was short and snow was on the ground, Rachel Carter Craighead, a normally generous woman then living in her parents' fine house at the corner of Sixth and Union, wrote in her diary: "Mrs. Walker sent over to get a scuttle of coal. We need it ourselves."[21]

The majority of Nashville's civilian population seethed under the military governorship of Andrew Johnson. Beginning his rule by demanding that all municipal officers take a special oath of allegiance to the United States, the governor had soon locked up a large number of the most prominent people of Nashville in the state penitentiary because they refused to comply. Union men were appointed to take their places. More and more arrests had followed. Six of the clergymen of the city were first thrown into prison and later expelled from Nashville. The plants of the daily newspapers and of the Methodist and Baptist publishing houses were confiscated. By the fall of 1862 Truesdail's secret police were operating in a high-handed manner and a 9:00 P.M. curfew was being enforced.[22]

The oppressive military presence was especially and literally brought home to Rachel Carter Craighead when she came home from a neighbor's house to find Yankee soldiers emptying every drawer and chest in the house. They had heard, they said, that she had a Confederate flag and were searching for it. Even worse, she wrote, "I was cleaning . . . when Tom [her husband] came up

[21]Davis, "Box Seat," April 1979, 11.

[22]Horn, "Nashville," 12. Mrs. Roy C. Avery, "The Second Presbyterian Church of Nashville Duing the Civil War," *Tennessee Historical Quarterly*, Dec. 1952, pp. 356, 368-70..

and said Pa and Mr. Herriford were arrested and sent to the penitentiary." Rachel's father had been arrested in his bank and the vaults robbed. "The Yankees have taken possession of the keys of the bank and everything in the safe," she said, "because Pa would not take the oath of allegiance to the Union." Her father was eventually paroled, but it was not long before he was arrested again. The arrest and parole syndrome continued for a long time, as he refused to take the oath of allegiance.[23]

Nashville's citizens longed for the appearance of the Confederate army that they hoped would save them from the hated Federals. On November 6 and 7, Morgan and Forrest, supported by some of Breckinridge's infantry from Murfreesboro, had made a demonstration in force against the defenses of Nashville. It created great excitement in the city — among the citizens as well as the Union troops. Word spread that the Confederates would be in Nashville in forty-eight hours. The Rebel fire brought on a furious bombardment from the batteries in forts Negley and Casino. Actually the Rebel movement was of no particular military importance and the result of the fighting was of no consequence, but it was the only action even resembling an attempt to storm Nashville during the Union occupation. Nashville's citizens, tremendously excited for the moment, soon realized that their hopes for relief were in vain.[24]

Life under the occupying army continued, symbolized by the cannons on the battlements encircling the impressive acropolis, crowned by the city's Greek temple capitol. Rough and filthy streets were barricaded with cotton and earthen parapets. The tramp of enemy soldiers and the rumble of cannon wheels echoed in the cold stone roads. Markets were bare and money scarce. Most of the able-bodied male population was gone to war. And there had been mourning in many of the families.

But in the midst of evil and misery the Nashville Theater was thriving. Literally every day the *Dispatch* reported that the theater was crowded and, prominently printing the play titles for the coming evening, the paper urged those who planned to attend to go early or purchase their tickets in advance. Always, regardless

[23]Davis, "Box Seat," April 1979, 8; March 1979, 32.
[24]Horn, "Nashville," 14, 15.

even of bad weather, the theater-goers were "numerous and enthusiastic," the building was "still crowded and everybody pleased," there was a "full house and happy people," or some such jubilant expression indicating that, as always in a wartime environment, some people were managing to have a good time.[25]

Undoubtedly most of the soldiers, however, would have preferred to be elsewhere. Some of them were disappointed when they first saw the city. Mead Holmes, Jr., was attracted to the capitol building, "the finest of the kind in the South," he said, but he thought the rest of Nashville was not impressive. "The streets were very narrow, but seemed well kept. The buildings are high, some seven stories, and well finished; yet, as a whole," he concluded, "I did not like the appearance of the city." Another Yankee agreed, as did many in his regiment. "Most . . . expressed themselves surprised and disappointed in regard to Nashville. It is not so large or so fine a city as we anticipated," he wrote. "Its buildings are old, dirty and dilapidated. The streets are narrow, rough and decidedly filthy. The State House is a large, extravagant institution."[26]

J.T. Gibson said his experience as a provost guard afforded "an opportunity of seeing the worst part of city life. . . . The guards at the [L&N] station were in demand every night to settle brawls in disreputable places in that section of the city." And in the Seventy-third Illinois, a unit known as "the Preacher Regiment" (a group strictly set apart from the rest because no card playing was tolerated among its members), W.H. Newlin wrote that the men were "much disappointed" in the appearance of Nashville. "Nothing but the State House seemed to meet the expectations. . . . It is visible from distant prominent points, and also affords a fine view of the city of Nashville and the surrounding country." Also among those fascinated by the capitol building was Henry A. Castle, who said that "the beautiful white marble capital, in so lofty an eminence, was a sight ever to be remembered."[27]

[25]Nashville *Dispatch*, Dec. 2–23, 1862.

[26]Holmes, *Soldier*, 119, 120. L.G. Bennett and William M. Haigh, *History of the Thirty-Sixth Regiment Illinois Volunteers, During the War of the Rebellion* (Aurora, Ill., 1876), 305.

[27]J.T. Gibson, *History of the Seventy-Eighth Pennsylvania Infantry* (Pittsburgh, 1905), 46, 47. W.H. Newlin, *A History of the Seventy-Third Regiment of Illinois Infantry Volunteers* (n.p., 1890), 111, 116.

Perhaps the Northern soldiers were more impressed by the countryside than by the city. An Iowa boy wrote to his sister that the soil in Tennessee was not deep, but it would raise good corn or wheat and would do even better with cotton. An Indiana soldier remarked that "a more beautiful country than middle Tennessee would be hard to find anywhere on the map of the U.S."[28]

As Christmas approached, the Federal army at Nashville, of course, had less chance for contact with family and friends than did the Confederates at Murfreesboro. Perhaps for that reason the writings of Union soldiers seem more solemn and dreary. John Chilcote, a member of the Ninetieth Ohio Infantry, recorded in his diary, "This is Christmas, and what a contrast between *our* Christmas and those who are at home in good, comfortable houses, with plenty to eat and good beds to sleep in, and good nurses when sick. . . . The measles, mumps, chicken pox, small pox and about everything else has broken loose and taken hold of the boys. . . ." One phrase was all that Eben Hannaford, a young Ohioan who would be severely wounded, shot through the base of the neck on the first day at Stones River and nearly dying, devoted to Christmas Day: "a warm and listless Christmas," he wrote.[29]

For some soldiers Christmas meant work as usual. An Indiana soldier wrote that "Christmas was a beautiful day; and we put it in with a Foraging expedition and had some sharp skirmishing." An Ohio soldier said, "Christmas day was no holiday for us. After breakfast we received orders to march with another foraging expedition at 8 o'clock. We took a road leading south from the Nolensville pike . . . and filled our wagons by 3 o'clock. Near the place . . . was a house where Christmas dinner had been prepared for some of our enemies, and some of our men either confiscated it or paid for it with counterfeit Confederate Script."[30]

Convinced that he had just completed a foolish march, David Lathrop of the Fifty-ninth Illinois Infantry entered in his diary on

[28]Catton, *Hallowed Ground*, 218.

[29]H.O. Harden, *Ninetieth Ohio Infantry* (Stoutsville, Ohio, 1902), 38. E. Hannaford, *The Story of a Regiment: A History of the Campaigns and Associations in the Field of the Sixth Regiment Ohio Volunteer Infantry* (Cincinnati, 1868), 291. Also see Eben Hannaford, "It Seemed Hard To Die of Suffocation," *Civil War Times Illustrated* (June 1967).

[30]Hartpence, *Fifty-first Indiana*, 93. Alexis Cope, *Fifteenth Ohio Infantry* (Columbus, 1916), 228.

Christmas Day: "Here we are in camp again. After loading our traps in the wagons we lay around promiscuously until yesterday noon, when we marched about five miles toward Nolensville, right about faced, and marched back again to the very spot we started from. 'Strategy, my boy!' "[31]

Other Union soldiers were in a reflective mood. John Beatty wrote, "At an expense of one dollar and seventy-five cents, I procured a small turkey and had a Christmas dinner; but it lacked the collaterals, and was a failure. For twenty months now I have been a sojourner in camps, a dweller in tents, going hither and yon, at all hours of the day and night, in all sorts of weather, sleeping for weeks at the stretch without shelter, and yet I have been strong and healthy. How very thankful I should feel on this Christmas night!"[32]

"Last night was Christmas Eve," recorded Henry Freeman. "It brought to my mind a thousand recollections of the past. The contrast is great. I sat up late in the evening at the fire, after attending to drawing rations, for we were under marching orders for this morning at five o'clock. A grand movement seems to be at hand. About eleven o'clock at night I heard heavy firing in the front. Where will the next Christmas Eve find me?"[33]

The Union army knew that a battle was at hand. All the signs were present, even if orders to move out on Christmas morning had been postponed until the day after Christmas. Hilarity there was, to be sure, but it seemed a bit subdued. A more solemn and somber feeling was pervading the army as the time for battle drew near.

[31]David Lathrop, *The History of the Fifty-Ninth Regiment Illinois Volunteers* (Indianapolis, 1865), 186.

[32]John Beatty, *Memoirs of a Volunteer, 1861–1863* (New York, 1946), 150.

[33]Henry V. Freeman, "Some Battle Recollections of Stone's River," *MOLLUS, Illinois Commandery* (1895), 229.

5

Rosecrans Moves South

The very epitome of the Union army's attitude to get on with the bloody business at hand was its commander, Major General William S. Rosecrans — although Washington would not have so thought. Like General Buell, "Old Rosy" had not shown what the national administration considered a proper appreciation of an East Tennessee campaign. Rosecrans was disturbed by the immense supply problems associated with moving an army into that part of the state. Besides, the enemy's main army was only thirty miles away at Murfreesboro. There was the proper point of attack — there, astride the railroad where the Union army, if victorious, could implement a campaign carrying into Chattanooga and Atlanta — right into the heart of the deep South.[1]

But President Lincoln, Stanton, Halleck, and others in the capital felt that Rosecrans was wasting time even in moving out against Bragg and the Army of Tennessee. After frequently urging action via telegraphic messages, General-in-Chief Halleck suddenly lost patience and told "Old Rosy" in early December that if he remained one more week in Nashville, "I cannot prevent your removal." Halleck said that already he had twice been asked to designate a successor for the Nashville commander. Rosecrans was not moved, but his temper flared. "I need no other stimulus to make me do my duty," he curtly informed Halleck, "than the

[1]Stephen E. Ambrose, *Halleck: Lincoln's Chief of Staff* (Baton Rouge, 1962), 105–6. Lamers, *Rosecrans*, 181–201.

knowledge of what it is. To threats of removal or the like I must be permitted to say that I am insensible."[2]

By mid-December Halleck had cooled off and wrote Rosecrans that he had never intended to threaten him but only desired to convey Lincoln's "great anxiety" about the Middle Tennessee stalemate. Halleck reminded Rosecrans that the British parliament would be convening in January and its pro-Southern members might find in the current situation strong arguments for intervention in the American conflict — a policy which France was known to be urging upon the English. Rosecrans tried to sound encouraging to his superior, but still he waited in Nashville rather than moving out against the enemy.[3]

Several matters were of concern. Due to abnormally dry weather, the Cumberland River, which encloses Nashville on the west, north, and east, had been too shallow to serve as a dependable supply line. The Louisville & Nashville Railroad needed to be repaired in places and some of its garrisons strengthened. Also, Rosecrans hoped to lull Bragg into a false sense of security, that all the Federals intended was to go into winter quarters.

A few days before Christmas the situation was turning in Rosecrans' favor. The general was pleased to see the Cumberland River rising. It was not yet high enough, however, to defy the prayer of the Confederate preacher in Shelbyville who had sanctimoniously intoned, "O Lord, let the rain descend to fructify the earth and to swell the rivers; but O Lord, do not raise the Cumberland sufficient to bring upon us those damn Yankee gunboats!"[4] But with five weeks' store of rations now accumulated at Nashville, the Cumberland had risen enough to provide the means of rapidly and safely augmenting this supply, even if the railroad were broken again by the Rebel cavalry.[5]

Furthermore, Rosecrans had learned that an entire division had been detached from Bragg's army and, equally good, Morgan's cavalry had been dispatched into Kentucky and Forrest's cavalry into West Tennessee. The raiders might do considerable

[2]*OR*, XX, pt. 2, 117, 118.
[3]Lamers, *Rosecrans*, 195, 196.
[4]*Ibid.*, 194.
[5]Hannaford, *Sixth Ohio*, 390.

harm on these forays (and indeed they did) but they would not be in range to render assistance to Bragg. Rosecrans' own army was in excellent condition. Now, he determined, was the time to strike! Becoming animated at a conference with his corps commanders, the effervescent Rosecrans finally sprang to his feet, slammed his mug of toddy down on the table, and, with face glowing, spoke rapidly and with intense feeling: "We move tomorrow, Gentlemen! Press them hard! Drive them out of their nests! Make them fight or run! *Fight them! Fight them!* Fight, I say!"[6]

Already the Union commander had been carrying on a heated verbal clash with his Confederate counterpart. The trouble stemmed from an alleged violation of a flag of truce. According to Union reports, a party of rebels bearing a flag of truce was waiting to receive an answer from the headquarters of Major General Horatio P. Van Cleve when a body of Confederate cavalry suddenly dashed upon a group of unsuspecting Federal cavalry, killing and capturing some of them. An "outrage of the grossest character," Rosecrans angrily wrote to Bragg, "has been perpetrated by your troops, in the presence of your own flag. . . . Such barbarous conduct, hardly paralleled by savages," Rosecrans continued, required that the Confederate commander must make some kind of reparation.

Bragg's response, couched in similar tone to Rosecrans' protest, gave a quite different version of what had occurred. According to Bragg, the problem developed solely because of "the reprehensible and criminal conduct of some of your subordinates." The bearer of the flag of truce had been arrested, kept for twenty-four hours, and, when finally permitted to leave, Bragg said, had been menaced and insulted by soldiers with drawn weapons. "To claim that a truce existed while my flag was forcibly detained by you is preposterous," Bragg concluded, stating that he was the one "entitled to apology and reparation." Perhaps the sharp exchange between the two army commanders on the eve of battle was fitting, symbolically, as their forces girded themselves for the struggle.[7]

Rosecrans' army, as it moved out toward Murfreesboro on December 26, was divided into three corps, led by Major Generals

[6]Lamers, *Rosecrans*, 201.
[7]*OR*, XX, 82–85.

Alexander McDowell McCook, Thomas Leonidas Crittenden, and George Henry Thomas. A thirty-one-year-old graduate of the United States Military Academy, ranking thirtieth in a class of forty-seven, McCook had served on the frontier, in Indian fighting, and as a tactical instructor at West Point. Being something of a wag, he irritated many people. "General McCook prides himself on being General McCook," observed one Union soldier at Nashville. A reporter described him as "an overgrown schoolboy," and after his command was near demoralization and ruin at the battle of Perryville, some Federals felt that the general had gotten just what he deserved.[8]

Crittenden was the son of the distinguished Kentucky senator who had tried so hard to work out a compromise between North and South in the critical weeks before Fort Sumter. Born in 1819 in Russellville, Kentucky, he was the younger brother of Confederate General George B. Crittenden. A lawyer in Kentucky, he fought in the Mexican war, serving part of the time as an aide to General Zachary Taylor. Afterward consul to Liverpool and a businessman, Crittenden commanded a division, as did McCook, in General Buell's army on the second day of the Battle of Shiloh. According to one observer, he had a "thin, staring face, and hair hanging to his coat collar — a very wild-appearing major-general, but quite a kindly man in conversation."[9]

Crittenden would be breveted for gallantry at Stones River, only to see his command routed in September at Chickamauga, after which Rosecrans would prefer charges against him, also against McCook and Brigadier General James S. Negley, in an effort to transfer some of the responsibility for that disaster to other shoulders. After an exhaustive investigation at Nashville, all three were formally exonerated.[10]

Undoubtedly, General George H. Thomas, born in Virginia and graduated from West Point in 1840, twelfth in a class of forty-two, was the best corps commander in Rosecrans' army. As a defensive fighter he was probably unsurpassed in either army and,

[8]Boatner, *CWD*, 526. Lathrop, *Fifty-Ninth Illinois*, 192. Foote, *Civil War*, I, 728.
[9]Boatner, *CWD*, 208.
[10]Ezra Warner Jr., *Generals in Blue: Lives of the Union Commanders* (Baton Rouge, 1964), 100.

while some evaluated him as a bit slow, others have felt his conduct of the Battle of Nashville indicated an equal capacity for offensive warfare. His later exploits would earn him such sobriquets as "the Rock of Chickamauga" and "the Sledge of Nashville." With experience in the Second Seminole War, garrison and frontier duty, the Mexican war, and as an artillery and cavalry instructor at the Point, Thomas had been an army man all his adult life. A severe wound in the face from an arrow only accentuated the fact. When Buell had retreated to Louisville, Thomas was directed by Washington to supersede him in command, but he declined saying that Buell had already issued orders for the offensive. Thomas did feel hurt when Buell's job was finally given to Rosecrans.[11]

Thomas' command was to constitute the center of the Union army, with Crittenden and McCook on the left and right wings, respectively. The army's overall strength in the Nashville area was about eighty thousand, but nothing like that many soldiers marched to Murfreesboro. Each of the three commands was well below its normal strength because of guard detachments to protect Nashville and other points along the lines of supply and communication. With no way of knowing where Forrest and Morgan or some other raider might eventually strike, the Federals felt such detachments were absolutely necessary.

The Confederate cavalry was, in fact, so superior to the Federal at this time that Rosecrans had been able to get very little accurate information about the exact location and extent of Bragg's army. The country toward Murfreesboro invited delaying action by small forces. Winding macadamized turnpikes were intersected by transverse ridges. Cleared patches of ground alternated with woodland and dense cedar brakes, while thickets of evergreen or brush formed ideal nests for enemy skirmishers. Uncertain where the Confederates might decide to make a stand, Rosecrans speculated that Stewart's Creek, a stream several miles west of Murfreesboro with steep banks that offered natural defensive advantages, might be the site. Regardless of where the confrontation came, he decided to march his columns along different roads in such a manner that they could support one another if necessary.

[11]Warner, *Generals in Blue*, 500, 501. Boatner, *CWD*, 836. Catton, *Hallowed Ground*, 235. Lamers, *Rosecrans*, 182.

Crittenden, on the left, moved out the Nashville–Murfreesboro turnpike through La Vergne, with a force of about 14,500 men. McCook's corps of about 16,000, the largest of the three, was farther to the west, marching through Nolensville and Triune. Thomas's 13,500 started out the Franklin road, tramping almost due south until they reached Brentwood, then swinging eastward across McCook's rear to eventually come into position as the center of the Federal force. Altogether, General Rosecrans would be marching into battle with about 44,000 troops, enjoying an advantage of some 7,000 over the Rebels.[12]

The weather was miserable. An Illinois soldier said that the march "began in a drenching rain." It created, he thought, "the worst mud I ever walked in," and that night he "went to bed without much supper at midnight, spreading my poncho in the mud." The next day, he wrote, was no better, "a dark, stormy day, drizzling rain."[13] An Indiana soldier reported that "it began to rain and continued the balance of the day. The hitherto dusty pike was converted into a sloppy sea of mud. . . . A cold rain fell the greater part of the night, and, as we were not permitted to have fires, we were very uncomfortable." Still another Federal, commenting on the terrible weather, also said that between Nashville and Murfreesboro "is a perfect wilderness waste." Many houses were burned, with only chimneys left to mark the spot, and the little town of La Vergne, he continued, seemed to have suffered more than any other place along the march.[14]

As the Union army pressed its advance, there was heavy skirmishing and sometimes small-scale fighting that terrorized unfortunate civilians who found themselves in the path of destruction. Near Espey's Chapel, one mile northeast of the village of Smyrna, lived Dr. Nimrod W. Thompson. The story was later told that when a shell crashed through his house, the doctor broke for the woods, urging his wife to follow. "Hold on," she yelled, "let me get

[12]Livermore, *Numbers and Losses*, 97. Union soldiers present for duty are listed at 44,800, with effectives estimated at 41,400; Confederates present for duty are given as 37,712, with effectives estimated at 34,732.

[13]Freeman, "Battle," 230.

[14]John J. Hight and Gilbert R. Stormont, *Fifty-Eighth Indiana Infantry* (Princeton, Ind., 1895), 110. William Ogburn to aunt, Jan. 22, 1863, Ogburn letters in possession of Susan Knight, Nashville.

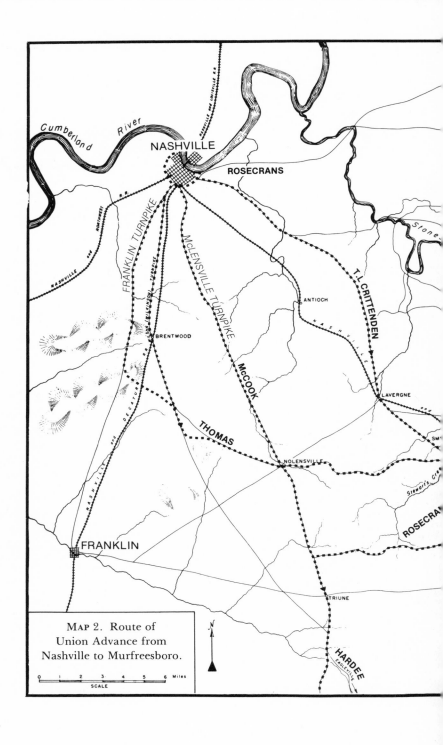

MAP 2. Route of
Union Advance from
Nashville to Murfreesboro.

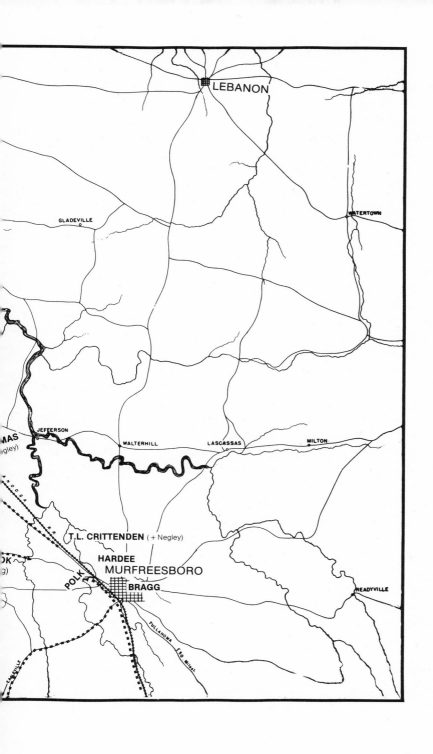

the baby!" "Forget the baby!" cried the panic-stricken doctor as he continued his frantic flight to escape danger. Presumably, in the horror of the moment, Dr. Thompson must have thought that they could get another baby.[15]

Most disturbing to Rosecrans' advance, probably, was the Rebel cavalry. Forrest and Morgan were gone, but Bragg still had about four thousand troopers under the leadership of twenty-six-year-old Joseph "Fighting Joe" Wheeler, recently appointed commander of all the cavalry in the Army of Tennessee. It was an assignment not especially appreciated by the older and widely acclaimed non–West Pointers, Forrest and Morgan. Wheeler had first screened the concentration of the Confederate infantry in his rear and held up the advance of the Yankees on his front. Then on the night of December 29 he struck.

Riding north, afterward swinging west and south, he completed a two-day ride around Rosecrans' whole army. The results were the capture of about a thousand Federals, the burning of parts or all of four wagon trains (McCook was hardest hit, a Yankee reporting that the turnpike "as far as the eye could see, was filled with burning wagons"), the acquisition of enough weapons to arm a brigade, and remounts for his men who needed fresh horses.[16] Not least among Wheeler's accomplishments was the adverse psychological effect that the trail of devastation left upon the Union commander. Although such can not be measured, Rosecrans' confidence, however bold a face he may have presented, could not have been strengthened by the Rebel troopers' circling his entire army.

While Wheeler rode, the Confederate infantry, about thirty-seven thousand strong, was concentrating and awaiting the approach of the Yankees at Murfreesboro, spread out along the banks of Stones River. Bragg had his army divided into two corps. The right, or northern wing, was led by Lieutenant General William J. Hardee. "Old Reliable," as he became known in Confederate legend, was already famous as the author of *Rifle and Light*

[15]Walter K. Hoover, *A History of the Town of Smyrna, Tennessee* (Nashville, 1968), 395.

[16]John P. Dyer, *From Shiloh to San Juan: The Life of "Fighting Joe" Wheeler* (Baton Rouge, 1961), 65–68. Edwin C. Bearss, "Cavalry Operations in the Battle of Stones River," *Tennessee Historical Quarterly,* June 1960, is an excellent account. Foote, *Civil War,* II, 85.

Infantry Tactics, commonly referred to simply as Hardee's *Tactics*, a manual of arms by which many of his soldiers had drilled. A West Point graduate, class of 1838, in which he ranked twenty-sixth out of forty-five cadets, Hardee had distinguished himself in the Mexican war, continued in the old army, and held the rank of lieutenant colonel when the Civil War began. He had led his corps well at Shiloh and was disgusted with Bragg after the Perryville battle. "If you choose to rip up the Kentucky campaign," he had told Polk, "you can tear Bragg into tatters."[17]

It was Polk — Bishop General Leonidas Polk — like Hardee recently promoted to lieutenant general, who commanded the southern or left wing of the Rebel army. The fifty-six-year-old Polk was a graduate of West Point, eighth in a class of thirty-eight, who resigned his army commission to study theology. He had been a missionary bishop to the southwest, the Episcopal bishop of Louisiana, and founder of the University of the South at Sewanee, Tennessee, before casting his lot with the Confederacy. Like Hardee, he led a corps at Shiloh and, also like "Old Reliable," harbored doubts about Bragg. Summoned to Richmond after the Kentucky campaign, Polk went armed with documents that he believed would exonerate him and, to say the least, present questions about Bragg's leadership. But Davis persuaded him to lay them aside, return to the army, and perform his duty, duty presumably made more palatable when the president handed him his promotion to lieutenant general.[18]

Now, as the battle of Murfreesboro approached, there were more reasons to question Bragg's leadership. A critic could well start with the general's decision to hold the position at Murfreesboro. The advantages usually cited are not impressive when carefully appraised. The normally rich Stones River valley had already been depleted of much food and cattle by Buell's army and the Yankee garrison at Nashville. Although the Confederates at Murfreesboro were astride the Nashville & Chattanooga Railroad, leading to the Rebel supply base at Chattanooga, a Federal advance necessitated a supply line, whether by pike or rail, of only

---

[17]McDonough, *Shiloh*, 70. Foote, *Civil War*, I, 774. Boatner, *CWD*, 374.
[18]Boatner, *CWD*, 657. McDonough, *Shiloh*, 70. Foote, *Civil War*, I, 774.

thirty miles from their Nashville base, while the Confederate rail link with Chattanooga was one hundred miles long, and there was no direct pike for wagon transportation.

But worst of all, Murfreesboro could be easily flanked. The only approach route readily blocked was the Nashville & Chattanooga Railroad. The Lebanon Pike, which led due north from Murfreesboro, was a very good possible route for a Federal flanking attack — and there was still another road into the town northeast of the pike to Lebanon. The west and south sides of Murfreesboro were also vulnerable, via the pike from Nashville through Triune. From Triune an army might march upon Murfreesboro by the road from Franklin, or swing farther to the southeast and then approach along the Salem road.

The Rebel force, spread over a forty-mile-wide front when the Federal advance began, was too thin, a dispersal made to protect all road approaches to Murfreesboro. Hardee's corps, except for one brigade at Triune, was at Eagleville on the Nashville–Triune–Shelbyville Road. Polk's corps at Murfreesboro was nearly twenty-five miles away, and Brigadier General John McCown's lone division was twelve miles east of Murfreesboro at Readyville, on the road to McMinnville. Thus, while attempting to cover the roads into Murfreesboro, part of the army was vulnerable to being cut off and defeated in detail.

If Rosecrans had been uncertain about Bragg's plans, the Rebel commander had experienced a worse quandary in evaluating the intentions of the Union general. Bragg had not expected the Federals to advance in the first place. Seemingly overconfident and lacking any well-organized group of scouts, he had relied for intelligence upon such dubious sources as reports from citizens, newspapers, and rumors. His intelligence reports were confusing and misleading. When the Yankees began moving out of Nashville the day after Christmas, Bragg groped for information, not yet sure this was anything but a demonstration in force, rather than a major campaign. As the cold drizzle soaked the ground in the dawn hours of December 27, the general, still uncertain of Rosecrans' aim, realized his army was in a perilous position and began drawing it together.

For about three days, Bragg did not know where Rosecrans'

army was or from which direction the Federals would approach. His cavalry was too badly scattered to provide the necessary information. When at last he succeeded in concentrating his army, Bragg's position west of Murfreesboro left much to be desired. "The field of battle," wrote Hardee in his frank report, "offered no peculiar advantages for defense. . . . The country on every side was entirely open and accessible to the enemy." Stanley Horn has suggested that the terrain was, in fact, "peculiarly unsuited to fighting." The ground was rough and uneven, interspersed with outcroppings of limestone ledges broken by deep crevices. The country was wooded to a great extent, interspersed by farm lands, especially corn and cotton fields with rail fences surrounding them. The forests were mostly composed of the Tennessee red cedar, growing in dense brakes or "glades," with limbs to the ground. The general area provided exceptionally difficult obstacles in the way of cavalry maneuvers or artillery fire.

Probably worst of all, potentially, was the split in half of Bragg's line by Stones River, which flowed north and then slightly northeast just west of Murfreesboro. Because of a bend in the river northwest of the town, the Nashville Pike and the Nashville & Chattanooga Railroad ran parallel to the river for some distance before crossing the river into Murfreesboro. In order to block the Nashville Pike, Bragg had to place a part of his army on each side of the river, an awkward position with the river rising.[19]

Regardless of the misgivings concerning Bragg's leadership that troubled Hardee and Polk, he was their commander. And by some strange quirk of fate, both Bragg and Rosecrans, in their rather blind groping, decided upon the same strategy. Rosecrans determined to send Crittenden's corps across Stones River, presumably slashing in on Bragg's right flank, driving it out of the action, opening the road into Murfreesboro, and taking the Rebel left in reverse. Bragg planned to leave Major General John C. Breckinridge's division on his right, to hold the high ground on the east bank of Stones River, while the rest of Hardee's corps massed on the left of his line, west of the river, and smashed into the Yankee's right wing.

[19]Connelly, *Autumn*, 23, 24, 42, 45-49. Horn, *Army*, 197, 198. McWhiney, *Bragg*, 346, 347.

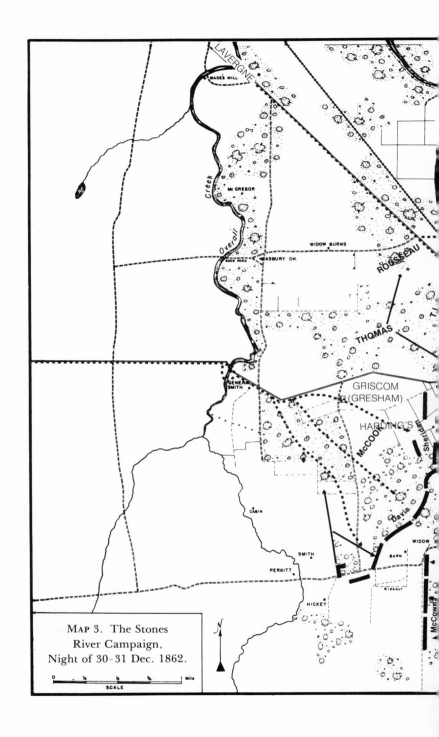

MAP 3. The Stones
River Campaign,
Night of 30–31 Dec. 1862.

SCALE

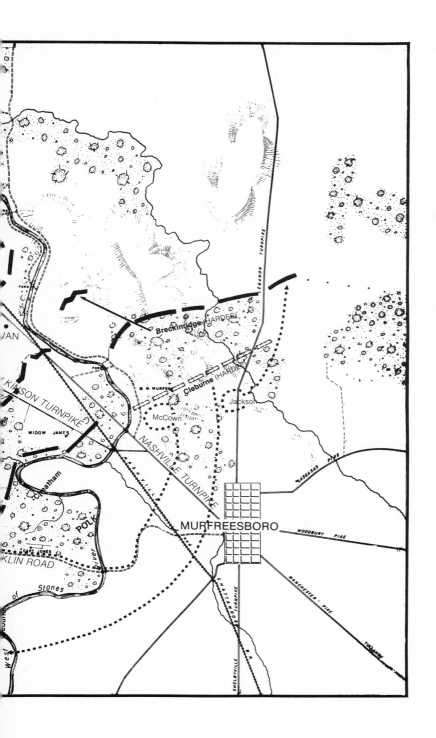

Rosecrans decided he would deceive Bragg, making him think the Federal right was longer and stronger than was actually the case, to insure that Bragg would not strengthen the northern end of his line. Thus he ordered that campfires be built for hundreds of yards beyond McCook's right. The strategy worked, but the result was not what Rosecrans had intended. Bragg believed and simply ordered his attacking columns to sweep more widely to the west; consequently, when they struck, they came in at a more advantageous angle, extending far beyond McCook's flank. Both commanders planned their attack for the morning of December 31.[20]

The thirtieth of December was a dreary day. "Rain had fallen almost constantly," reported A.M. Crary of the Seventy-fifth Illinois Infantry, "and the soldiers were saturated with water. Toward night the wind swept coldly from the north, and . . . no bivouac fires were allowed. . . ." A soldier in the Ninetieth Ohio Infantry said that some of the men, "having lost their blankets and knapsacks, suffered terribly from the cold."[21]

Just as the men were preparing to get what sleep they could, one of the strange events of the war took place. In the stillness of the winter night, the military bands of both armies began to play their favorite tunes, and the music became something of a contest. "Yankee Doodle" was answered by "Dixie," and "The Bonnie Blue Flag" brought out a resounding version of "Hail Columbia." Ultimately, a Federal band struck up the familiar "Home Sweet Home," and a member of the Nineteenth Tennessee Infantry wrote: "Immediately a Confederate band caught up the strain, then one after another until all the bands of each army were playing 'Home Sweet Home.' And after our bands had ceased playing, we could hear the sweet refrain as it died away on the cool frosty air on the Federal side." It was a strange prelude to one of the bloodiest battles of the war.[22]

A Federal soldier remembered that Brigadier General Joshua W. Sill came in from the cold to see his aide, who had been severely wounded during the day's skirmishing. The Yankee's attention

[20]*OR*, 184, 663, 664, 255.
[21]A.M. Crary, *Seventy-Fifth Illinois Infantry* (Herrington, Kan., 1915), 63. Harden, *Ninetieth Ohio*, 39.
[22]Womack, "River," 7.

was fixed upon the general. "Just before leaving," he said, General Sill "stood for a while leaning on his sword, wrapt in deep thought, and I imagined a shade of sadness on his fine face. The next morning, when he was killed almost instantly at the opening of the battle, I wondered whether some sad presentment of his fate was not passing through his mind as he stood the evening before, gazing silently upon his wounded aide."[23]

While several officers sat perched on fences, warming themselves at nearby fires, Colonel Julius P. Garesché, the assistant adjutant general (chief of staff) to Rosecrans, kept apart from the rest. His cold hands partially covered by a greatcoat, the twenty-one-year-veteran of the regular army who had refused a commission as a major general after Fort Sumter, saying he would earn his stars on the battlefield, was reading Thomas a Kempis' *Imitation of Christ*. This battle was to be his baptism of fire. The half-mystic, half-saint, whom many loved but few if any understood, remembered that years ago an old woman in Washington had predicted that he would be killed in his first battle. Garesché showed no evidence of fear, but he did not expect to survive the next day's engagement.

Over in the Rebel army, Private Hardaman Tucker was no doubt thinking much of the time about his fiancée, "Duck" Lanier, whom he planned to marry soon. Tucker was rather despondent. Unable to obtain leave, he had been trying to hire a substitute so he could go home and marry. If Tucker could have looked twenty-four hours into the future, he would have known that his plans would no longer matter. He would be dead.

One wonders how two men who participated in this fight would have felt if they could have seen nearly four-score years into the future. Lieutenant Richard Beard marched in the Confederate ranks, while Lieutenant Arthur MacArthur fought on the Union side. The strange fact is that Beard's granddaughter, Jean Marie Faircloth from Murfreesboro, would one day marry young MacArthur's son, the brilliant and flamboyant twentieth-century general of the United States Army, Douglas MacArthur.

Shortly after the men settled down for the night, Confederate

---

[23]Bennett and Haigh, *Thirty-Sixth Illinois*, 332.

Captain D.C. Spurlock of the Sixteenth Tennessee Infantry made his way to a hotel on the south side of the town square, where his mother and father waited for him. The Spurlocks had lost a son at Perryville and had made the trip to Murfreesboro in a wagon to see the captain before he entered the battle. After a few hours with his parents, Spurlock left the hotel and returned to his regiment on the bank of Stones River; it was only a short time before daylight — and the captain had only a few hours to live.[24]

[24]Lamers, *Rosecrans*, 209. Enoch L. Mitchell, ed., "Letters of a Confederate Surgeon in the Army of Tennessee to his Wife," *Tennessee Historical Quarterly*, March 1946, p. 77. Ruth White Cook, Confederate Scrapbook, TSLA. Douglas MacArthur, *Reminiscences* (New York, 1964), 7, 8. Womack, "River," 7.

6

"Shiloh!" Again!

Dawn of December 31 was cold, wet, and miserable. Union soldiers struggled to arouse themselves from the deadening effect of the night's sleep. On the army's right, McCook's Federals gazed upon the dismal, winter landscape of dark cedar thickets and forlorn cotton and corn fields. Breakfasts were prepared and coffee was boiled as drowsy men blinked the sleep out of their eyes and wondered if the year's end would bring the long, red day of slaughter that everybody anticipated was close upon them.

Despite the confidence of Rosecrans that his planned attack against the Confederate right wing would relieve any potential danger to McCook's corps, some of McCook's soldiers had been very uneasy about the signs of Rebel activity just beyond their lines. Brigadier General Philip H. Sheridan had been up most of the night, inspecting his brigades and conferring with his subordinate officers. He was troubled about the Union right, which seemed to him the logical place where the Confederates might attack. Another of the worriers was an officer in Sheridan's division — General Joshua W. Sill, commanding Sheridan's First Brigade, camped on the division's right.[1]

Sill was a vigilant, competent Ohioan who impressed one Yankee observer at Murfreesboro with his "coolness and skill as an officer and soldier." After his graduation from West Point in 1853, ranking third in a class of fifty-three that included such notable

---

[1] *OR*, 348. J.H. Woodard, "General A. McD. McCook at Stone River," *MOLLUS, Los Angeles Commandery* (Los Angeles, 1892), 11, 12.

persons as Sheridan, James B. McPherson, John M. Schofield, and John B. Hood, he had served at various arsenals and ordinance depots, and taught at the Point and a Brooklyn college before entering the Civil War as colonel of the Thirty-third Ohio Infantry. Advanced to the rank of brigadier general, he commanded at Battle Creek, Tennessee, and fought at Perryville. "A fearless and able soldier" was the evaluation of another Federal who served beside Sill at Stones River, and Sheridan, who knew him well, said he was modest, courageous, and a practical military leader.[2]

Although General Sill would not survive the battle to make a report, J.H. Woodard was with Sill at his headquarters sometime before midnight; Woodard later wrote that as he looked east and south from Sill's headquarters, large bodies of enemy troops could be detected in the distance passing across the Union front toward the right of the Yankee army. General Sill said the movement had been going on since dark and probably indicated that the Rebels were massing in force for a strike against the Federal flank. Fascinated, Sill continued to watch, his vision aided by a few enemy campfires flickering in the background and sometimes illuminating the marching Confederate soldiers. His apprehension mounted steadily. Three times Sill sent warning messages to Sheridan, advising him of the enemy movement; finally, he mounted up and rode to Sheridan's headquarters.[3]

Sheridan was awake and he too was concerned. Sill spoke in deadly earnest and strongly urged his division commander to accompany him to McCook's headquarters, where they could impress upon the corps commander's mind the danger of the gray-clad army's attacking the Federals on the right flank at dawn. Sheridan agreed and the two went to consult McCook. They found him asleep on some straw in a fence corner. It was Sheridan who aroused him and reported the general condition on the front of the line.

McCook did not seem impressed. The corps commander said

    [2]Woodard, "McCook," 12. Boatner, *CWD*, 762. James L. McDonough, *Schofield: Union General in the Civil War and Reconstruction* (Tallahassee, 1972), 5. *Harper's Encyclopedia of U.S. History* (New York, 1902), VIII, 186. Bennett and Haigh, *Thirty-Sixth Illinois*, 332. P.H. Sheridan, *Personal Memoirs*, 2 vols. (New York, 1888), I, 208, 209.
    [3]Woodard, "McCook," 11, 12. *OR*, 348.

that the Rebels were gathering in force on the Union army's right, but Rosecrans still held firmly to the belief that his own attack upon the Confederate right in the morning would be so vigorous that the Rebels could not launch an assault, instead being compelled to withdraw the troops sent to McCook's front in an attempt to sustain the northern end of their line.[4]

Rosecrans and McCook may have been satisfied. Certainly Sheridan and Sill were not. Long before daylight, about four o'clock that chilling winter morning, Sheridan had his division assembled under arms and the cannoneers at their pieces. Henry Castle, a sergeant in the Seventy-third Illinois Infantry, said that "Sheridan came along the line, on foot and unattended. . . . He called for the major, ordered him to arouse his men quietly, have them breakfast and form in line of battle at once. He personally visited each of his twelve regiments and saw that his orders were executed. . . ."[5]

Unfortunately for the Union, McCook's other division leaders, Jefferson C. Davis and Richard W. Johnson, did not take the same precautions. And this was not because they had failed to receive a warning. Shortly before daylight McCook seemed to have second thoughts and sent a message to both men saying he was apprehensive that an attack would be made upon his lines at daybreak. He instructed that their men be under arms and on the alert. But all Johnson and Davis did was relay the order to their brigade commanders. They did nothing to insure that the order was obeyed.[6]

One of Johnson's three brigadiers, General August Willich, had been disturbed a few hours earlier by noise upon his front. About three o'clock in the morning, Willich sent Lieutenant Colonel Fielder A. Jones out on a reconnaissance with Company B of the Thirty-ninth Indiana Infantry. Jones' small band of less than a hundred men patrolled the woods some six hundred yards in front of the Yankee picket line. Tramping back from the perilous night mission, Jones reported that he had discovered no indications of the presence or purposes of the Rebels.

By five-thirty in the morning everything was quiet, Willich was

[4]Woodard, "McCook," 11, 12.
[5]Richard O'Connor, *Sheridan the Inevitable* (Indianapolis, 1953), 90.
[6]Woodard, "McCook," 13.

Photograph by Rudy E. Sanders

This winter scene on the battlefield today, looking northwest across a typical rail fence, shows the alternating open and timbered terrain which characterized the area of conflict.

eating his breakfast and, according to a Yankee officer who shared it with him, the general's apprehension of an attack seemed to have vanished. He said something to the effect that the Rebels were so quiet that he guessed they must not be there anymore! Willich's attitude was characteristic of the scene on the Federal right, where men who may have been a little worried earlier had relaxed and become more confident that the Confederates were not likely to do anything more than annoy the Yankee army. And then, in the gloomy twilight, shortly after six o'clock, they saw the Rebels coming.[7]

Confederate skirmishers were out in front, preceding a long gray double line of infantry that stretched as far to both right and left as the eye could see in the foggy half-light of the early morning. There was something eerie about the way they came—quietly emerging from the clumps of black cedars, forming into battle lines and, still making no sound, charging toward the Federals on the run. Only when they actually smashed into the Union line did they break out yelling and screaming.[8]

They hit with pile-driving force, ten thousand of Hardee's Rebels stampeding into the Union camps. McCook had sixteen thousand soldiers in his corps, but mentally, and in some cases tactically, they were not prepared to receive an attack. The onslaught was so startling and appalling that Federal soldiers, officers and enlisted men alike, supposed the enemy's assaulting force must be twenty-five thousand or even thirty-five thousand strong. Colonel William H. Gibson, commanding the Forty-ninth Ohio Infantry regiment, said it was "an assault which no troops in the world could have withstood." Surprise and momentum were the decisive factors and these the Confederates firmly possessed.[9]

Gates P. Thruston, aide to General McCook, heard the heavy firing of rifled-muskets and rode rapidly to the front. He arrived in time to witness what he described as an unforgettable sight, the advancing line of Hardee's corps, "an overwhelming force," sweeping over Johnson's division. It was a "thrilling spectacle that

---

[7]OR, 313, 919, 921, 923–24. Woodard, "McCook," 13. Edwin W. Payne, *History of the Thirty-Fourth Regiment of Illinois Volunteer Infantry* (Clinton, Iowa, 1903), 43.
[8]Lamers, *Rosecrans*, 221.
[9]OR, 296, 304.

a soldier might see once in a lifetime of military service," Thruston said, but it was also an appalling sight filling him with dismay as he watched the Federal lines crumble.[10]

Another Union soldier, J.H. Woodard, reported: "It seemed . . . that the whole Confederate army burst out of a piece of woods immediately on the front, and just beyond an open field." On came the Rebel columns, "cheering as they advanced, and sweeping through the field," wrote a Federal medical attendant. "The truth was," he candidly acknowledged, "we were surprised and 'Shiloh!' was the word we exchanged when we had time to reflect."[11]

It was nine months since the Rebels had shocked the Union army early on a beautiful Sunday morning at Shiloh, Hardee's corps then too spearheading the charge that intially overwhelmed the startled Federals. The onslaught at Shiloh had come from the same direction, the south, at the same time of morning, and had resulted in panic, many Yankees fleeing from the front lines. It was only natural that the thought "Shiloh!" would have popped into the minds of Union soldiers who had heard so much about that great battle and who, in some instances, had fought on that bloody field.

Rebel Major General John P. McCown had three brigades of infantry in the Confederate's advance division as he drove in and hit the Federal flank near the junction of Gresham's lane running north from the Franklin road. Major General Patrick R. Cleburne's division was to his rear, following McCown's line at a distance of about five hundred yards, ready to send support wherever needed. McCown took two of his brigades, those led by Brigadier Generals Mathew D. Ector and Evander McNair, directly across the Franklin road, charging straight into the camps of Brigadier General Edward N. Kirk's Union brigade.[12]

These Federal troops, facing east and south near the Franklin road, were aligned, from right to left, in the following order: the Thirty-fourth Illinois regiment, the Twenty-ninth and Thirtieth

---

[10]Gates P. Thruston, *Personal Recollections of the Battle in the Rear at Stone's River, Tennessee* (Nashville, n.d.), 6, 7.

[11]Bennett and Haigh, *Thirty-Sixth Illinois* 335–36.

[12]*OR*, 774, 844, 912.

Indiana regiments, and the Seventy-seventh Pennsylvania. Captain Warren E. Edgarton's Company E, First Ohio Light Artillery, rested in the left rear of the Thirty-fourth Illinois. The Thirty-fourth's line, formed on the brigade's southern flank, extended across the Franklin road and then, sweeping west, bent back to the north, recrossing the road.

General Kirk's men were up and under arms with a picket line covering their front and flank. About daylight a half-battery of horses from Edgarton's artillery was unhitched and taken to water at a small stream approximately one hundred yards to the rear. The horses had barely reached the water when the yelling Confederates came swarming into the brigade's camp. Their picket line had been virtually worthless for detecting or delaying the Rebels and General Kirk simply did not have time to react effectively. He ordered the Thirty-fourth Illinois to support Edgarton's battery, but the Confederates' rapidly advancing line, bayonets glistening, came in like an avalanche. Shouting and shrieking, the men in gray quickly overpowered the Federal defenders. Although his objectivity is questionable because of the criticism arising from the captain's having part of the horses watered at the time of attack, Edgarton reported that his infantry support gave way in disorder "almost with the first volley." The ground was quickly strewn with dead horses and dead or wounded men. The whole battery was captured and Kirk's brigade was rapidly driven back onto the brigade of General Willich. Kirk himself was mortally wounded in the first few minutes of the fray.[13]

Carried to a house on the Wilkinson Pike about two miles to the rear where a Yankee doctor had established a regimental hospital, the painfully wounded but excited general demanded that his bearers keep going and shouted at the doctor and his attendants that they had better get out at once or they would all be captured. Almost as soon as Kirk was gone Confederate cavalry pounded up to the house, and Dr. F.G. Hickman made his escape only by abandoning surgical instruments, uniform, and sword, and dashing across the fields toward the Nashville Pike.[14]

The Rebels' advance was like a huge tidal wave. An Illinois sol-

[13]*Ibid.*, 255, 256, 264, 300, 301, 304, 320. Payne, *Thirty-Fourth Illinois*, 43.
[14]*Confederate Veteran*, III, 162.

Union Brigadier-General Edward N. Kirk was mortally wounded during the first few minutes of the Confederate attack against the Federal right wing.

dier remembered, as characteristic of the scene, that the Thirty-fourth Illinois poured volley after volley into the oncoming Confederates, while at the same time skirmishers of the Twenty-ninth and Thirtieth Indiana and Seventy-seventh Pennsylvania directed an oblique fire on the advancing enemy, but the grayclad column rolled forward like an automaton, seemingly invulnerable to the Yankee firepower. He watched a Federal battery that had been firing canister and which started to limber up to withdraw to better ground; the Confederates, he said, swept it with one unbelievable volley, killing seventy-five horses and leaving the men unable to move a single gun. The surviving artillerists fled for the rear.[15]

Because of the great pride attached to both the national and regimental colors, the Confederates were determined to cut down the Federal's flags. The strife over the colors of the Thirty-fourth Illinois was terrible and bloody. Five color-bearers fell in quick succession, but as fast as they fell the flag was raised aloft by someone else and flaunted in the face of the attackers. The entire color guard was finally killed or wounded and the colors were dragged through the mud and triumphantly borne off the field by the surging Rebels.[16]

Even less prepared for the Rebel attack than Kirk's command was Willich's brigade, consisting of the Thirty-ninth and Thirty-second Indiana regiments, the Fifteenth and Forty-ninth Ohio, and the Eighty-ninth Illinois. Willich had allowed his men to stack arms and make coffee while he had ridden to the headquarters of his division commander, Brigadier General Richard W. Johnson, located in the rear. Thus when the Confederates struck, there was no one present at the point of assault above the rank of regimental commander. Concerted action by the brigade was impossible.

As his soldiers vainly attempted to resist the Rebel onslaught, dismay and panic swept Willich's command, made worse by the terrorized men of Kirk's brigade who, racing headlong for the rear, ran directly through the ranks of Willich's brigade, trampling some of his men into the ground. An Indiana regiment remembered with bitter amusement a captain who had been so afflicted

[15]Payne, *Thirty-Fourth Illinois*, 44.
[16]*Ibid.*

with rheumatism that he could walk only with great difficulty, with the help of a cane. Caught up in the rout, he dropped the cane and went to the rear at a breakneck run. His men, whom he rapidly outdistanced, pointed and cried out in derision: "My God, look at the captain run!"[17]

Willich himself, hearing the sounds of battle and shocked by the realization that disaster might be upon him, rode quickly into the confused lines, drawing up and shouting orders in his German accented English to those whom he mistakenly supposed were his troops. Instantly, somebody shot his horse and one of the soldiers to whom Willich had been giving orders curtly informed the general that Confederate commanding officers wore a different colored uniform from the one that he had on! Unknowingly, Willich had dashed into the Rebel lines and now found himself a prisoner, as disorder, fear, and horror gripped many of his Union troops.[18]

The Confederates, animated by their charge, seemed disdainful of death. Colonel John C. Burks, leading the Eleventh Texas, was mortally wounded but still boldly advanced, shouting to his men to come on and follow him. Burks finally fell, exhausted and dying, but still at the head of his command. The flag-bearer of the Tenth Texas, Sergeant A. Sims, saw a Union color-bearer endeavoring to rally his regiment. Sims dashed forward, seized the Yankee standard, and grappled with his Federal counterpart for its possession. The struggle ended with both men shot, collapsing in a bloody heap in the midst of the colorful silk.[19]

Meanwhile, McCown's third Rebel brigade, under Brigadier General James E. Rains, had marched directly west, staying south of the Franklin road, then turned sharply north, sweeping across the road and around the right flank of the Union position. Also swinging around the Federal right wing and vigorously slashing at their right and rear was Brigadier General John A. Wharton's cavalry brigade, which succeeded in capturing about fifteen hundred prisoners, a four-gun battery, several hundred wagons, and gen-

[17]C.C. Briant, *History of the Sixth Regiment Indiana Volunteer Infantry* (Indianapolis, 1891), 194–95.
[18]*OR*, 304. John G. Parkhurst, "Recollections of Stone's River," *MOLLUS, Michigan Commandery* (Detroit, 1890), 8, 9.
[19]*OR*, 774. *Confederate Veteran*, XII, 118.

erally spreading havoc behind the front line. One of the Federal commanders said he saw cavalry on his right, infantry assailing his left, and heavy masses rushing to assault his front. The only alternative to annihilation or capture was to beat a rapid retreat.

Yankee division commander Johnson, who later estimated the attacking force as thirty-five thousand strong, watched as two of his three brigades were overwhelmed. Leaving their artillery in the hands of the enemy, the brigades broke up and streamed back to the northwest. As they made for the rear, discarding their weapons as they ran, some of them were shouting, just as they had under Buell about three months earlier, "We are sold! Sold again!" Nevertheless, when Johnson made out his After Action Report of the battle, dated January 8, 1863, he asserted that "every arrangement" had been made to receive an attack, and "every precaution" had been taken against surprise.[20]

Many of the Rebels who had stormed through part of McCook's camps were elated by their triumph. One Confederate soldier wrote: "We swept everything before us. . . . We struck the enemy by surprise while arms were stacked and their breakfast was being prepared." "The coffee pots and frying pans were on the fires steaming as we went through their camp," recalled J.A. Templeton, a member of G Company, Tenth Texas Cavalry Dismounted. Another Confederate, P.R. Jones, later wrote, "Many were still in their 'pup' tent asleep and were killed while lying there. The onslaught was so sudden and the slaughter so great that they retreated in . . . confusion, every fellow for himself and the devil take the hindmost." Some of the Rebels, overcome with curiosity, were exploring the enemy tents, rummaging through the possessions of those they had just killed or driven off. "They had abandoned everything in order to get away," said Jones, but then he realized his statement was not completely true; he stumbled upon one Yankee who, even in death, was still holding firmly to his pot of coffee.[21]

[20]OR, 264, 296, 966, 967. Colonel W.D. Smith, "The Battle of Stones River, Tennessee, December 31, 1862–January 2, 1863" (Washington, D.C., 1932), 26. Stanley F. Horn, "The Battle of Stones River," Civil War Times Illustrated, Feb. 1964, p. 5. Foote, Civil War, II, 87.

[21]Confederate Veteran, XVI, 391; XII, 24; XXXI, 341.

Everyone seemed to be yelling and shouting. The Rebels were pressing in with fury and driving the Yankees on McCook's right, but they were paying a heavy price in blood and life. As Rains' brigade slashed into the Union lines the general himself was shot, falling from his horse mortally wounded. A Captain McCauley watched spellbound, then turned to tell one of his men that Rains had been hit, only to feel a sudden numbing stab as a bullet ripped through his rib cage, and he too was on the ground. McCauley could not move his right leg and, terrified, he struggled to drag himself along the ground, hoping to find some shelter from the storm of bullets tearing through the air.[22]

Another captain in Rains' brigade, Meredith Kendrick, took a severe wound in the thigh and lay with his head propped up against a tree, pale from the loss of blood. Private W.D. Clark, rushing past but seeing his captain's condition, stopped and offered to help him to the rear. Kendrick waved him on; almost at the same instant, a bullet struck Clark in the neck and as blood and flesh spattered everywhere, he fell dead at the feet of the disabled captain. In spite of the Rebel losses, which were many, it must have seemed to the Federals, at this time, that nothing could arrest the surging Confederates.[23]

The grayclad line of Cleburne's division, composing the second wave of Rebel attackers and buoyed up by the overwhelming success of the lead division, now bore in against the collapsing Union flank. Cleburne had four brigades under his command, directed by Brigadier Generals St. John R. Liddell, Bushrod R. Johnson, Lucius E. Polk, and Stirling A.M. Wood. Following Hardee's orders, Cleburne swung his line gradually to the north as he advanced and moved Wood's brigade forward from its rear position to connect with the next Confederate division advancing on his right, that of Major General B. Franklin Cheatham.[24]

Matters did not develop according to plan for Cleburne. McCown, like Cleburne, was supposed to swing his division gradually to the right as he moved forward. Instead McCown had continued northwestward while Cleburne was turning to the north. Within a

[22]*Ibid.*, X, 172.
[23]*Ibid.*, XVI, 391.
[24]*OR*, 774, 844.

few moments enemy skirmishers were firing all along Cleburne's front and the general realized that McCown's division had disappeared. Suddenly, rather than being a second supporting line for the lead division, Cleburne's soldiers had become the foremost line on that part of the field. Putting skirmishers forward immediately, Cleburne's division swept onward for three hundred or four hundred yards across ground obstructed by numerous fences and thickets and raked by musketry. Then they broke into a solid line of Federals, some waiting in a large cedar brake and others positioned in an open field.[25]

Cleburne's infantrymen crashed into a part of the Yankee line held by the second of McCook's three divisions. The unit's commander was a brigadier general with the unlikely name of Jefferson C. Davis. It had only been three months since the thirty-four-year-old Davis, a dangerous man to cross, had gunned down Major General William "Bull" Nelson in a Louisville hotel hall, a murder for which the Indianan was never punished, being soon restored to active duty, partly because of his military ability and partly on the political influence of Indiana Governor Oliver P. Morton.[26] But now Davis was fighting for his life and that of his division. He got assistance from Richard Johnson's reserve brigade, led by Colonel Philemon P. Baldwin, which came up from its bivouac at division headquarters, about one mile to the northwest. Firing from behind natural breastworks of limestone rock in the cedar brakes and taking cover behind portions of fence, depressions in the ground, whatever offered a little protection in the open field, the Union soldiers made a stubborn defense along the whole front of Cleburne's advance.

In the midst of this bloody struggle, at least one Confederate in Cleburne's division was worried about being shot from behind — by his own men. John M. Berry remembered that the Federal fire pinned down his company in an open field. The Rebels would lay on their stomachs, fire, and then roll over on their backs to reload, trying to keep as low as possible. Berry was shooting right over the head of Dick Jones, who turned and said, "John, you'll shoot me!"

[25]*Ibid.*
[26]Boatner, *CWD*, 226.

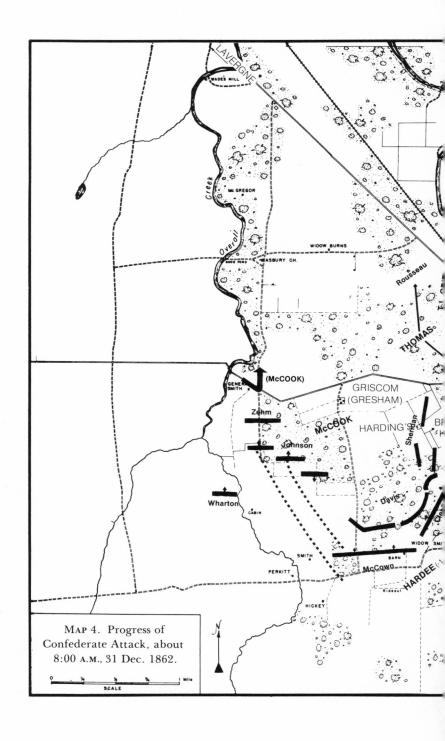

MAP 4. Progress of
Confederate Attack, about
8:00 A.M., 31 Dec. 1862.

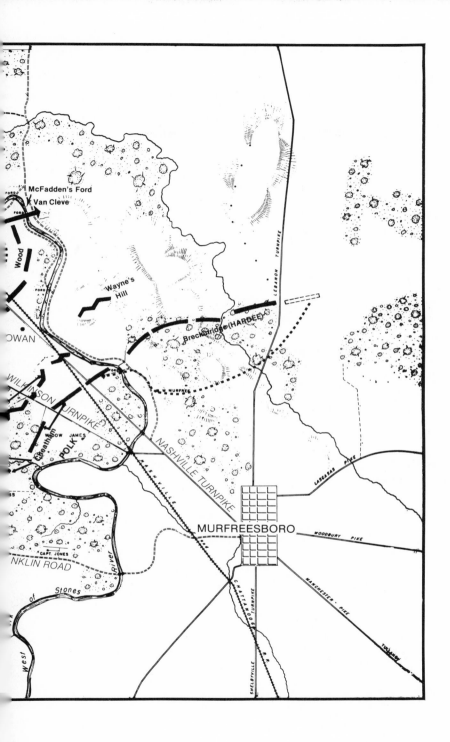

McFadden's Ford
Van Cleve
FORD
FORD
Wood
FORD
Wayne's
Hill
OWAN
Breckinridge (HARDEE)
WILKINSON
TURNPIKE
MURFREE
NASHVILLE
Cheatham
WIDOW
JAMES
POLK
LEBANON TURNPIKE
NASHVILLE TURNPIKE
LASCASAS PIKE
CAPT. JONES
NKLIN ROAD
MURFREESBORO
River
WOODBURY PIKE
of Stones
MANCHESTER PIKE
West
CHATTANOGA TURNPIKE
SHELBYVILLE PK
TURNPIKE

"No I won't, if you keep your head down," responded Berry and and fired again. Jones was then so deafened and alarmed that he turned again, lashing out at Berry with protests accented by oaths, apparently ready to attack his comrade-in-arms. Perhaps fortunately for Berry, another Confederate command assaulted the Union troops from an angle, forcing them to retreat and relieving the pressure on those pinned down in the field.[27]

The fury of the Rebel onslaught was at last too great. After a fierce and bloody struggle the larger part of the Federal line under Davis was overwhelmed. "We gave them one of the heaviest volleys of musketry I ever heard," remembered Captain Robert D. Smith of the Second Tennessee Infantry, "and the fighting," he continued, "was more desperate than anything I ever witnessed." The Yankees fell back for several hundred yards where they once more contested the enemy's onrush, fighting across woods, pastures, and open fields. Again the Confederate pressure was too much and the Federals continued to retreat with Cleburne's division in rapid pursuit.[28]

Some Confederates pursued almost too rapidly. General Liddell had halted his brigade and dispatched J.M. Dulin of the Sixth Arkansas to bring up the ammunition wagons before resuming his advance on the enemy. Hurrying forward with two four-horse ordnance wagons and anxious to renew the pursuit of the Yankees, Dulin discovered the brigade was not where he thought. He supposed that Liddell had continued the advance, yelled to his drivers to "come on," and plunged ahead into a corn field. The rush of the teams and the crashing and cracking of the dry stalks spread terror among several rabbits that sprang up and raced to find other cover. But rabbits were not all that Dulin flushed out of the corn field. A whole line of blueclad Yankees broke cover and scampered for the rear area, leaving Dulin with the distinction of being the only man in the army who could say that he had charged the enemy with two ordnance wagons.[29]

As panic-stricken Yankees raced away from the fight, a Rebel prisoner named J.T. McBride, captured in a skirmish shortly be-

[27]*Confederate Veteran*, VIII, 73.
[28]Smith, "Confederate Diary," 43. *OR*, 264, 270, 271, 280, 281.
[29]*Confederate Veteran*, V, 220.

fore the battle, watched in disgust. Then he stood up and shouted to the Federals, "What yer running fer? Why don't yer stand and fight like men?" McBride seemed to be doing his best to stop the fleeing Union soldiers until a fellow prisoner interrupted him, saying: "For God's sake, Joe, don't try to rally the Yankees! Keep 'em on the run! Do anything to continue the demoralization, and let's make our escape!"[30]

The Confederate divisions of McCown and Cleburne in double line of battle now drove the Union soldiers, with great slaughter on both sides, for nearly two miles through the cedar brakes toward the Nashville Pike until the Federals finally took up a new line, manned by infantry and artillery, along the Wilkinson Pike. In doing so, the Rebel advance had gradually lost coordination and momentum. Various factors slowed the drive. Intermingling of units was a problem. General Liddell, leading the brigade on the left of Cleburne's division, became separated from Cleburne by following the movement of McCown's command. Key personnel were lost. When General Rains, directing the advance of his troops against an enemy battery, had fallen, shot through the heart, his brigade recoiled in confusion. Many of the men in butternut were fatigued and their ammunition exhausted. Time was lost both in replenishing supplies and in reorganizing. And the Yankees, realizing the possibility of imminent disaster to their whole army, were fighting furiously to keep from being driven back across the Nashville Pike.[31]

The Rebel attack was experiencing more problems and confusion on Cleburne's right. Here General Leonidas Polk, before the battle, had rearranged his corps command structure because of the rugged terrain and the length of his front line. Originally Major General Jones Withers was to take charge of the first attacking line and Major General B. Franklin Cheatham the second. Under the new plan General Cheatham was to direct the two left brigades in Withers' front line and his own two left brigades in the supporting line. Withers would lead the two right brigades of his division plus the two right brigades of Cheatham's command.

[30]*Ibid.*, II, 229.
[31]*OR*, 775, 845. *Confederate Veteran*, VII, 550.

This revamping, on the eve of battle, probably contributed to the confusion that characterized the Rebel assault.

Cheatham's attack was not coordinated. Colonel J.Q. Loomis, directing the far left brigade on Cheatham's front, was late moving forward. The time was about seven A.M. when Loomis surged across a corn field and open woods and ran head-on into the left wing of McCook's corps, consisting of the remaining brigade of Davis' division, under Colonel William E. Woodruff, and Joshua Sill's brigade of General Sheridan's division.[32]

Here the Confederates encountered the stiffest resistance thus far in the battle. Woodruff's brigade was posted on the edge of a woods on the south side of a rise. General Sill's brigade of Sheridan's division was on Woodruff's left, facing east and making a sharp angle with Woodruff's line at the top of the wooded slope. Expecting an attack, Woodruff had ordered his men to sleep on their arms without fires. Sheridan, as previously noted, had also anticipated an attack and brought forward two regiments from his reserves to reinforce Sill's brigade. And he had the entire division under arms with the cannoneers at their pieces. Furthermore, the fierce fighting on the army's right flank at dawn fully alerted both Sheridan and Woodruff to expect the Rebel assault momentarily. The clash was bruising and cruel.[33]

Loomis drove in and hit the Yankee line held by Woodruff. As the Confederates moved into the open and struggled up the incline, they were swept by a galling musketry fire mixed with artillery. The Union infantry was partially sheltered behind a rail fence and fought with the coolness of veterans. The Yankee artillery, posted on Woodruff's left, enfiladed the Rebels with terrible effect. Loomis' brigade was decimated, its commander wounded, and the unit collapsed and retreated in disorder over the dead and wounded.[34]

Most of Loomis' regiments consisted of Alabama troops, and as they fell back through Cheatham's division that was about to go into the fight against Sheridan, the Alabamians took a lot of jeering from Colonel A.J. Vaughan's Tennesseans and Texans. One

[32]*OR*, 687, 706, 734, 754-55.
[33]*Ibid.*, 288, 348.
[34]*Ibid.*, 348, 706, 754-55.

of the Alabamians stared at a hooting Tennessean and pointedly replied, "You'll soon find it the hottest place you ever struck!" He was probably right. And undoubtedly, regardless of the front they put up, there were a lot of men, Rebels as well as Yankees, who would have liked to escape from the terrible scenes of slaughter. An unknown Confederate soldier watched a scared rabbit jump from its hiding place and, with its white tail elevated, scamper to the rear. Gazing wistfully at the little animal, his sad remark was perhaps characteristic of the feelings of a great many others: "Go it Molly Cottontail, go it! I'd run too if I didn't have a reputation to sustain." Confederate Lieutenant Charles King's slave Cad rode up on a gray horse to deliver something to his master. Fierce fighting was raging all about and Cad questioned Lieutenant King, "Marse Charles, hadn't I better take this horse back?"[35]

Making the situation worse for the Rebels was the failure of the brigade on Loomis' right, that of Colonel A.M. Manigault, to advance until eight A.M. Consequently, Cheatham had to commit both of his supporting brigades, led by Colonel Vaughan and Brigadier General George Maney, in the first hour of the fight.[36]

Vaughan took his men across the same difficult ground in front of Woodruff's brigade where Loomis had gone and found the same murderous fire being poured into his front. Charging furiously up the gentle grade, some Rebels penetrated the Union line briefly, even driving the gunners away and, for an instant, capturing two of the Federal cannon. But as the raking fire that enfiladed the Confederates from their left took a heavy toll, the butternuts were thrown back. Colonel Vaughan's order to retreat was not heard by Colonel W.H. Young and his Ninth Texas regiment, who continued to fight and, finding some cover in a wooded area, gradually worked their way around the Federal flank until they were able to deliver a continuous harrassing and enfilading fire that took its toll among the Yankee defenders.[37]

Then while Loomis' brigade, now under direction of Colonel J.G. Coltart after Loomis was disabled by a large limb sheared

[35]*Confederate Veteran*, XVII, 449; VII, 550. Ruth White Cook, Confederate Scrapbook, TSLA.
[36]*OR*, 706.
[37]*Ibid.*, 706, 744.

from a tree, and Vaughan's command were being organized to assault the Union position again, Sheridan's batteries were able to wheel to their right and pour a devastating fire into the right flank of Cleburne's division to the west. It was imperative that the Confederates break the Union stronghold at this point of the battlefield.[38]

Vaughan and Coltart again advanced to the attack. Manigault's brigade had come up on Coltart's right, with Maney's brigade supporting it. In spite of all the confusion and piecemeal attacks, the Confederate assault was now being driven home with grim determination. Indeed, one Rebel regiment, earlier quarantined because of a smallpox case and its guns distributed to other commands, was so confident from the initial Confederate success that, despite its lack of firepower (and some even claimed the unit had no guns at all!), the regiment charged and overwhelmed a sector of the Yankee line, supplying itself by taking the guns of the enemy.[39]

As Manigault's brigade moved forward to join in the fight, a conspicuous act of heroism led to one of the rare events on any battlefield of the Civil War — promotion on the field for distinguished gallantry. Company A of the Tenth South Carolina Infantry was deployed as skirmishers when a squadron of Yankee cavalry swept in from the flank, capturing the company's commander, Lieutenant C. Carrol White, and several of his soldiers. Although a prisoner, Lieutenant White called out to the rest of his men in a loud voice, "Company A! Rally on the right!" The men rallied quickly but hesitated to fire, fearing that they would kill their own soldiers who were prisoners. White shouted, "Don't mind us. Commence firing!" White and his fellow prisoners dropped to the ground, his order was instantly obeyed, and the deadly fire from several score Enfield rifled-muskets was sent into the enemy's ranks, emptying many of their saddles. Rising up quickly from the ground, White and the others grappled with their captors, who soon found that they had become the prisoners. Lieutenant Francis S. Parker, aide to General Bragg, happened to be on that part of the field and observed White's unusual example

---

[38]*Ibid.*, 706.
[39]*Confederate Veteran*, XXVIII, 19, 46, 78, 406, 407.

of both presence of mind and courage. Parker reported the incident to Bragg and the general immediately ordered Lieutenant White's promotion to a captaincy.[40]

The main force of Manigault's attack fell upon Sill's brigade. These Yankees, ensconced in a thick cedar grove, many protected by limestone outcropping, were well prepared for the Rebel onset and dealt out a crushing frontal fire.

Sheridan described the carnage: "The enemy . . . continued to advance until they had reached nearly the edge of the timber, when they were opened upon by Sill's infantry, at a range of not over 50 yards. The destruction to the enemy's column, which was closed in mass, being several regiments in depth, was terrible. For a short time they withstood the fire, wavered, then broke and ran."[41]

As the Rebels retreated, thirty-one-year-old General Sill launched a spirited counterattack, driving the enemy across the open ground and shouting encouragement to his men, when he was killed instantly by a shot through the head. The Federal troops, momentarily demoralized by the loss of their commander, pulled back to their defensive position. Manigault rallied, re-formed his brigade, and boldly advanced to the attack a second time. Torn again by an iron storm of bullets, his lines recoiled once more in the midst of confusion and death.[42]

Manigault's plight was made worse from a devastating fire on his right flank inflicted by two Yankee batteries. Situated about six hundred yards apart, one battery was positioned on a ridge across open ground toward a brick kiln and the Harding house, and the other rested in a wooded area farther to the east. They were positioned so that if a single regiment attempted to rush one of the batteries, the other poured a flanking fire into the attackers. Manigault conferred with Maney and the two agreed upon a simultaneous assault, Maney going for the battery toward the Harding house, while Manigault changed front to the right and engaged the battery in the woods.[43]

The plan seemed simple enough; its execution proved otherwise.

[40]*Ibid.*, XIII, 17; XV, 263; XXXIV, 46.
[41]*OR*, 348.
[42]Sheridan, *Memoirs*, I, 223.
[43]*OR*, 734.

Battles and Leaders of the Civil War

Photograph by Rudy E. Sanders

(*Above*): General Joshua W. Sill, West Point graduate and vigilant brigade commander, played a key role in alerting Sheridan's division to the likelihood of a Rebel attack. Sill was killed in action on the first day of battle. (*Below*): Broken artillery pieces, laying amidst the numerous limestone outcroppings, graphically show the role of terrain on the course of the battle. Here the men of General Philip Sheridan beat back several Confederate attacks, their delaying action giving Union troops time to form a new line along the Nashville Pike.

Maney called upon his First Tennessee and Fourth Tennessee regiments to storm the battery on the ridge and the Tennesseans at once moved to the attack, but unfortunately for the Rebels, Manigault had not finished re-forming his brigade for its supporting role. When the Tennesseans, a skirmish line in front, had advanced several hundred yards and were nearing the brick kiln, the Union battery in the woods opened up a raking fire on their right flank. Colonel H.R. Feild, commanding the First Tennessee, thought the fire was coming from a Rebel battery, as did many of the men in his regiment. Feild ordered his soldiers to lie down and the Tennesseans were soon raising a frantic shout, directed toward the Federal gunners, "Cease firing, cease firing, you are firing at your own men!"

Out on the skirmish line, Sam Watkins of Columbia, Tennessee, watched in frustration and anger as he heard his comrades yelling and saw them being shot. Watkins realized that the men behind those guns were Federals and he screamed over and over to his buddies, until it made him hoarse, "They are Yankees; shoot, they are Yankees!"[44] But Colonel Feild sent forward Lieutenant R. Fred James, a young lawyer from Murfreesboro, to tell the gunners that they were firing on their own troops. James had approached to within about fifty yards of the battery when he was shot down by its infantry support—killed very near his mother's farm.[45] Still convinced that a Rebel battery was doing the firing, Feild next sent Lieutenant John Marsh toward the guns. Marsh rode to within forty to fifty yards, the Union infantry sent a volley crashing toward him that fortunately missed its mark, and he wheeled his horse and tore back to the Confederate position. "Then I became convinced it was the enemy," wrote Feild when he made his report of the action.[46]

James A. McMurry, commanding the Fourth Tennessee, had also thought the battery was friendly until Sergeant Oakley, color-bearer of the Fourth, had conspicuously risked his life by marching a considerable distance in front of his regiment and holding the flag aloft for several minutes until the heavy fire he received

[44]Watkins, "Co. Aytch," 93.
[45]Ridley, Battles and Sketches, 156. Watkins, "Co. Aytch," 93.
[46]OR, 737.

assured everyone that they faced a Union battery. The story of Oakley's flaunting of death was awe-inspiring and quickly spread through the army, later leading General Leonidas Polk to seek out the sergeant, saying, "I must shake hands with you," and declaring that he was proud to be in the presence of so great a man.[47]

The Rebels of the First and Fourth Tennessee, certain at last that an enemy battery had been blasting them, opened fire with vigor and drove the Federals from their guns. Vividly describing this action, one of the Confederates who participated in the charge said: "We raised a whoop and a yell, and swooped down on those Yankees like a whirl-a-gust of woodpeckers in a hail storm, paying the blue coated rascals back with compound interest; . . . every man's gun was loaded, and they marched upon the blazing crest in solid file, and when they did fire, there was a sudden lull in the storm of battle, because the Yankees were nearly all killed. I cannot remember . . . ever seeing more dead men and horses and captured cannon, all jumbled together, than that scene of blood and carnage. . . . The ground was literally covered with blue coats dead; and, if I remember correctly, there were eighty dead horses."[48]

Explanations may be offered for the tragic confusion during which the First Tennessee took most of its casualties in the battle of Murfreesboro. Probably General Maney and Colonel Manigault did not have a clear understanding about the coordination of their attack. Maney may not have adequately briefed his regimental commanders concerning the tactical situation. Possibly the noise of thousands of rifled-muskets and artillery fire, the smoke-enshrouded atmosphere, and unfamiliarity with the terrain contributed to the fiasco.

Sam Watkins had another explanation. "It was Christmas," he wrote. "John Barleycorn was general-in-chief. Our generals, and colonels, and captains, had kissed John a little too often. They couldn't see straight. . . . They couldn't tell our own men from the Yankees."[49] His account has a touch of both amusement and bitterness, but Watkins may have been partially right. He was not

[47]*Ibid.*, 737, 738. *Confederate Veteran*, II, 68.
[48]Watkins, "*Co. Aytch*," 94.
[49]*Ibid.*, 93.

the only one who noted the effects of large amounts of whiskey among the Rebels.[50]

A Union soldier from Illinois, Charles Doolittle, whose division was driven back in the early fighting, volunteered to stay behind and assist the wounded. Soon the Rebels overran the improvised hospital and "such cursing of the Yankees you never heard," reported Doolittle in a letter to a friend. "A great many of them had been drinking," continued Doolittle, "and the whiskey served . . . to increase their hatred and bitterness." P.R. Jones, Tenth Texas Cavalry Regiment (dismounted), recalled that "just before daybreak . . . some whiskey was passed down the line, of which more than half of my company did not drink a drop, but others imbibed freely. It was not given to the soldiers to inspire courage," Jones explained, "but to warm them up after long exposure to the rain and cold weather." It would be surprising indeed if this were the only such instance throughout the Confederate ranks.[51]

Regardless of what role whiskey may have played in some parts of the army, the Rebel lines were still going forward. Manigault's brigade, making three charges in its sector of the battle, sustained a very heavy loss in officers and men. In Vaughan's brigade the horses of every officer of the field and staff, except one, and the horses of all the officers of the field and staff of every regiment, except two, were killed. One-third of the entire force of Vaughan's brigade was lost in this effort.[52]

Among the losses was Dr. W.A. Lowe who, when the war began, had just finished his medical training and was about to enter practice. Enlisting as a private in the One Hundred and Fifty-fourth Tennessee, he had been wounded at Shiloh and now fought at Murfreesboro, side by side with his brother James. While he was reloading his rifled-musket a bullet gored his right eye, passed through his skull, and came out at the base of the brain. His

---

[50]Thomas Malone said he saw generals "manifestly somewhat excited by drink" and could not tell when to depend on their judgment; quoted in Womack, "River," 9. Hardee reported to Bragg that Cheatham was drunk and unfit for duty on Dec. 31 and Bragg said he reported this to Polk and the latter claimed he had received the same information. McWhiney, *Bragg*, I, 354.

[51]Charles Doolittle to Mollie, Feb. 6, 1863, Charles Doolittle Papers, Knox College Library, Galesburg, Ill. *Confederate Veteran*, XXXI, 341.

[52]*OR*, 706–7, 734–45, 744, 754–56.

brother, distraught by the ghastly spectacle but seeing that the doctor was still alive, picked him up and carried him toward the rear. Before they were beyond the range of the Federal bullets, Lowe recovered consciousness and demanded that his brother abandon him to his fate and return to the battle. He was so insistent that James at last complied. Making his brother as comfortable as possible on the cold hard ground, James then trudged back through the debris of war and into the heavy pall of gunsmoke that engulfed the front lines.[53]

The Rebels paid an awful price, but at last they mustered sufficient manpower. Confederate brigades of Coltart, Vaughan, Maney, and Manigault were hammering relentlessly at the Yankee stronghold, as the units led by Brigadier Generals J. Patton Anderson and Alexander P. Stewart advanced to attack Sheridan's left, posted south of the Wilkinson Pike, and Brigadier General James S. Negley's division north of the pike.

General Cheatham had come up, calling on the men to "give it all you've got!" "Come on boys and follow me," he yelled as he personally led the charge. The general made such an impression on one Rebel soldier that, although he was wounded in the arm, he dragged himself to his feet muttering, "Well, General, if you are determined to die, I'll die with you," and joined again in the attack. General Cheatham had a well-deserved reputation as one of the most profane men in the army. At some point about midmorning of this awful day, General Leonidas Polk, Cheatham's corps commander, was close at hand while Cheatham was shouting to his men, "Give 'em hell! Give 'em hell!" Apparently feeling compelled to join in with some encouragement of his own, the former Episcopal bishop of Louisiana responded with, "Give 'em what General Cheatham says, boys. Give 'em what General Cheatham says!"[54]

Fighting seemed to be swirling in every direction and the Union position was crumbling. Woodruff's brigade was finally flanked on both sides as one of Sill's regiments that had protected Woodruff's left began falling back. The Rebels pressed their advantage

[53]*Confederate Veteran*, VIII, 368, 369.
[54]Watkins, "*Co. Aytch*," 93-94. Foote, *Civil War*, II, 88.

and Woodruff's entire brigade retreated. With his right flank now exposed, Sheridan began withdrawing Sill's brigade and the supporting regiments that he had called forward earlier. Sheridan's left brigade under Colonel George W. Roberts was under heavy attack by Anderson and Stewart. The first Rebel assault on Roberts was beaten back, and Roberts made a counterattack before he also retreated to join the rest of Sheridan's command.[55]

Sheridan tried to establish a new line stretching east from the Gresham house and bending back to the north, where Roberts' brigade held its position just south of the Wilkinson Pike. But the strength of the Rebel attack was too great. Roberts' brigade, for example, threw back three infantry attacks while an artillery duel raged at a range of no more than two hundred yards. In the midst of the struggle, as Roberts' brigade fought savagely to hold its ground, a young corporal came up to Lieutenant Colonel Nathan H. Walworth of the Forty-second Illinois and made what seemed to be a strange statement: "Colonel, I come to return my gun to you, for I suppose that I shall go on furlough now." The puzzled colonel wondered what the man meant but then saw that a hole was blown in his abdomen from which his intestines were trailing out. Assaulted from the east, south, and southwest, running low on ammunition, and with Colonel Roberts killed in this bloody melee, the brigade retreated again.[56]

Another of Sheridan's brigades, led by Colonel Frederick Schaefer, was out of ammunition. And Sheridan's right flank was unsupported as the rest of McCook's corps had already been driven farther to the north. Once more Sheridan's division fell back to find a new line of defense in the cedars north of the Wilkinson Pike.[57]

Thus, by ten o'clock in the morning, McCook's corps had been forced out of its line of battle and sent reeling back through the cedars. Only Sheridan's division had been able to conduct a fighting retreat and remained in action. Davis' and Johnson's divisions had been driven for three miles, all the way back to the Nashville

---

[55]*OR*, 281, 288, 349. Henry M. Cist, *The Army of the Cumberland* (New York, 1882), 109–11.

[56]*OR*, 349. Womack, "River," 8.

[57]*OR*, 349, 407.

Pike, where their remnants were now being regrouped between the railroad and the pike. Two-thirds of the Federal right wing had been wrecked and the center had also fallen back. Surprise, which Napoleon liked to say was one of the three most important elements in warfare, had been achieved and if Bragg could follow up this initial advantage with a judicious use of his forces, victory was within his grasp.

7

"This Battle Must Be Won"

Behind the Union lines, near the left or northern flank of the Federal position, General Rosecrans had first supposed that the distant noise of musketry on the army's right wing indicated the carrying out of his instructions. The general was confident that McCook, just as intended, was firmly holding the Confederates' attention with a spirited demonstration on the right while the Yankees' principal attacking force, consisting of three divisions, was crossing Stones River on the army's left wing. Not even the arrival of an excited lieutenant, sent from Captain Elmer Otis, who commanded the Fourth U.S. Cavalry, informing Rosecrans that the right wing was broken and the enemy was driving it back, changed the Union commander's faith that his plan was unfolding perfectly. Rosecrans placed more credence in a courier from McCook, galloping up about the same time and reporting that McCook's corps was being assaulted and must have reinforcements.

"Tell General McCook to contest every inch of ground," Rosecrans instructed the courier, repeating his previous orders. "If he holds them we will swing into Murfreesboro with our left and cut them off." Still confident, he assured his staff, "It's working right."

McCook had neglected to report the rout of Kirk's and Willich's brigades and the withdrawal of Davis' division, thus misleading Rosecrans about the actual situation on his right. For a while General Rosecrans continued to think that all was well. When news came that General Sill had been killed, Rosecrans looked grim but said, "We can not help it. Brave men must be killed." At the news of Willich's capture, he urged, "Never mind, we must win this fight."[1]

But the rising din of battle on the army's southern flank, coming continually closer, was obviously more than the sounds of a holding action. The hellish, ear-splitting noises were diminished by distance and atmospheric peculiarities, which may help to explain why the battle raged for more than an hour before Rosecrans realized not only that his plan was not working but that the army was facing imminent disaster. With two of his three divisions routed, McCook, far from being able to conduct an inch-by-inch defense, had hardly been able, as Shelby Foote has written, to conduct a defense that was mile-by-mile.[2]

Having firmly concluded, at last, that the Rebels were launching an all-out attack against his right flank, and surmising that the probable objective was to cut off the army from the Nashville Pike, Rosecrans canceled his own attack plans. He ordered General Crittenden to have Brigadier General Horatio P. Van Cleve's division recross the river. Two brigades of Brigadier General Thomas J. Wood's division (Harker's and Hascall's), then en route to the ford, were ordered to reinforce the collapsing right at once. Wood's other brigade (Wagner's) and Brigadier General John Palmer's division were to hold their ground between Stones River and Thomas' corps.

As Wood spurred his horse in the direction of the fight, which was swelling louder and louder, he yelled back, "We'll all meet at the hatter's, as one coon said to another when the dogs were after them!" Considering both Rosecrans' lack of humor and the frazzled condition of his army, it is exceedingly unlikely that he found Wood's remark amusing. The general next prepared to form a new defensive line. It would be at a right angle to the old line, thus cutting across the path of both the Federal fugitives who were trying to escape and their Rebel pursuers.[3]

The scene before Rosecrans, as he rode toward the fighting,

---

[1]Kenneth P. Williams, *Lincoln Finds A General: A Military Study of the Civil War*, 5 vols. (New York, 1949–59), IV, 267, 268. Lamers, *Rosecrans*, 219, 220, 223. Foote, *Civil War*, II, 89, 90.

[2]Freeman, "Battle," 232. Foote, *Civil War*, II, 90.

[3]Foote, *Civil War*, II, 90. Lamers, *Rosecrans*, 223, 224.

must have been disheartening. Hundreds of men, even thousands, were retreating. Many of them were fleeing from the battlefield. Colonel Frederick Knefler, leading the Seventy-ninth Indiana Infantry as it struggled to help establish the new line, wrote, "May you never see such a spectacle." The field of Shiloh, the colonel claimed, was a "pleasant sight compared to this. Infantry, cavalry, artillery, came flying in inextricable confusion, horror on their faces. Our line was torn and trampled down. We were compelled to fix bayonets to preserve ourselves. No human voice could have been heard over the tumult. At last the fugitives cleared our front, and as far as we could see the Rebels were coming in solid columns, howling and yelling."[4]

Henry Castle was one of the Federals who watched it happen. "If there was anything more disgraceful at Bull Run than the scenes I witnessed in those cedars, I have not seen it described," he said. "All around us, and often breaking through us, was a yelling mob; officers weeping or swearing, soldiers demoralized and shivering."[5]

Another Federal gave an absorbing account as he watched from behind General Thomas' corps. Saying that it was the first and only time he ever witnessed the rear of a partially defeated army and that it was impossible to describe the scene adequately, Henry Freeman wrote, "The debris was drifting back rapidly. . . . Cannon and caissons, and remnants of batteries, the horses of which had been killed, were being hurriedly dragged off by hand. There were men retiring with guns, and men without their guns; men limping, others holding up blood-stained arms and hands; men carrying off wounded comrades; and faces blackened with powder, and in some cases stained with blood. . . . Riderless horses dashed out of the woods which still partly hid the combat, ran for a distance, and stopped and stared back at the tumult. . . . Among the disorganized men falling back, there were some crying and some cursing. Over all arose, near at hand or more faintly from the distance, the yells of the Rebel victors. . . ." The din of thousands of rifled-muskets firing and the roar of cannon and explosion of shells, approaching nearer and nearer, sounded "as if some mighty power was breaking and crashing to the ground every tree

[4]Lamers, *Rosecrans*, 224.
[5]Newlin, *Seventy-Third Illinois*, 132.

in the forest."[6] Some Federals compared it to the rising of a great wind ushering in a storm. Others said the sound rose like the distant, magnified rumble of many heavy wagons.

Colonel John G. Parkhurst was commanding the Ninth Michigan Infantry, assigned to General Thomas as the provost guard of the army's center corps. Parkhurst had rejoined the regiment only the day before Christmas, having been in a Confederate prison most of the time since July 13, when he was captured by Forrest's troopers at this very same town. Perhaps he wondered if his recent history was about to be repeated. In the midst of reading to his regiment Rosecrans' dramatic and stirring address, designed for the eve of the Yankee attack, Parkhurst's attention was suddenly diverted as alarming evidences of the raging battle streamed toward him. Stragglers, wounded, riderless horses, and men crying "All is lost!" were leading the way to the rear. Then came cavalrymen, teams cut loose from wagons, with the galloping mules bearing two or even three riders each, and, finally, panic-stricken infantrymen.

Parkhurst sent out details of soldiers to stop the terrified troops but quickly realized that his entire regiment would be needed to stop the fleeing men. The Ninth Michigan was immediately placed in line of battle across the Nashville Pike, its flanks extended widely in order to block as much ground as possible. "Cavalry, artillery, infantry, suttler's and camp followers came rushing with the force of a cyclone," said the colonel, "and the Ninth Michigan was ordered to fix bayonets and charge upon this panic-stricken mass of men." The charge was made, checking the stampede, and the fleeing troops in that sector were at last halted. Other Union regiments were also employed in this nasty work of stopping their own panic-stricken comrades in arms from running away.[7]

As the Rebel drive had swept northward, leaving a wake of smoke-enshrouded, mangled humanity, there were sometimes unexpected scenes of pathos. John M. Berry, Seventh Arkansas, came across a Yankee suffering from a ghastly looking wound in the knee. At the Federal's request, Berry stopped and placed a piece of wood under his leg in an attempt to make him rest more

[6]Freeman, "Battle," 233, 234.
[7]Parkhurst, "Recollections," 7.

comfortably. Then Berry remarked that he was "nearly dead for water" and was surprised as the Federal offered him a canteen. Berry declined to take it, telling the Yankee that he himself would need all his water. But the wounded man insisted and Berry then took a few swallows of what he recalled was some of the best water he ever drank. And, he added, if the man were still living, he would like to meet him again.[8]

There were also Yank-Reb meetings involving the wounded that turned out quite differently—that seemed about as bitter as the worst fighting. Dave Sublee of the First Tennessee stumbled across a wounded Union soldier who asked for a drink of water. Looking down at the man, Sublee asked him the name of his regiment. After answering the question the Federal added, "A damned good regiment too; and if we had many such you wouldn't have been here." "Well," replied Sublee, his temper flaring, "but you are here, and you want a drink of water. Well, I won't give you a drop, for I have no doubt that when you are home you live near a running creek or a big spring and, damn you! that's where you ought to be now!"[9]

Besides the wounded and the Rebel cavalry, there were other people in some of the rear areas. Seventeen-year-old Bromfield L. Ridley, who lived near the little town of La Vergne, about ten miles from the battle ground, had joined the so-called Seed Corn Contingent, a group of boys under eighteen years of age, too young to be called upon for regular service in the Confederate army. This band of Southern teenagers was in the rear areas of the Union army busy picking up Yankee stragglers, whom they found fleeing in every direction. Ridley said the Seed Corn Contingent bagged more than two hundred prisoners and the prized one, caught four or five miles from the battle area, was a lieutenant colonel. Elated by the rout of the Federal right wing, young Ridley thought the whole Union army would have suffered the same fate if Bragg had vigorously followed up his dawn assault.[10]

Ridley may have been right, but General Rosecrans was taking effective action to stop the Rebel onslaught. He sent fresh regi-

[8]*Confederate Veteran*, VIII, 73.
[9]Womack, "River," 9.
[10]Ridley, *Battles and Sketches*, 148–49, 152–53.

ments from his left and center into his new line. Staff officers were instructed to reform the stragglers and use them, along with the reserves and units retreating in some semblance of order, to strengthen the new defensive position. The remaining artillery was strategically placed to support the line, commanding the southern approaches from which the Confederates were coming. Rosecrans' new position, if successfully defended, would save his wagon trains in the rear and enable the Union army to hold the Nashville Pike as well as the railroad.[11]

But the general was also concerned about his left flank, where he feared the Confederates might try to follow up the Federal withdrawal in that sector. Having already ordered that one brigade of Van Cleve's division be left to guard the ford across Stones River, Rosecrans, accompanied by his assistant adjutant general (chief of staff), rode to the river bank position and inquired who commanded the brigade. Stepping forward was Samuel W. Price, a Union colonel from Kentucky. "Will you hold this ford?" Rosecrans demanded. "I will try, sir," replied Price. Rosecrans was not satisfied and repeated his question. Then the colonel answered firmly, "I will die right here." The answer was still not what the general desired and for the third time he addressed Price, "Will you hold this ford?" Price responded with two words, "Yes, sir." At last Rosecrans had the simple, determined answer he sought. "That will do," he said, and turning his horse, galloped off toward the tumult of battle.[12]

Rosecrans seemed to be everywhere, trying to see personally to all his dispositions. Those who saw him in the heat of the fight at Stones River were impressed. Henry Freeman remembered him as "every inch a soldier," and as the general passed with a part of his staff riding to the front, Freeman said that "the crisis seemed to rouse his every energy." Rosecrans was "the embodiment of strength, courage, coolness and determination."[13] Surgeon Eben Swift recalled him as "moving calmly, cheering and inspiring our faltering

---

[11]*OR*, 192–93. Lamers, *Rosecrans*, 223–25. Williams, *Lincoln*, IV, 267–68. Wilson J. Vance, *Stone's River: The Turning Point of the Civil War* (New York, 1914), 48–49.

[12]Clarence C. Buell and Robert U. Johnson eds., *Battles and Leaders of the Civil War*, 4 vols. (New York, 1887–88), III, 623. Lamers, *Rosecrans*, 225–26. Foote, *Civil War*, II, 90.

[13]Freeman, "Battle," 234.

troops, . . . and wherever the battle raged most fiercely, General Rosecrans bore his charmed life." Wearing his old blue overcoat, with a cigar stump clamped between his teeth, wrote J.L. Yaryan, "he left the position usually occupied by the Chief, came to the line of battle, and by his presence and words cheered and encouraged the men of the center and left." Whitelaw Reid said that "when disaster had enveloped half the army . . . Rosecrans was magnificent. He grasped in his . . . hands the fortunes of the day" and "stemmed the tide of retreat. . . ."[14]

Rosecrans' assistant adjutant general and highly respected companion, Lieutenant Colonel Julius P. Gareschè, thought the general was recklessly exposing himself to death and pleaded with him to be more careful. "Never mind me," Rosecrans replied. "Make the sign of the cross and go in." The only way to be safe, he said, was to destroy the enemy. "This battle must be won," he kept repeating.[15]

Later in the morning Rosecrans found Sheridan leading back some of the survivors from his cut-up division. Sheridan's face was darkened with black powder. His ammunition was gone and, forced to retreat, he was angry and swearing furiously. "Watch your language," Rosecrans said as he cut short the tirade. "Remember, the first bullet may send you to eternity." Sheridan protested, "I can't help it. Unless I swear like hell the men won't take me seriously." Then he pointed to his broken ranks. "This is all that is left, General." Rosecrans assured him that ammunition was available because Crittenden's wagon train was still intact and, he continued, the Union army must resist the Rebel advance as stubbornly as possible. The momentum of their attack had to be arrested. "Replenish your ammunition," the general concluded, "and get your men back into the fight."[16]

Rosecrans was now in the midst of the battle, hurrying up ammunition that was needed at many points, planting Captain James H. Stokes' Chicago Board of Trade Battery on a rise of ground, and placi..g the Pioneer Brigade in position for its support, the first battalion on the left and the others on the right of the battery.

[14]Lamers, *Rosecrans*, 226, 227.
[15]*Ibid.*, 225. Foote, *Civil War*, II, 91.
[16]Lamers, *Rosecrans*, 227. Sheridan, *Memoirs*, I, 232-33.

He rode from place to place; posted other batteries; directed the formation of new lines; conferred with his corps, division, and brigade commanders; and observed the terrain and enemy positions. Sometimes he was up front, right on the battle line, as when, later in the day, the Rebels struck Van Cleve's position and Rosecrans directed a counterattack. An orderly had already been struck and killed beside him, but the general seemed totally without fear. Staff officers were waving hats, shouting encouragement to the line, and flashing their swords. Then Rosecrans shouted, "Now, let the whole line charge!" "Shoot low! Be sure of your aim!" he admonished, as a cheer rose, bugles blew, and the Union line moved forward, pushing the Rebels back in that sector.[17]

At such times the general was more nearly performing the role of a division commander than an army commander, but his obvious presence at the front, as he probably realized, helped to reanimate the hard-pressed Yankee soldiers. Rosecrans seemed infused with the grim determination that comes when one is shocked, almost sickened, by the realization that he is on the verge of being beaten, and then begins to fight back with everything that he has. Undoubtedly his example, as well as his decisions, were factors in steeling the Federal forces to fight, regardless of the consequences, to stop the Rebel avalanche—or die trying.

But, late in the day, in spurring from one part of the field to another, the general narrowly escaped being hit by a cannonball that decapitated one of the men riding with him. It was his friend Garesché. According to a witness of the gory scene, the headless body rode on for almost twenty paces as the horse plunged forward, and then it slid off. Rosecrans' coat was bespattered by the blood, causing many people who saw him afterward to assume that he was wounded. "Oh, no," he would say, "That is the blood of poor Garesché." Regardless of how heartsick he may have felt, there was no time to stop.[18]

At mid-morning the Union forces were working desperately to form a last line of defense to cover the railroad and the Nashville Pike, while two key divisions carried the brunt of the battle, struggling to stave off disaster. Those Federals that grimly fought against

[17]Freeman, "Battle," 234. Vance, *Stone's River*, 49. Lamers, *Rosecrans*, 230.
[18]Lamers, *Rosecrans*, 232. Vance, *Stone's River*, 49. Foote, *Civil War*, II, 91.

(*Above*): Federal forces fight to hold the pike and the railroad to Nashville as the seemingly triumphant Rebel army drives toward these lines of retreat. (*Below*): Colonel Samuel Beatty's brigade advanced with determination to sustain the right side of the Union line in the bloody struggle of December 31, 1862.

the full fury of a driving enemy that saw victory within its grasp were Sheridan's emaciated division, which had relocated in the cedars north of the Wilkinson Pike and west of a farm (today's Van Cleve Lane), and Brigadier General James S. Negley's division of Thomas' center corps, which linked up at a right angle with Sheridan's left and extended northeastward toward the Nashville Pike. Colonel John F. Miller and Colonel Timothy R. Stanley's brigades were in the front line of Negley's division. From right to left, Sheridan had Sill's brigade, now led by Colonel Nicholas Greusel, then Colonel Frederick Schaefer's brigade, and finally Roberts' command, now led by Colonel Luther P. Bradley. The Yankee situation largely depended upon whether there would be time for a part of Thomas' corps, plus reinforcements from Crittenden's left corps and the stragglers who could be regrouped, to re-form so that the Union line would be bent back—"refused," in the language of Civil War dispatches—along the southern side of the Nashville Pike.[19]

As Sheridan's brigades made one more stand, completing what was probably a decisive fighting retreat that saved the Federal army at Stones River, and one that was possibly never surpassed during the Civil War, Rosecrans had instructed Thomas to order Major General Lovell H. Rousseau's division southwest into the cedar brakes, coming up on Sheridan's right and rear. Rousseau would thus be in position to protect the rear of both Sheridan and Negley; he must also help stop Hardee's rampaging Confederates from reaching the Nashville Pike. Rosecrans ordered Van Cleve's division to come up on the right of Rousseau, while Colonel Charles G. Harker's brigade from Wood's division was sent still farther to the right of Van Cleve. On the other end of the Federal line, Brigadier General John M. Palmer's division from Crittenden's corps was in position to the left of Negley's soldiers. Palmer's line extended northeastward across the Nashville Pike and toward the river. Colonel William B. Hazen and Brigadier General Charles Cruft's brigades were in the front line, Colonel William Grose's in support. Finally, Colonel George D. Wagner's brigade of Wood's

---

[19]*OR*, 349-50, 407-8, 193-94, 356-57, 370. O'Connor, *Sheridan*, 92-95.

division completed the left of the Union line, anchoring it on the river.[20]

As a result of all the stopgap improvisations, enacted amid the confusion of retreat, there was much intermingling of units and a resultant loss of control by division and corps commanders. Part of Crittenden's corps anchored the left of the line, but another part was on the Union right. Wood's division was likewise split, Wagner's brigade on the left, Harker's on the right of the line, and Brigadier General Milo S. Hascall's in reserve (although it would soon be ordered to reinforce Palmer). Sheridan's division rested between Thomas' two divisions of Negley and Rousseau. And reformed units from McCook's corps were inserted wherever reinforcements were needed.

As Rousseau's division, Lieutenant Colonel Oliver H. Shepherd's brigade on the right front with Colonel John Beatty's brigade on the left and Colonel Benjamin Scribner's unit in support, moved southwest into the dense cedar brake, it slammed into McCown's re-formed Rebel division. These elated Confederates, just resupplied with ammunition after driving McCook's Yankees for two miles, tore into Rousseau's troops with vengeance, confident that they could destroy the Union army.[21]

Colonel John Beatty recalled that General Rousseau had ordered him into this bloody affair with the demand that he hold his position "until hell freezes over." Beatty described the action as the Rebels desperately strove to overcome the Federals: "I take position. An open wood is in my front; but where the line is formed, and to the right and left, the cedar thicket is so dense as to render it impossible to see the length of a regiment." Then came the initial Confederate assault. "The roar of the guns," wrote Beatty, "sounds like the continuous pounding on a thousand anvils. My men are favorably situated, being concealed by the cedars, while the enemy, advancing through the woods, is fully exposed." With a terrible slaughter, the Rebels were finally forced back. But, with barely time to replenish its supply of ammunition, Beatty's bri-

---

[20]*OR*, 193–94, 574, 502, 517, 527, 544–45, 493.
[21]*Ibid.*, 378, 383, 373.

gade could see the Confederates coming again. This charge was made with still more fury and lasted longer, before it too was at last repelled.[22]

Beatty's men were holding their ground, but on his right the Grayclads had driven in the right side of Shepherd's brigade, forcing him to retire, fighting as he did so. Discovering that both Shepherd's and Scribner's brigades had retreated, unable to contact General Rousseau, and seeing troops falling back on his left also, Beatty concluded that hell must be about to freeze over.

Meanwhile, farther to the Union right, Van Cleve's troops, supported by Harker's brigade on their right, had advanced to the southwest through the cedars and across the open fields until Cleburne's Rebel division, still rolling rapidly toward the Nashville Pike, drove into them. A furious fight ensued. Then a gap in the Yankee line gave the Confederates an opportunity. The Grayclads charged into the opening between Colonel James P. Fyffe's brigade of Van Cleves' division and Harker's brigade. Fyffe was outflanked on his right and fell back as Cleburne's men applied pressure all along Van Cleve's front, forcing the rest of his division to retreat.[23]

As troops from Rousseau's and Van Cleve's divisions retreated toward the Nashville Pike, Henry Freeman of Captain James St. Clair Morton's Pioneer Brigade, supporting the Chicago Board of Trade Battery, was in the Yankee position formed as a last line of defense. Freeman dramatically described the scene: "Crossing the railroad to the open space between it and the Nashville Pike we filed to the right and formed line of battle. 'Battalion, lie down!' was ordered, and the line lay prostrate, each man keenly peering into the thicket in front. . . ." A hail of bullets was passing over the Federals and many missiles were smacking into the ground, throwing dirt into the faces of the crouching men. "On came the sounds of battle," wrote Freeman. "Then . . . the line of struggling blue-coats slowly falling back came into view through the trees. They were loading and firing as they retired. But their am-

[22]Beatty, *Memoirs*, 153. Richard O'Connor, *Thomas: Rock of Chickamauga* (New York, 1948), 211.
[23]*OR*, 502-3, 574, 597-98.

munition was about exhausted, and they passed over our prostrate line and laid down behind it." Freeman remembered that the order "'Battalion, rise up!' came like an electric shock!"

Then Morton, the brigade commander whose long brown hair made him obvious for all to see, rode to the front and called out to the ranks, "'Men, you haven't got much ammunition, but give 'em what you have, and then wade in on 'em with the bayonets!' The Confederates were near at hand," continued Freeman. "Suddenly their line seemed to burst through the thicket just in front. 'Commence firing!' rang out, and men on both sides were cut down by a storm of bullets. Some were screaming, 'Give 'em hell.'" Others were urging, "Pour in the shot, boys!" Everyone seemed to be yelling. Freeman could see the Rebel flag moving forward, then wavering, and finally, it was going back! Then an officer was shouting "Forward, Forward!" and the Union line pressed after the retreating Confederates for a short distance before stopping to re-form, and then it pushed forward again.

Dead and wounded lay everywhere. Freeman heard someone call his name and recognized Sergeant Post of the Seventy-fourth Illinois, his leg torn and mangled by three bullets. A smile spread over Post's face as Freeman extended his hand and the sergeant grasped it. There was only time for the hurried pressure of a hand clasp as the advance was stopped and the Federals prepared for the next Rebel attack.[24]

Farther to the southeast, at the bloody angle formed by Sheridan and Negley's divisions, the battle was building to another climax. Again the decisive pressure was on Sheridan. His men, he said, gave no sign of faltering but cried for more ammunition. All but two regiments of Schaeffer's brigade had now run out of cartridges. The corps' ammunition train had disappeared in the first assaults of the day, and it was thought to have been captured. Actually, it was saved by the heroic efforts of Captain Gates P. Thruston, whose men cut a path through the cedars and reached the Nashville Pike just in time to avoid capture and to supply the new Union line.

[24]Freeman, "Battle," 234–36.

Sheridan had to pull back his men or see them overrun. He ordered Schaeffer's two regiments to counterattack, hoping to give the rest of his division time to withdraw. The Rebels were forced back, but Colonel Schaeffer was killed, Sheridan's third brigade commander to die within about three hours of fighting.[25]

Private Henry A. Castle penned a moving account of some of the action, concluding with Schaeffer's death:

I saw a Rebel battery come up. I started promptly for the center of the regiment to notify the major, but heard that he had just been carried off wounded. I then ran to the right to find the adjutant, and learned that he, too, had retired for the same reason. I assumed the responsibility of marching the company double-quick out of the defile, trusting the rest to follow, which they did with alacrity, as just then the shells came shrieking through the straight and narrow gorge with a venom that would have left few unscathed in five minutes more. I then notified the four remaining captains that they were without a commander. Being of equal rank, they sent me to the brigade commander, sitting on his horse 200 yards to the rear, with a request to settle the matter of procedure. I started toward him, but before I had made half the distance he, the last of our brigade commanders, was shot before my eyes and fell to the ground a corpse.[26]

Sheridan's division had lost more than one-third of its fighting force and, without ammunition, had to counterattack with bayonets to keep the Confederates off its flanks as the unit withdrew. Eight guns had to be abandoned, but the rest of the artillery was hauled through the forest by hand. The retreat must have been, as Richard O'Connor has suggested, "a ghastly procession of powder-stained, exhausted, bloody-bandaged men; youth made weary and sick in a few hours of killing and maiming in the dark forest."[27]

But it was still not over for Sheridan's men. General Rosecrans galloped up and ordered Sheridan to replenish his ammunition, marching one regiment at a time to the rear. Roberts' brigade, now led by Colonel Bradley, would be taken to the right where it would fight again under the direction of General McCook, and

[25]*OR*, 350.
[26]O'Connor, *Sheridan*, 94.
[27]*Ibid.*, 95.

Schaeffer's brigade, now commanded by Lieutenant Colonel Bernard Laibold, would see action once more on the left of the Union line.

It was about eleven o'clock when Sheridan withdrew from the cedars, leaving a gap between Rosseau and Negley which the Rebels soon exploited. This had compelled Colonel Beatty to pull back his brigade as the Confederates began pressing into his rear. The withdrawal of Sheridan also forced the withdrawal of Negley, whose division soon came under a heavy converging fire, with the enemy coming around his right flank.

In retiring, Negley had to drive the Rebels from his path at the same time that he held back a column that was pressing his rear. After a terrific fight, Negley at last reported with his two brigades — less some guns left behind — to General Thomas who then had his corps together. The right of Palmer's division also had to withdraw to avoid being enveloped, but his left brigade — Hazen's command — continued to hold its strong position on a wooded knoll astride the railroad.[28]

All along the line a spectrum of frantic and often sickening events was unfolding in the midst of the continuing violence. One Confederate soldier remembered that the Rebels had just overrun the Harding house, which the Yankees had been using for a hospital. A number of Federal wounded were left behind, lying on the floor. Suddenly a shot from one of the Union batteries crashed into the house and C. Irving Walker saw five of the wounded Yankees torn and killed by the missile as blood, flesh, and muscle spattered all over the room.[29]

Another Confederate, J.H. Nichols, charging toward the Federals, was keenly aware that men all around were being cut down by the enemy fire. Then a sudden pain struck Nichols, his legs folded, and he too was on the ground. His right leg was paralyzed. "For some minutes," Nichols recalled, "I lay on the ground watching the maneuvering of the enemy," and then the full realization

[28]OR, 407-8, 373, 544-45, 517. Williams, Lincoln, IV, 269. Wilbur Thomas, General George H. Thomas: The Indomitable Warrior (New York, 1964), 293-94. Alexander F. Stevenson, The Battle of Stone's River (Boston, 1884), 81-89. O'Connor, Sheridan, 94-95.

[29]Confederate Veteran, XV, 263.

This battle sketch graphically depicts the prolonged and bloody fighting that characterized the intense fight along the banks of Stones River.

of the "great danger to which I was exposed" came over him. Frantically, he began struggling to drag himself along the ground away from the carnage.[30]

One Union soldier, whose wound had been dressed by a surgeon and who had the use of his hands, was sent to build a fire for the rest of the wounded. Before he could start the fire, he was struck again, a bullet ripping through his arm, and he returned to the doctor. Perhaps he may have wondered if he were jinxed because, within a matter of minutes, the Rebels swept through the area and he had become a prisoner.[31]

A Rebel sergeant, Joseph Thompson, of Company I, Nineteenth Tennessee Infantry, dashed far out into a clearing, captured a Yankee prisoner, and was returning in triumph when a shell burst above his prize, killing the Federal instantly. With a grim determination, Thompson turned around, charged once more toward the Union lines, captured still another Federal, and succeeded in bringing him safely back to the Confederate lines.[32]

As Sam Watkins, struck in the arm by a fragment of a shell, headed back toward a Confederate field hospital, he overtook a man whose left arm had been entirely torn off. The soldier was, Watkins recalled, "as white as a sheet." Dazed with shock, the wounded man moved toward the rear while Watkins, in wonder and horror, watched the ghastly sight of bloody, mangled flesh where once had been an arm. All at once the man dropped down and died, without a struggle or a groan.[33]

Across the way in the Union lines, J.H. Haynie of the Nineteenth Illinois, fighting in Negley's division, described how the battle looked from the Yankee side. He wrote, "Our comrades were falling as wheat falls before the cradling machines at harvest time. We could hear the hoarse shriek of shell, the . . . rattle of musketry, . . . the impact of solid shot, the 'chug' when human forms were hit hard, the yells of pain, the cries of agony, the fearful groans. . . . Struck horses, no longer neighing or whinnying, were

[30]*Ibid.*, X, 162.
[31]Bennett and Haigh, *Thirty-Sixth Illinois*, 334.
[32]W.J. Worsham, *The Old Nineteenth Tennessee Regiment, C.S.A.: June, 1861–April, 1865* (Knoxville, 1902), 72.
[33]Watkins, *"Co. Aytch,"* 95.

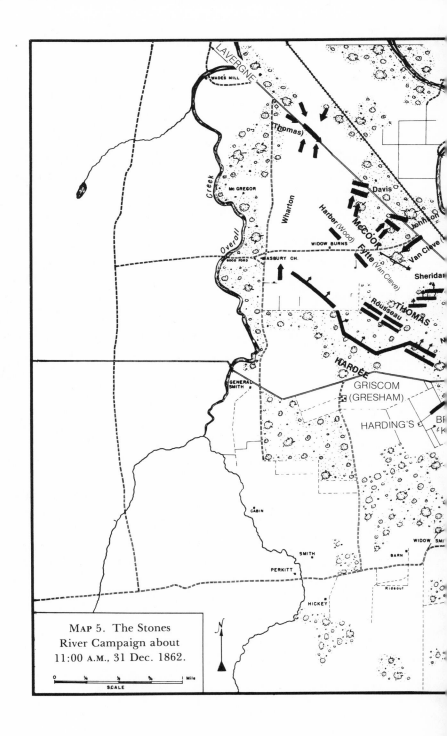

MAP 5. The Stones River Campaign about 11:00 A.M., 31 Dec. 1862.

SCALE

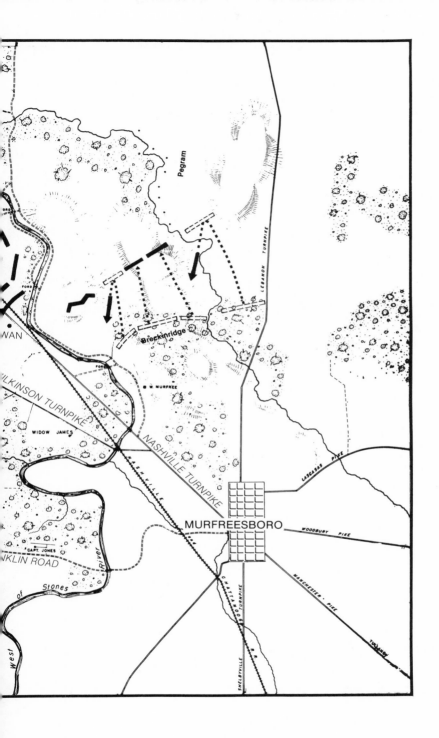

Pegram

LEBANON TURNPIKE

Breckinridge

W. MURFREE

WILKINSON TURNPIKE

NASHVILLE TURNPIKE

NASHVILLE R.R.

WIDOW JAMES

LASCASAS PIKE

MURFREESBORO

WOODBURY PIKE

CAPT. JONES

FRANKLIN ROAD

WEST FORK of Stones River

CHATTANOOGA TURNPIKE

MANCHESTER PIKE

SHELBYVILLE R.R.

TURNPIKE

agonizing in their frantic cries. Cannon balls cut down trees around and over us, which falling crushed living and dead alike. . . ."[34]

Alexander F. Stevenson was another Yankee who recalled the gruesome scenes amidst the dead and dying and wounded as the armies frantically grappled. Death and blood seemed to be everywhere, he said. The commander of the Twenty-seventh Illinois, Colonel Fazilo A. Harrington, was struck by a piece of shell that tore the jaw away from his face. Lieutenant Colonel Francis Swanwick, of the Twenty-second Illinois, was so badly wounded that he could not be moved, while Captain Charles Houghtaling was carried away barely alive, the blood, as it flowed from his wound, leaving a dark track on the cold stones. Stevenson remembered Lieutenant R.C.M. Talliaferro, who had seemed completely unafraid as the fight raged furiously, shot dead between his cannons, and Houghtaling's men, refusing to leave their guns, concluded Stevenson, fought with revolvers, sabers, and even ramrods before the Rebels finally overwhelmed them.[35]

A Confederate soldier remembered coming upon a dead Yankee colonel and said, "he had on the finest clothes I ever saw, a red sash and fine sword. I particularly noticed his boots. I needed them, and had made up my mind to wear them out for him. . . . I took hold of the foot and raised it up and made one trial at the boot to get it off. I happened to look up, and the colonel had his eyes wide open, and seemed to be looking at me. He was stone dead, but I dropped that foot quick. It was my first and last attempt to rob a dead Yankee."[36]

These and countless more were the awful, strange, sometimes grimly humorous, and often tragic occurrences up and down the lines as the battle raged. The struggle involved every type of man — most were dirty, darkened by gunpowder, their adrenalin flowing freely. Furiously they fought in a heavy, gloomy haze of stifling gun smoke, amidst the deafening noise of musketry and artillery, the terrifying crash of cannon projectiles tearing through the branches of the trees, and the horrifying sight of the gruesomely mangled wounded men, often writhing in agony, struggling but

---

[34]J. Henry Haynie, *The Nineteenth Illinois* (Chicago, 1912), 186.
[35]Stanley F. Horn, ed., *Tennessee's War, 1861–1865* (Nashville, 1965), 142.
[36]Watkins, *"Co. Aytch,"* 95.

unable to escape the scene of carnage. Everywhere lay dead soldiers and dead and maimed horses; the ground was littered with thousands of lost, broken, or abandoned accoutrements of war. Many wanted to turn and run—and some did. Some overcame a natural revulsion to the ghastly horrors of war with the belief that their cause was right. Others fought only for their unit, their comrades, during these intense, violent hours when no one else really mattered, when the rest of human kind was blocked out of mind. Still others fought merely because they were there, cruelly trapped in a particular time and place from which there was no escape. A few would even say, later, that they were glad they were in it. Probably many of their realistic comrades would not have believed them.

By noon the Federals had been forced back to what turned out to be their final defensive position. If the original Union line were compared to a gigantic jack knife with the blade open and pointing south and slightly west, the blade would now be more than halfway closed. And the point where the blade bends back from the handle would be the wooded knoll astride the railroad and close to the Nashville Pike.

But the Rebel successes thus far were more apparent than actual. True, the Confederates had surprised, mauled, and driven most of the right side of the Union line for nearly three miles. Nevertheless, Sheridan's division of the Yankees' right-wing corps, in one of those intangibles of war, had made an unusually stubborn defense, complicating and delaying the Rebel assault. The Confederates had not gained either the Nashville Pike or the railroad. Thus Bragg's plan to cut off the Federals from their Nashville base was unrealized. The Rebel drive had gradually lost momentum. Their wheeling tactics, improperly executed, whether due to difficult terrain or faulty leadership, resulted in inefficient use of manpower and subjected some units to costly flanking fire. In order to plug the gaps in the line, the Confederates had already committed their reserves in the attacking force to the battle. And Bragg had made no provisions for bringing any reinforcements to strengthen his assaulting columns.

As the Confederates made desperate onslaughts to break the Yankees' line at the Nashville Pike and complete a dazzling triumph for the Southern cause, they came up against fresh Union brigades, assisted by regrouped units from the early morning struggle, all favored by terrain and supported by strategically placed artillery. These Yankees were fighting as if they believed what their commander was saying, "This battle must be won!"

8

"Hell's Half Acre"

Now the Rebels prepared for the final attack, the assault on the sharp salient at the center of the Yankee line that protected the railroad and the Nashville Pike. Within this salient, slightly northeast of the pike and on both sides of the railroad, was a thick, circular clump of cedars covering about four acres of rocky, moderately elevated ground. After Action Reports referred to it as "Round Forest," the name by which local citizens knew it. Several hours before the day was over, however, it had become known to the soldiers who fought there by a new name, "Hell's Half Acre."

This point, where the V-shaped Union lines came together, was initially weak, the most exposed part of the Yankee position, being subject to enemy crossfire. But directly in its rear, immensely strengthening the salient, Generals Rosecrans and Thomas had concentrated more than fifty guns, artillery of all calibers, ready to unleash a withering fire over the heads of the Union infantry and strike into the ranks of the oncoming Rebels. The weak became strong and the salient was then fraught with destruction and death for Blue and Gray alike.

The infantry posted in the Round Forest were men from Colonel William B. Hazen's and Brigadier General Charles Cruft's brigades, supported by Colonel William Grose's brigade, all from Palmer's division, and Brigadier General Milo S. Hascall's and Colonel George D. Wagner's brigade of Wood's Division. When fully formed, this last Union defensive alignment, looking from Palmer's and Wood's focal divisions to the right and back to the northwest, was in the following order: Negley's and Rousseau's divisions of Thomas' corps, then Morton's Pioneers; next came Harker's brigade from Wood's division and, finally, the re-formed divisions of Davis and Johnson. Holding the Union line to the left and northeast of Palmer was Wagner's brigade from Wood's division.[1]

Here at the Round Forest, with Palmer's and Thomas' soldiers bearing the brunt of the Confederate attack, the surging Rebels were brought to a halt. Ironically, it was the hard-charging Confederates who had forced the Federals back into the Round Forest from their earlier position several hundred yards southeast in the cotton fields around the recently burned Cowan house. Once the Yankees were firmly ensconced in the wooded position, it seemed that nothing the Grayclads tried could shake them loose.

Twice in the late morning the Rebels attacked up the axis of the Nashville Pike and railroad, trying to drive them out of the clump of cedars. The first Confederate assault on Round Forest was made by Brigadier General James R. Chalmers' brigade of Mississippians, who had been waiting forty-eight hours in shallow trenches and without fires. These veterans of Shiloh knew what was expected of them and charged across the cotton fields, bellowing out the Rebel yell. The time must have been a little after eleven o'clock.[2]

Reaching the Cowan house, they were met by a barrage of artillery fire, massed Yankee cannon, staggering the Gray ranks with an awful slaughter. Still they advanced, some plucking cotton and stuffing it in their ears to diminish the deafening noise. Then the Union infantry concealed in the cedars and posted in the field south of the Pike opened fire with rifled-muskets, cutting down the Mississippians by the dozens. General Chalmers was struck in the head and carried from the field unconscious. Some regiments lost a half-dozen color-bearers. The Federals said it was like a shooting gallery; they could not fire amiss as they mowed down the struggling Rebels. The Confederate lines wavered, became disorganized, and finally fell back, leaving a third of their strength dead or wounded in the open fields.[3]

[1]*OR*, 373, 377-78, 407-8, 460-61, 517, 544-45, 574-75.
[2]*Ibid.*, 756.
[3]Foote, *Civil War*, II, 92. *OR*, 756. Horn, *Army*, 203. Buell and Johnson, *Battles and Leaders*, III, 629.

Photograph by Rudy E. Sanders

Looking southeast from the Stones River National Cemetery, a lone artillery piece marks the position of the Yankee infantry defending the Union center and right, stretching back along the Nashville Pike to the west. The gun points in the direction from which the Rebels were attacking.

Next came Brigadier General Daniel S. Donelson's brigade of Tennesseans from Cheatham's division. One of the regiments in Donelson's brigade was the Eighth Tennessee. Lieutenant Colonel John Anderson reported that before the assault the regiment lay for twenty minutes behind the flimsy rail and log fortifications just vacated by Chalmer's brigade when it charged. Anderson said that a hail of bullets was passing above the men, many missiles smacking into the logs, and some were coming underneath the logs. The Eighth Tennessee lost fifteen or twenty killed and wounded while waiting in this position. Following the awful wait was the disconcerting spectacle of Chalmers' brigade pouring back in retreat, its squads and companies trampling over the Eighth's crouching soldiers, after which came their turn to attack.[4]

It was about noon when Donelson's men surged across the very same ground where Chalmers had failed. And the Cowan house, with its yard and garden fences, split the line into separate forces, Colonel John H. Savage's Sixteenth Tennessee and three companies of Colonel John Chester's Fifty-first Tennessee going to the right and the rest of the brigade to the left. Savage's Tennesseans straddled the railroad as they attacked, two companies on the north side of the tracks and eight companies on the south.[5]

Leading one of the companies to the north of the tracks was Captain D.C. Spurlock, who had been visiting his mother and father only a few hours before the battle. He had not advanced far, one account said less than fifteen yards, when he was shot and killed. In fact, by the time Spurlock fell, every officer in the company had been killed and Private Wright Hackett assumed command and led the men on toward the enemy. The Yankee fire was at its concentrated worst. In a bitter rage, Colonel Savage was crying out at General Donelson, accusing him of putting the Sixteenth Tennessee in a position to get them all killed. Savage saw his brother, acting Lieutenant Colonel L.N. Savage, fall before the steady stream of Yankee fire, but he continued trying to press forward. Then the acting major of the regiment, Captain Jim Womack, who said the space between the two lines was "now an unobstructed plain of only about 100 yards," took a hit, his right arm

[4]*OR*, 715.
[5]*Ibid.*, 711, 717, 707.

badly broken, and went down writhing on the ground in pain as the carnage continued.[6]

At last the punishment was too much. To Savage it seemed that he did not have the expected support on his left. The Rebels were facing "such a fire," one of them remembered, "as I do not suppose men were ever before subjected to"; apparently every man in the regiment would be cut down if they continued (over one-half were killed or wounded), so the Sixteenth Tennessee retreated.[7]

Advancing from the left side of the Cowan house were the Eighth and Thirty-eighth Tennessee regiments, along with most of Colonel Chester's Fifty-first Tennessee. Yelling and shrieking, these Rebels moved at a double-quick pace across the open fields and into the face of a raking Yankee fire. Colonel W. L. Moore was out in front, leading the Eighth Tennessee. As Colonel John Anderson watched, he saw Moore's horse fall and thought that the colonel himself had been killed. The Eighth's color-bearer, J.M. Rice, was shot down, but he determinedly crawled forward on his knees, still holding the colors aloft, until a second bullet killed him.

The Rebels were paying a horrible price, but onward they charged toward the cedar brake south of the Round Forest. At last across the open fields, they were plunging into the Yankee-filled woods when Colonel Moore overtook his regiment. Unharmed, he had freed himself after being pinned under his dying horse and then dashed madly after his regiment. Now, sword in hand, he was once more boldly urging his men forward when he went down, shot through the heart.

Sweeping into the woods, the Confederates crashed into the Federal's first line, which gave way before the elated attackers. A second Union line was brought forward; neither could it stem the hard-driving Tennesseans. The men in Gray had gained a temporary success, driving back Negley's division and Cruft's brigade, capturing about one thousand prisoners and eleven guns.

It was, however, a heartbreaking, pyrrhic victory. The Eighth Tennessee went into the battle with 425 men, of which 306 became casualties, most of them in this devastating assault. In one of its companies, out of twelve officers and sixty-two men engaged,

[6]Womack, "River," 8. Womack, *Diary*, 77.
[7]*OR*, 715.

only one corporal and twenty men escaped unhurt. What happened to the Eighth Tennessee had also happened to the rest of Donelson's brigade. A strong Union counterattack soon drove them away from this blood-bought soil and everything, except for the dead and wounded, was just as it had been before the attack was made.[8]

If the Yankee salient were going to be broken, the Confederate high command had to find reinforcements. General Bragg decided to use Breckinridge's five-brigade division, the largest in the army, still stationed on the east bank of Stones River. About one o'clock he ordered the division across the river, except for Brigadier General Roger W. Hanson's brigade, which was to hold Wayne's Hill, considered strategic in the defense of the Confederate right and rear. Breckinridge's troops could have been used to advantage much earlier, but Bragg, Breckinridge and cavalry Brigadier General John Pegram had inadvertently joined in a mass of confusion that cost the Rebel army about three hours of time—and possibly the battle.

Soon after ten o'clock Bragg had realized that the Rebel attack had lost momentum; some units were out of ammunition, others were disorganized, and many soldiers exhausted. At that time he reached Breckinridge, but what he intended the Kentuckian to do is not clear. Perhaps, with some of Breckinridge's troops, Hardee's drive against the Union right could be reinforced, or maybe Bragg meant to strengthen Polk's divisions then attacking the Federal center. In his official report Bragg said that he ordered Breckinridge to reinforce Polk. His order was not written, however, being verbally conveyed by Major William Clare, Bragg's assistant inspector general. Clare, whose account is supported by two of Breckinridge's staff officers, later recounted that the order was merely for Breckinridge to move forward, that is, to advance his division on the east side of the river.

But Breckinridge, the victim of some poor cavalry reconnaissance, refused to move and reported to the army's commander that the Federals, in heavy force, were coming toward him. The Kentuckian's alarm came from an early morning report of Pe-

[8]*Ibid.*, 711, 715, 718-20, 689-90.

gram's cavalry, saying that a large body of enemy soldiers had crossed the river well upstream and were headed in his direction. Pegram had sighted Van Cleve's Yankees, some of whom were across the stream. These Federals, of course, were withdrawn shortly after the cavalrymen sighted them, but unfortunately for the Confederates, this important fact went unreported and apparently unnoticed for a long time. For several hours, in fact, Breckinridge was content to rely on Pegram's reports, evidently never sending staff officers to determine what the Union force was doing.

Galloping back to Bragg, Major Clare reported the conversation with Breckinridge. Probably, although again there is uncertainty because of conflicting reports, Bragg ordered Breckinridge to first be certain that Yankees were in his front and, if so, to attack them before they advanced. Clare had barely completed relaying this message to Breckinridge when Colonel J. Stoddard Johnson rode up bringing another message from the army's commander. Now Bragg too, like Breckinridge, had received information from Pegram's cavalry that Yankees were crossing the river, information he considered reliable. Bragg ordered the Kentuckian to attack!

Breckinridge alerted his units and moved forward for about a half-mile when new instructions came from Bragg, ordering him to pull back on the defensive and send help for Polk's corps. The time was about eleven-thirty. Bragg called, according to his own account, for two brigades, but Breckinridge said the request was discretionary, asking for one, or two if another could be spared. And the accounts of Breckinridge's staff only serve to further muddle the issue.

Regardless of the truth on this point, the brigades of brigadier generals Daniel W. Adams and John K. Jackson were at once ordered to cross the river and march to the support of General Polk. Then Bragg changed his mind again. His most recent reports, including one from Breckinridge, convinced the commanding general that a Federal force still threatened him on the east side of Stones River. Countermanding his orders for Adams and Jackson to reinforce Polk, he now contemplated strengthening Breckinridge with two brigades from Polk! Then, in a short while, the perplexed general vacillated once more.

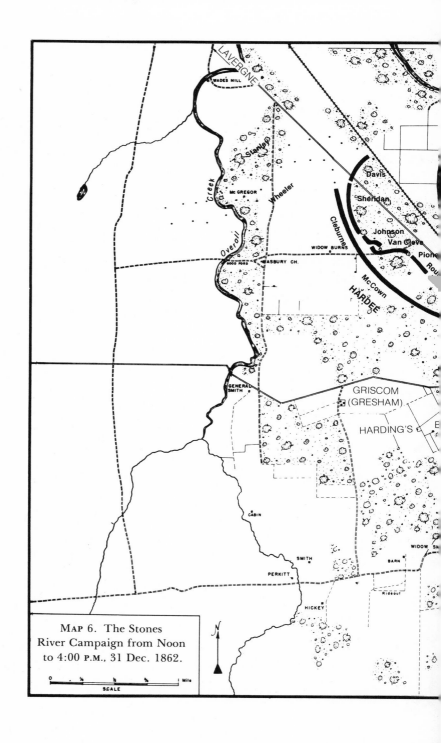

MAP 6. The Stones River Campaign from Noon to 4:00 P.M., 31 Dec. 1862.

SCALE

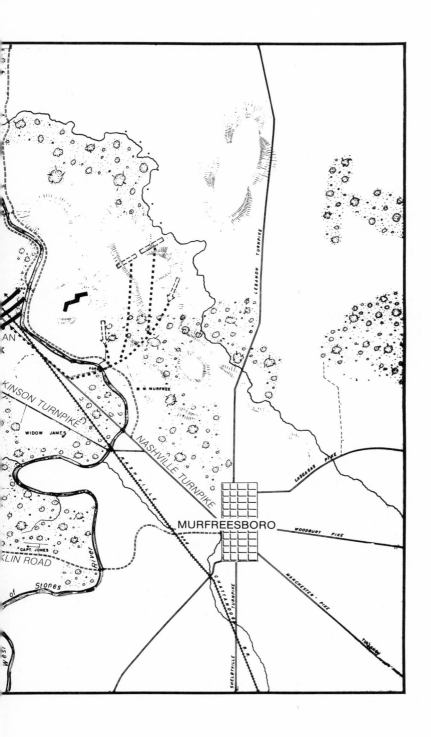

His own scouts were reporting that General Pegram's information was wrong. No Federals were across the river except a few sharpshooters. Certainly no heavy infantry force was about to advance on Breckinridge. And another message from Breckinridge seemed to support this conclusion. Thus, about one o-clock, Bragg ordered Breckinridge to send four of his brigades across the river at once. Polk was at last to be reinforced. The Kentuckian gave word for Adams and Jackson, who had already started, to continue their march, while he followed with the brigades of Brigadier General William Preston and Colonel Joseph B. Palmer.[9]

Bragg's attention was by this time stubbornly fixed upon the Round Forest. He ordered Polk, when the brigades from Breckinridge arrived, to drive the Union left center by throwing all the force he could collect against Hell's Half Acre. Even if the assault failed, Bragg thought it would force Rosecrans to withdraw enough men from the Union right to allow Hardee to reach the Nashville Pike.

Poor leadership, such as by Bragg and Polk, was disheartening and severely limited the chances for a Rebel victory. It should have been evident, after the failure of Chalmers and Donelson, that piecemeal assaults, one brigade after another, could not succeed against the Yankee salient. By the time Breckinridge's soldiers started coming on the field, the Union had been given significant time, an hour or more, in which to strengthen their alignments in the Round Forest and resupply the ammunition for the artillery posted just behind it.

Nevertheless, when Adams and Jackson arrived from across the river, sometime between one-thirty and two o'clock, they were ordered forward, one after another, right across the fields strewn thickly with the dead bodies and seriously wounded of those Confederates who had earlier tried to crush the Union left center. Adams formed his regiments with the Thirteenth and Twentieth Consolidated Louisiana on the right, next the Sixteenth and Twenty-fifth Consolidated Louisiana, and, on the left, the Thirty-second Alabama. Then the mass of Grayclad troops, in excellent

[9]*Ibid.*, 665-66, 694, 702-3, 782-83, 789. Connelly, *Autumn*, 59-60. William C. Davis, *Breckinridge: Statesman, Soldier, Symbol* (Baton Rouge, 1974), 336-37. Mc-Whiney, *Bragg*, I, 357-60.

order, moved steadily toward the wooded rise of ground. The Union soldiers watched them come and one of the Yankees said "it was a magnificent brigade," and "this assault was . . . the most daring, courageous, and best-executed attack which the Confederates made. . . ."[10]

Shells and shots plowed through the Rebel ranks, but still they advanced in near-perfect alignment. Closer and closer they came, their speed increasing. Suddenly the Federals could see, by the glistening flashes, that the Confederate line had brought its arms to a "charge bayonet" and were running forward with a tremendous cheer.

Then rang out, up and down the Union line, the loud commands, "Commence firing! Commence firing!" and volley after volley of rifled-musketry crashed from the Federal line, tearing into the Rebel ranks. They fell by the scores, but their line still moved on as if, some of the Yankees thought, with irresistible force. A part of the Union line melted away, falling back before the attack. But officers were strengthening the weak spots, urging their men to stand and fight, and most did.

And then, very quickly, it was over. The Rebel line had suffered terribly; it was broken and falling back. General Adams was wounded, hundreds of soldiers in his brigade were killed or wounded, and the gallant effort had failed.[11]

Jackson's Georgia-Mississippi brigade following Adams', also charging furiously, was shocked by the murderous Yankee fire. His assault bogged down, with the tide of survivors rolling back. Again Jackson's men formed and charged a second time, only to meet with the same fate. By this time Jackson had lost more than a third of his men, and all of his regimental commanders were killed or wounded.[12]

At this point Breckinridge arrived on the field to find that Adams and Jackson had already been sent in against the enemy without waiting for his other two brigades. He rode forward to rally Adams, only to learn that the general was wounded and Colonel Randall L. Gibson was in command. Then Polk ordered

[10]*OR*, 793, 795, 800, 801. Stevenson, *Battle*, 111–13.
[11]Stevenson, *Battle*, 112–13.
[12]*OR*, 838–39.

Breckinridge to take the Round Forest as soon as his men could finish crossing the river and forming in position for the attack. The Kentuckian determined to lead his troops in person.[13]

William McKay, of the Eighteenth Tennessee Regiment of Prestons' brigade, remembered how his regiment had moved at double-quick time to reinforce Polk, crossing the river in water from knee to waist deep, and Spencer Talley, of the Twenty-eighth Tennessee, said, "We made no halt but plunged right through the river and soon after crossing our pants were frozen . . . and darkness was fast coming on us." It was about four o'clock when the two brigades moved out across the fields of cotton and toward the Yankee salient, Preston on the right and Palmer on the left. "In the fading light," recalled Spencer Talley, "the sheets of fire from the enemy's cannon looked hideous and dazzling. . . ."[14]

The Twentieth Tennessee was on the right of Preston's brigade and struck a picket fence as it advanced. The regiment's colonel, Thomas B. Smith, gave the command, "By the right flank, tear down that picket fence, *March!*" "This command," said W.J. Mc-Murray, "caused a great deal of laughter . . . , but," he added, "it was the last laugh that many of those brave fellows ever had."[15]

Farther to the left, the Fourth Florida, with the Sixtieth North Carolina, a regiment that had never been in an engagement before, advanced toward the Cowan house ruins. They encountered the same yard and garden fences that had earlier split up first Chalmers' and then Donelson's brigade, and also hampered the early afternoon attackers. The two regiments were thrown into considerable confusion. Staff officers and brigade commanders saw the trouble, soon re-formed the ranks, and resumed the advance.[16]

One of the Federals who witnessed the assault said, "The gallantry of this advance is indescribable. . . . The Confederates had no sooner moved into the open field from the cover of the river bank than they were received by a blast from the artillery. . . . Huge gaps were torn in the Confederate line at every discharge. . . ." And Colonel Hazen, in command of the foremost Union brigade

[13]*Ibid.*, 783, 818.
[14]William McKay memoirs, Confederate Collection, TSLA. Womack, "River," 8.
[15]McMurry, *Twentieth Tennessee*, 233.
[16]*OR*, 784.

Said to be the nation's oldest Civil War memorial, the Hazen Monument was erected in 1863 by members of Colonel William B. Hazen's Union brigade as a memorial to fifty-five of their fallen comrades.

at the tip of the salient, was apprehensively waiting and watching the Rebels' steady advance. He wrote:

About 4 P.M. the enemy again advanced upon my front in two lines. The battle had hushed, and the dreadful splendor of this advance can only be conceived, as all description must fall vastly short. His right was even with my left, and his left was lost in the distance. He advanced steadily, and, as it seemed, certainly to victory. I sent back all my remaining staff successively to ask for support, and braced up my own lines as perfectly as possible. The Sixth Kentucky had joined me from the other side some time previously, and was posted just over the embankment of the railroad. They were strengthened with such fragments of troops as I could pick up until a good line was formed along the track. A portion of Sheridan's division was also but a few hundred yards in rear, replenishing their ammunition boxes. A portion of General Hascall's troops was also on the right of the railroad.[17]

Onward rolled the Grayclad wave of attackers, as the sun sank lower behind the cedars and Yankees questioned if they could hold their line one more time. Rebels wondered if this final, sacrificial effort before darkness engulfed the field would prove to be the decisive assault.

It was not to be. Halfway across the four hundred yards of open space General Breckinridge realized that the Union line was not parallel to the Confederate line as supposed; instead the Rebel right and the Union left, at point of contact, would form an acute angle, subjecting the attackers to an enfilading fire. Already, the Twentieth Tennessee was being pinned down on the Rebel right. Private McMurray remembered that "it got so hot for us we were ordered to lie down, with nothing to protect us but cotton stalks. The Yankee infantry had now turned loose on us; we couldn't go forward without reinforcements and they could not be gotten up to where we were, and we didn't want to go back, so we stayed there until it was useless to stay any longer." Finally, Colonel Smith gave the order to fall back, every man for himself and, said McMurray, "if ever you saw a lot of men get out of a place in quick

[17]Horn, *Tennessee's War*, 144. *OR*, 545.

time, the Twentieth Tennessee Regiment did it, I being one of the foremost!"[18]

Lying beside McMurray was a neighbor boy, John Crocker, with whom he had gone to school. When the order to retreat was given, they sprang up together, but a bullet struck Crocker in the upper thigh, shattering the bone and he fell into the hands of the Federals. Crocker survived the wound but McMurray did not see him again until the war was over.[19]

The Twentieth Tennessee's colonel was wounded; J.M. Smith, a color-bearer and brother of the colonel, was dead; a large number of the regiment was left in the cotton field either killed or wounded, and the unit was in a state of confusion. At that point Major Fred Claybrooke, who was mounted on a very large horse, rode forward. He took Issac Hyde, one of the color-bearers, up behind him on the horse with the colors prominently displayed; in spite of the enemy fire, he rode up and down the line, rallying the men until he restored order. Then he faced them by the right flank and double-quicked them under a bluff of rocks at the river edge, out of the line of fire.[20]

Like the Twentieth Tennessee, Preston's entire brigade was being roughly handled by Federal artillery and musketry, but finally he rallied and, along with Palmer, did force the Federal infantry back from the forest. Breckinridge's attack had come nearer to success than those before, but the strength of his assault was spent. His advance stopped in the cedars and the Yankee defenders, although giving ground, were far from crushed. Soon afterward Hardee came up and he and Breckinridge rode along the line, concluded it was too weak to make another assault, and ordered the men to go into bivouac for the night.[21]

It has been written that the Rebels would have smashed the Yankees on December 31 if President Davis had not sent Stevenson's division to Mississippi some two weeks before the battle.

[18]*OR*, 784. Buell and Johnson, *Battles and Leaders*, III, 628–29. McMurray, *Twentieth Tennessee*, 223, 234.

[19]McMurray, *Twentieth Tennessee*, 234.

[20]*Ibid*.

[21]*OR*, 784. Nathaniel Cheairs Hughes, *General William J. Hardee: Old Reliable* (Baton Rouge, 1965), 144.

Bruce Catton has contended that the Southern army "almost certainly would have won decisively if Stevenson's missing division had been there to help."[22] Perhaps, but Bragg's conduct of the battle does not warrant optimism that he would have used Stevenson's division effectively. Probably he could have won the battle on December 31 with the troops at hand, if he had employed them to the best advantage.

The Rebels missed several opportunities. Wharton's cavalry drove to the Nashville Pike in the furious morning attack and, with proper support, which could have been supplied by Wheeler's command, might have held it. But Wheeler, making his spectacular attention-grabbing ride around the Union army, did not arrive on the field of battle until early afternoon. Then he did not support Wharton, instead riding off in a different direction; Wharton was finally beaten back from the pike. A united cavalry command might well have cut Rosecrans' supply line to Nashville.[23]

Another possibility would have been to use Breckinridge's brigades to reinforce Hardee, rejuvenating the original Confederate thrust against the Yankee right and occupying the Nashville Pike in McCook's sector. The Confederates would thus have been continuing to pound the weakest part of the Union line, where there was a good chance of decisive action by rolling up the right and driving it back upon the center. After the shock and devastation of the early morning attack it is doubtful that the Federal army could have withstood another strong assault on that weakened flank.

The importance of the Nashville Pike, from the Federal point of view, is told by Alexander F. Stevenson:

If the Confederates had succeeded in taking and holding the Nashville pike there can be little doubt that the battle would have been lost, and a large part of the army captured. Near the Nashville pike were our ammunition trains, which would have fallen into their hands. The pike was the only road that connected us with Nashville, our base of supplies, and, in case a retreat was necessary, the only road on which the army could fall back. But more important still, it would have enabled the Confederates to enfilade General Thomas' corps, and to fire on Palmer's

[22]*Never Call Retreat* (New York, 1965), 43.
[23]Edwin C. Bearss, "Cavalry Operations," 118-25. Connelly, *Autumn*, 57-58. Dyer, *Shiloh to San Juan*, 68.

Battles and Leaders of the Civil War

The Nashville Pike out of Murfreesboro, here looking northwest, was desperately defended by the Federals as the Confederates sought to sever the Yankee communications with Tennessee's capital.

and Wood's divisions from the rear as well as from the front. Under the demoralizing influence of the defeat of Davis' and Johnson's divisions, but few troops could have stood a double fire like this. . . . A more serious state of affairs cannot be contemplated. . . .[24]

It is an established maxim in military tactics that an attacker should always press his advantage. The commander of the Union left, General Crittenden, later wrote: "Every time the right was driven in I thought (and I now think) that nothing but a most extraordinary blunder on the part of a soldier of the experience of Bragg hindered him from breaking Rosecrans' army in two and leaving me standing with my troops looking at Murfreesboro. . . . Bragg had the advantage; all that he had to do . . . was to pursue it. . . ." Hardee, who did attack the Union right three times in the afternoon, was of the same opinion. "If . . . a fresh division could have replaced Cleburne's exhausted troops," the general contended, "the rout of Rosecrans' army would have been complete."[25]

But Bragg said that by the time Breckinridge's brigades crossed the river it was too late to send them to reinforce Hardee. On this point Bragg was probably right. Breckinridge's troops would have had to follow a winding route around the rear of the entire army. Such a move would have exhausted them and consumed still more time. A reserve to reinforce Hardee should have been provided, but when Breckinridge finally came across the river it was too late. Decisive action by Bragg to assist Hardee would have been required no later than mid-morning.

Whether Breckinridge's brigades were used to reinforce Hardee, or against the Union salient at the Round Forest, entirely too much time was expended in making the decision to bring them across the river. The Federal right was allowed time to recover from the shock of attack and the left center was given too long to be strengthened.

But perhaps the worst Rebel mistake was the piecemeal manner in which Breckinridge's units were fed into the slaughter. One can freely acknowledge the benefit of hindsight and still marvel that

[24]Major Joseph Cumming reminiscences, Joseph Cumming Papers, Southern Historical Collection, Univ. of North Carolina. T.B. Roy, "Hardee Sketch," in Hardee Papers, Alabama State Department of Archives and History, Montgomery. Stevenson, *Battle*, 102–30.
[25]Buell and Johnson, *Battles and Leaders*, III, 633. *OR*, 777.

Bragg and Polk, after their experience at Shiloh against the Hornets' Nest, were making the very same mistake again. Colonel G.C. Kniffin, a Union staff officer, pointedly concluded, "The error made by General Polk in making an attack with the two brigades that first arrived upon the field, instead of awaiting the arrival of General Breckinridge with the remaining brigades, was so palpable as to render an excuse for failure necessary."[26]

Bragg was nearby and must certainly be censured too. As the commander of the army, his was the responsibility to stop a piecemeal attack if he did not approve. One respected student of the war, Kenneth P. Williams, has defended the generals, arguing that "there seems to have been room for no more than a two-brigade front, and how close one assault can follow another must always be a matter of dispute. A long interval favors the defender, but a short one can cause the second assault to be disorganized by men from the one that has failed."[27]

Williams makes an interesting point, but several of the assaults against Hell's Half Acre were not even of two-brigade strength! Chalmers' brigade attacked alone, as did Donelson's, and Jackson's brigade, the smallest in Breckinridge's command, with an effective strength of only 874, also made an unsupported assault. And it seems obvious that an hour and a half is too long between assaults. Yet this was the approximate interval between Donelson's attack and those of Jackson and Adams. Again, about this time passed before Palmer and Preston launched their attacks in the late afternoon.

When it is remembered that Donelson's single brigade supported on the left by Patton Anderson's and A.P. Stewart's brigades, drove the Yankees from the cedar brake south of Hell's Half Acre, even if only temporarily, and that one of Breckinridge's brigades did finally push back the enemy in the Round Forest (albeit retiring from the position in the early morning hours of January 1), then it seems possible that a massed attack with the majority of Breckinridge's reinforcements, numbering more than six thousand soldiers, might have crushed the Union left center and brought a sweeping victory.

[26] Buell and Johnson, *Battles and Leaders*, III, 626.
[27] Williams, *Lincoln*, IV, 273.

Still another good possibility for the Rebels would have been to order Breckinridge's troops to cross Stones River and, with a minimum of marching, attack the Yankee left. With the Federals off balance following Hardee's devastating assault on their right, this pincer movement might also have caught them by surprise. Whether or not surprise were achieved, such an action would have assured the protection of the Confederate right, about which Bragg was so concerned, and placed tremendous pressure upon the Yankees—perhaps decisive pressure.

But when a final analysis is made of the Rebel effort on December 31, it is evident that Bragg's attack was in trouble from the start and the success achieved, as Thomas L. Connelly has observed, "was more superficial than real."[28] For some strange reason Bragg selected McCown, whom Bragg considered his worst division commander, to lead the vital left-flank attack, where the battle opened, weighting him with the heavy responsibility of cutting the Yankees off from their Nashville base by driving through to the Nashville Pike and the railroad. McCown's advance soon carried too far to the left, which pinpointed another problem. Bragg had planned upon the attacking force's making an intricate wheeling movement of men touching elbows as they bore to the right. Such a movement, considering the rugged terrain around Murfreesboro, was impossible; the result was that units were too far spread and had flanking problems, the command suffered loss of control, reserve troops had to be committed too early, and, finally, heavy losses were incurred.

Probably nothing short of immediate, total destruction of McCook's corps was acceptable, if Bragg's plan were going to succeed without some significant adjustments as it unfolded. Grady McWhiney, modern biographer of Bragg, has concluded: "Bragg's plan was defective because, unless the Union army collapsed at the first onslaught, it would be pushed back into a tighter and stronger defensive position as the battle continued, while Confederate forces would gradually lose momentum, become disorganized, and grow weaker. Like a snowball, the Federals would pick up strength from the debris of battle if they retreated in good

---

[28]Connelly, *Autumn*, 55.

order. But the Confederates would inevitably unwind like a ball of string as they advanced."[29]

Actually, Bragg's problem was not so much with the attack plan itself, because no plan in war can be expected to work precisely without modifications, and the Confederate attack did take the Federals by surprise, but rather his abdication of command control once the battle was underway. Bragg either had not given sufficient forethought to coping with the type of situation McWhiney described, which did in fact occur, or assuming he had envisioned the whole spectrum of battle and considered the possible developments and his alternatives, then he lacked the necessary decisiveness to make a firm commitment in the heat of the fight.

Several Rebels later commented about never seeing Bragg throughout the course of the day's struggle. The general was present, but during the morning hours when critical, decisive actions might have been taken by a commanding general, Bragg could just as well have left the field. Having set the holocaust in motion, he simply allowed it to run its own course, taking no significant action until afternoon, when he brought Breckinridge's troops across the river for the piecemeal assaults against Hell's Half Acre.

[29]McWhiney, *Bragg*, I, 364.

9

New Year's Eve

The short winter twilight soon faded into darkness and a hush fell over the battlefield. Both sides, exhausted and badly mauled, seemed relieved as the night finally brought an end to the fighting. The ground was frozen, the wind was strong, and rain beat hard against the fields and glades. There were cities across the land where champagne corks popped and friends danced and wished one another "Happy New Year!" If they could have seen the horror and misery that the savagery of war produces, at that moment spread in hideous panorama west and northwest of Murfreesboro, most of them would have ceased their merrymaking.

"The cold night fell," wrote James K. Hosmer, "the winter heavens dimly lighting up groups shivering by the campfires, and the dreadful field with its burden of mutilation and death." One soldier, who remembered the day as "the longest I have ever spent in my life," said that when the night came, as he walked along "watching the men sitting on the rocks and cold ground shivering. . . , I could not help but think how little the people at home know of the suffering of the soldier." In the cedar thickets and among the limestone boulders tormented men spent an agonizing night; some of them froze to the ground by their own blood. All night long wounded soldiers, Rebel and Yankee, called out for help, for a fire, for a stretcher, for water—or for death.[1]

W.J. McMurray, from the Twentieth Tennessee, was detailed

[1]Lamers, *Rosecrans*, 234.

for picket duty and found "the ground was strewn with the dead and wounded." While making his rounds, about one o'clock in the morning, he discovered a wounded Federal from the Eighteenth U.S. Infantry. The soldier said that he was badly wounded, almost frozen, and asked that McMurray build a fire at his feet. The Rebel responded that a fire would only attract the Yankees' attention and their pickets might start shooting. Overcome by pain and the cold, the Union soldier was not concerned with the danger, pleading for McMurray to build a fire. "He begged me so pitifully, and as he was down in a ravine," wrote the Confederate picket, "I took the chances, and searched among the rocks and got some cedar limbs and made him a fire and gave him some water, placed his head on his knapsack and made him as comfortable as possible. . . . The poor fellow had bled and laid on the cold ground until life was nearly gone."

McMurray told him that if his line were not attacked or ordered away, he would come back again before daylight. When he returned, about two hours later, the Federal "had crossed over and was sleeping the soldier's sleep and I could do no more for him." At daybreak, while still on picket duty near the place where he had ministered to the dying Yankee, McMurray said he counted seventeen minié balls in one cedar tree that was not over twelve inches in diameter at a height of six feet, and twenty-two dead Federals lying within fifty feet of the tree.[2]

A Confederate soldier from the Second Tennessee Regiment remembered how the troops brought in all the wounded within reach, laid them in rows upon the ground, both friend and foe placed together, and then made fires between each row, in an attempt to prevent them from freezing to death.[3]

"The dead and wounded were thick all around us," wrote J.T. Tunnell of the Fourteenth Texas Cavalry (dismounted). There was a large lime sink four or five feet deep nearby. "This afforded protection from the wind, which was very cold, and we built fires in there, as they could not be seen by the enemy," he reported. "Among the wounded," Tunnell continued, "was a Yank quite

[2]McMurray, *Twentieth Tennessee*, 235–36.
[3]Smith, "Confederate Diary," 44.

young and intelligent, shot . . . through the breast. . . . We divided water and rations with him, and next morning our young Yank, with assistance to rise, could sit up awhile."[4]

Similar scenes were occurring on the Union side of the field. "No fires were permitted," recalled Henry Freeman who went on picket duty at midnight, "but the officer whom I relieved pointed out a crevice between two rocks, just wide enough to get into, at one end of which he had built a smouldering fire, not visible a few feet away. It made a good fireplace, with a comfortable seat, and here, after each round of the picket line, one could stop and warm up." Only a few feet away, Freeman continued, were "two severely wounded Confederates, for whom nothing could be done more than to supply water from my canteen to allay their thirst. One of them seemed very grateful. Both were dead when the morning of the new year, 1863, at length dawned. . . . Some kindly hand covered their faces with their hats and spread blankets over the . . . remains. . . ."[5]

Uncomfortable in the cold night that became still colder toward morning, and amid the wreckage and the corpses, another Federal remembered that "for a long time sleep fled my eyes; the past day seemed more like a month, when measured by events and especially by the contrast between my feelings and anticipations in the morning, and our actual condition at night. This was New Year's Eve, such a one as I had never before seen."[6]

Still another Yankee recounted how, on that bitter cold night when he had no blanket, a Rebel deserter came into the Federal lines, wrapped in a blanket which he gave to the grateful Union soldier. "It was stiff and glazed with blood and long use," the Federal said, "but it proved the most comfortable blanket I ever saw."[7]

Many people who lived near Murfreesboro, within hearing of the battle, were especially worried about their relatives in the Confederate army. James Foster, a wealthy planter who lived on the border between Rutherford and Bedford counties, had five sons in the Rebel army at Murfreesboro. All day December 31 he

[4]*Confederate Veteran*, XVI, 574.
[5]Freeman, "Battle," 239–40.
[6]Bennett and Haigh, *Thirty-Sixth Illinois*, 355.
[7]William B. Hazen, *A Narrative of Military Service* (Boston, 1885), 6.

paced the yard in the dim, dank cold, listening to the cannonade of the battle. Finally, at dusk, as the battle sounds diminished, he called one of his tenants and said, "Go hitch the mules to a wagon and go to Murfreesboro and bring back my dead and wounded boys." About midnight the man returned with an empty wagon. All five of the Foster boys had survived.[8]

As soon as he could find time, General Breckinridge sent his son Clifton — serving in the cavalry escort attached to his father's headquarters — into Murfreesboro to see his wife Mary and tell her that he and their sons had come through the battle unharmed.[9]

Few could hope to be so fortunate. Young G.B. Moon, who had a brother in the Twenty-third Tennessee of Cleburne's division, came from Unionville, in company with several friends, to see the battlefield. Arriving at sunset, he was appalled by the horrible sights of the wounded. Moon spent most of the night searching for his brother Richard, whom he learned was among the casualties, but could not find him. All the next day he continued the search, to no avail. And one woman who lived near Murfreesboro had four sons fighting in the Confederate army, all killed in this battle. B.L. Ridley later listed a number of soldiers in the Rebel army, all from around Murfreesboro, all either killed or wounded in the fight.[10]

For one reason or another some of the dead were given special attention. Colonel Hazen searched along the railroad tracks for the body of his friend, Julius Garesché. When he found it, the muscles in Garesché's hand contracted, Hazen thought, and the dead hand reached toward him. He grasped it, removed the West Point ring, picked up *The Imitation of Christ* by Thomas a Kempis that Garesché always carried, and sent a detail to remove the body to a less exposed place. Later in the night, on high ground at the rear of the Union left, Hazen watched a burial squad dig Garesché's grave.[11]

Under the cover of darkness the survivors of D.C. Spurlock's company of the Sixteenth Tennessee crept alongside the railroad and retrieved the body of their captain. When they reached the

[8]Interview with Robert McBride, descendant of the Foster family, May 2, 1978.
[9]Davis, *Breckinridge*, 338.
[10]*Confederate Veteran*, VII, 119. Ridley, *Battles and Sketches*, 155-56.
[11]Lamers, *Rosecrans*, 234.

Harper's Pictorial of the Civil War

In this night scene Union soldiers prepare a grave for Colonel Julius Ga-resché, assistant adjutant-general to General Rosecrans. The twenty-one-year-veteran of the regular army, decapitated as he rode beside his commander, had long believed that he would be killed in his first battle.

spot where he had fallen they wrapped his body in a blanket and carried it to the town square to be delivered to his parents. The next day the heartsick parents began the trip to McMinnville with the dead body of their son in the back of the wagon.[12]

Perhaps the most remarkable incident was the tribute paid by the Rebels to Union Colonel George W. Roberts, who had fallen while so conspicuously directing Sheridan's Third Brigade. The Confederates dug a grave among the rocks and cedars; Major Luke W. Finlay wrapped the body in his own military cloak and read the service of the dead over the remains; a military salute was fired and a bugler played taps. Last of all, a group of privates brought a large smooth stone and placed it on Colonel Roberts' grave, having chipped an inscription on the stone.[13]

Many of those soldiers who had not been wounded were ravenously hungry. A young woman who lived in Murfreesboro said that sometime after dark a mass of Confederate troops filed onto the front lawn of her home. The officer in charge promised that his men had been given strict orders not to touch anything. Then he turned to the mother of the house, saying, "We have had nothing to eat for —— " but she interrupted, calling to her cook with instructions to "put on both ovens and have them ready quick." Making dough and rolling it into the old-fashioned "journey cakes," she passed them out to the soldiers as fast as they could be cooked.[14]

Most men, the Blue and Gray, had to be satisfied with less appetizing food. A Federal soldier recalled: "In the evening some rations of 'shoulder' came up, and one box of hard-tack, sufficient to give one cracker to each man, which was distributed." Some men boiled coffee, in spite of the orders against building fires, and if they had a little bacon to go along with it, that was all for which they could reasonably hope.[15]

Perhaps the cold was more difficult to bear than the scarcity of

[12]Womack, "River," 9.
[13]Smith, "Twenty Fourth Tennessee," 88.
[14]*Confederate Veteran*, XX, 519.
[15]Freeman, "Battle," 239. Hascall, "Personal Recollections," 165. John L. Yaryan, "Stone River," *MOLLUS, Indiana Commandery* (Indianapolis, 1898), 170–71. Michael Fitch, *Echoes of the Civil War As I Hear Them* (New York, 1905), 107–8. Vance, *Stone's River*, 56.

food. Spencer Talley's commanding officer considered the plight of his men and ordered a barrel of whiskey brought to them. Talley's account follows: "A detail of one commissioned officer from each company was sent to this barrel of whiskey for his men. I was sent from our company and, having gathered a dozen or more canteens, started for the barrel which was three or four hundred yards away. When I got there I found the barrel setting on its end with the head out and a crowd around it on the same mission as myself. When my time came to fill up I would take a canteen in each hand and sink them into the liquor and they would say 'good, good, good,' until they were full. With the canteens swinging around my neck," Talley continued, "I started back, and found it was all I could do to walk; bending over the barrel and enhaling the fumes had made me drunk."[16]

Along the bank of Stones River many Rebels built fires and the heat from the outside and the liquor on the inside did much to relax the men and perhaps make the hideous night seem not quite so awful as they lay on the frozen ground and waited for the morning. Here and there men nonetheless woke up screaming with nightmares.

The number of dead and wounded in each army was about the same. Rebels could hear the rumble of wagons, northwestward along the Nashville Pike, and some thought it signified an attempt by the Federals to save their ammunition trains before the start of a general withdrawal toward Nashville. In reality, it was the sound made by a long caravan of Yankee wounded being taken back to the military hospitals in Tennessee's capital city. Provost Marshal John Fitch wrote of what he saw among the host of Union wounded: "Those who witnessed surgical operations at the noted 'Brickhouse Hospital' will never forget those scenes. There were the headquarters for cases requiring amputation; and at times three tables were thus in requisition. Human limbs and pieces of flesh cast outside the house, through the windows, 'would fill a cartload.' The floors 'ran rivers of blood,' and the surgeons and attendants resembled butchers at work in the shambles."[17]

In Murfreesboro, General Bragg ordered all churches and pub-

[16]Womack, "River," 9.
[17]Fitch, *Annals*, 292.

lic buildings converted into hospitals, and he triumphantly telegraphed Richmond, "God has granted us a Happy New Year." He
announced that Rosecrans had been "driven from every position
except his extreme left." Bragg seemed convinced that Rosecrans
would retreat to Nashville that night and telegraphed his theater
commander Johnston that he would pursue. He, however, went to
bed without inspecting his lines or formulating any plans for a
pursuit. In fact, he made no preparation for the next day other
than to send one brigade, Palmer's, of Breckinridge's battered
troops back to their original position east of the river.[18]

Perhaps the long hours of battle had left the forty-five-year-old
general as tired as his men who did the fighting, but more likely
his lethargy is explained by a confidence that the Federals would
retreat — a confidence shared by much of the army, both in the
high command and in the ranks. The tone of General Hardee's report conveys the feeling of triumph that had spread among the
Confederates: "For three miles in our rear, amid the thick cedars
and the open fields, where the Federal lines had been originally
formed, their dead and dying, their hospitals, and the wreck of
that portion of their army marked our victorious advance. Our
bivouac fires were lighted at night within 500 yards of the railroad
embankment, behind which their disordered battalions sought
shelter."[19]

Hardee made no comment in his report about whether or not
he expected the Union army to retreat, but the evidence that
many Rebels anticipated such is abundant.[20] Some years later, on
the other hand, Confederate General Liddell, whose brigade occupied a position on the extreme Rebel left, penned an account
that gave a different impression, as though he believed that offensive actions by the Southern army that night were imperative.
Claiming that a great chance to crush the Federals was lost, Liddell wrote, "in the evening Hardee came along and I took the opportunity to call his attention to the fact that we were in command
of the Railroad and Nashville Turnpike and by bringing up all reserves and driving Rosecrans toward Murfreesboro by attacking

[18]*OR*, 662, 665. Connelly, *Autumn*, 61. McWhiney, *Bragg*, I, 363–64.
[19]*OR*, 778.
[20]Connelly, *Autumn*, 61.

him in rear I had no doubt that success would be with us." Hardee, according to Liddell, would not listen, saying that he was "disgusted." What Hardee meant by such a remark Liddell did not presume to know. Liddell then continued to say that he had never forgiven himself for not going to see General Bragg and persuading him to come and look for himself at the opportunity before them.[21]

If his story is accepted at face value, Liddell hardly seemed to be expecting Rosecrans to retreat. His account is suspect, however, not only because it was written years after the battle, but also because neither his nor any other officer's report, Union or Confederate, suggested that the Rebels commanded the railroad or the Nashville Pike. Furthermore, there were no reserves to be brought up for reinforcement on the Confederate left.

While the Rebels bided their time, many of them expecting the Federals to pull out, Rosecrans and his officers discussed their situation. All three corps commanders were present, along with a number of their subordinates. Because of conflicting accounts, it is impossible to know either the precise sequence of events or which general, if indeed any single one, exerted a dominance of will in the decision not to retreat. One story credits the laconic Thomas, dozing through most of the conference but suddenly aroused by the mention of the word "retreat," with the determining voice as he stoically muttered, "This army does not retreat," and "I know of no better place to die than right here." Biographers of Thomas, and there have been several, usually favor this version.[22]

Credit has likewise been given to Sheridan who, picking up on General Thomas' remark, is said to have sprung to Thomas' side, speaking emphatically to the same effect and requesting for his division the honor of leading the attack on the next day. There are also accounts, one of which he himself penned about thirty years later, that General Crittenden was opposed to the retreat, saying that his men would be very much discouraged if they had to aban-

[21]McWhiney, *Bragg*, I, 362.

[22]O'Connor, *Thomas*, 214. W. Thomas, *Thomas*, 298-99. Francis F. McKinney, *Education in Violence* (Detroit, 1961), 195. Thomas B. Van Horne, *The Life of Major General George H. Thomas* (New York, 1882), 97. Henry Coppee, *Great Commanders, General Thomas* (New York, 1895), 100-101. Don Piatt, *General George H. Thomas: A Critical Biography* (Cincinnati, 1893), 211, 212. Yaryan, "Stone River," 173-75.

don the field. Rosecrans' own record of the conference, usually favored by his biographers, describes both Crittenden and Thomas as deferring to their general-in-chief's judgment and pledging their support whatever his decision might be, while McCook advised a retreat to Nashville. Afterward, Rosecrans claimed, he announced his firm resolve to fight. At least one other report supports Rosecrans' story in substance, saying that he concluded by stating, "Gentlemen, we have come to fight and win this battle, and we shall do it. Our supplies may run short, but we will have our trains out again tomorrow. We will keep right on, and eat corn for a week, but we will win this battle. We can and will do it."[23]

Yet another version is that Rosecrans, inquiring of surgeon Eben Swift if he had sufficient transportation to move the wounded, fully intended to retreat. Then, after riding out at midnight for an inspection of his lines and seeing firebrands moving in the night close to the Nashville Pike, the general concluded that he was surrounded and to withdraw was impossible. Actually Federal cavalrymen, suffering from the cold, had disobeyed orders against kindling fires, but Rosecrans assumed they were Confederates and were forming line of battle by torchlight. Only then, some have concluded, did he send word to his subordinates that the army must "prepare to fight or die."[24]

From all the accounts available it seems likely that McCook advised a retreat, fearing that if the Federal army was beaten at Murfreesboro, the road to Louisville and the Ohio region would be irrevocably opened to the Confederates. McCook could well have been edgy. It was his command that was mauled on the Union left at Perryville and now, on the right at Stones River, had been shattered. Probably Thomas, and perhaps Crittenden, counseled that the army stand firm. Whether Thomas played the dramatically decisive role with which several writers have credited him is a moot point. It is reasonable that Rosecrans would have sought the wisdom of all his corps commanders regardless of whether he was thinking primarily in terms of retreat or holding his ground. Maybe he thought he was surrounded and could not retreat; possibly he

[23]O'Connor, *Sheridan*, 97. Buell and Johnson, *Battles and Leaders*, III, 633. Lamers, *Rosecrans*, 235–37. Fitch, *Annals*, 677.
[24]Foote, *Civil War*, II, 95.

was influenced by others to maintain his position; perhaps he would have refused to retreat even if Thomas had not been present. The evidence is not adequate for drawing a firm conclusion.

While the generals made decisions the horrors of the night and early morning continued. Colonel W.D. Pickett of Hardee's staff was assigned the job of paroling the wounded Yanks who had been gathered at the Griscom residence on the Wilkinson Pike. According to Pickett, "There appeared to be about one thousand wounded in the house upstairs and downstairs, in outhouses, and on the grass surrounding the house. These wounded were in various stages of vitality—from the slightly wounded, who were cheerful and talkative, to the mortally wounded." While Pickett was attending to his duties at the Griscom house, he said, "the Federal litter bearers brought in the body of an officer (which was laid on the grass outside the house) clothed in a somewhat worn undress uniform without insignia of rank. He was of slight build, rather thin-visaged face, full sandy whiskers. His features were in perfect repose. His whole appearance impressed me as of no ordinary man. It was the body of Brigadier General Joshua Sill. . . ."[25]

In all the confusion and uncertainty of war some who were thought to have been killed were discovered still alive. John E. Gold, Company F, Twenty-fourth Tennessee of A.P. Stewart's brigade, had been rushing forward with a canvas bag of ammunition slung over his shoulder when a cannon ball, bounding along the ground, smashed into him. Gold's companion, James Davis, also detailed as an ammunition carrier, saw him fall and thought he was killed. Actually, the partially spent cannon ball struck his ammunition bag, which cushioned the blow, and Gold was only knocked unconscious. That night he rejoined his unit, to the pleasant surprise of all, especially Davis.[26]

Struck by a shot that tore through his right wrist was W.H. Peters, a Federal soldier. As he bent forward in pain, grasping the wrist and attempting to stop the flow of blood, there was a brief instant when the colonel of his regiment happened to glance his way and thought Peters was dying. That evening the colonel reported to a friend that Peters was killed, "shot right through the

[25]*Confederate Veteran*, XVI, 452.
[26]Gold narrative, Confederate Collection, TSLA.

belly." He had bled profusely and almost passed out from loss of blood, but the flow was finally arrested in time to save his life.[27]

Doubtless these men, and others like them, felt very fortunate to be alive. A Rebel bugler, with a minor wound, perhaps could have said that he owed his life to whiskey. Jake Schlosser was carrying a flask against his leg when a bullet passed through the flask, which absorbed part of the impact, before the bullet struck him in the groin. And there were soldiers whose luck on the first day of the battle would desert them on the last day. Wounded in the ankle by a piece of shell and sent to the hospital, Willis A. Jones of Company B, Twenty-fourth Tennessee, felt he could still fight. On the last day of the battle, January 2, Jones hobbled back to the line and, while he was reloading his gun, a shot struck the lock, drove the hammer through his lung, and killed him instantly.[28]

One Rebel soldier remembered being treated for a wound in his arm at a Federal hospital that had fallen within the Confederate lines during the day's fighting. He described the horrors of what he said was a veritable charnel house: "The next morning, January 1, 1863, with arm in sling, I strolled over the yard, where lay in rows hundreds of Federal dead, with narrow aisles between along which one might walk and read the name, company, regiment and State of each. Often times the simple word, 'unknown' was pinned upon the dead soldier's breast. On the outer edge of this yard a long ditch was being dug the size of a large grave, but of great length, to receive these unfortunate victims of war. While they were our enemies, my heart went out in sadness for their bereaved loved ones."[29]

Almost one hundred years after the battle, Tommie Clack would write of his father, M.M. Clack, of Company A, First Tennessee Cavalry, who had described to the son how he had been detailed to bury the dead at Murfreesboro: "This was accomplished by using poles that could be hooked into the clothing of the dead and dragging the bodies to trenches and then covering them with earth. . . ."[30]

[27]*Confederate Veteran*, XXVI, 93.
[28]Smith, "Twenty Fourth Tennessee," 87.
[29]*Confederate Veteran*, XVI, 391.
[30]Tommie Clack to Dan M. Robison, May 7, 1962, Confederate Collection, TSLA.

Many witnesses testified to the uproar in the town of Murfrees-boro. "Confusion reigned supreme," wrote a wounded Rebel. "Thousands of prisoners and wounded without number occupied the town, which was almost entirely set apart for a hospital for the wounded and dying. We saw . . . the long black casket contain-ing the body of our beloved General Rains, which cast a deep gloom over our spirits. His presence in battle had been equal to a regiment of men."[31]

A hospital had been set up in a church visited by a young Ten-nessean who had just been walking over part of the battlefield. "Here I saw more horrible sights, if possible," he reported, "than I had already seen. The groans and cries of suffering soldiers rang long in my ears." One soldier, obviously in agony, made a vivid impression, insistently calling out to him, begging that he take a knife and cut a bullet out of his hand. At last a doctor came up, took out the bullet, and dressed the wound.[32]

Colonel H.L.W. Bratton of the Twenty-fourth Tennessee was among the wounded, his left leg shattered by a piece of shell which passed on through his horse, killing it and wounding the colonel a second time in his right leg. There was no choice; the mangled left leg had to be amputated. Unable to be moved, Brat-ton would be left behind when the Rebels finally pulled out of Murfreesboro; he died a few days later.[33]

Also placed in a hospital in Murfreesboro was Captain Jim Wo-mack of the Sixteen Tennessee, his arm badly broken by a shot sustained in the charge against Hell's Half Acre. He was more for-tunate than most. "Here I fell into the hands of my brothers S.M. and B.R.," he recounted, "who procured a private house for me and carried me to it; where they also carried brother J.B. who was wounded a few moments before I was, but not so seriously."[34]

A lady who went into Murfreesboro in search of her son wrote, "On entering town what a sight met my eyes! Prisoners entering every street, ambulances bringing in the wounded, every place crowded with the dying. . . . Frank Crostwaite's lifeless corpse

[31]*Confederate Veteran*, XVI, 391.
[32]*Ibid.*, VII, 119.
[33]Smith, "Twenty Fourth Tennessee," 87.
[34]Womack, *Diary*, 78.

was stretched out on a counter. He had been visiting my house [just before the battle]. The churches were full of wounded, where the doctors were amputating legs and arms. I found my own safe, and, on being informed that another battle was expected to begin, I set off on my way home, and passed through our cavalry all drawn up in line."[35]

The early morning hours dragged on as the wounded suffered and died. Soldiers of both armies, if they were fortunate, wrapped themselves in blankets and huddled close to a fire. Many dreaded the dawn for they expected to have to fight again. After all, neither army had retreated and nothing had actually been decided by the battle thus far. True, some Federals expected a withdrawal, for a rumor to that effect made its way through the army. Certainly many in the Rebel army expected the Union forces to retreat. But it was unrealistic for the common soldier, if he really thought about it, to allow himself the luxury of anticipating anything other than another day of savagery like that just experienced. No private soldier could possibly see the whole field of conflict or know what the generals were thinking. If his sanity were to be maintained his mind had to be prepared for more of the same.

One wonders how many, Rebel or Yank, thought of the fact that this day, January 1, 1863, Lincoln's Emancipation Proclamation went into effect.

[35]Ridley, *Battles and Sketches*, 154.

10

Bragg Makes a Decision

Ew Year's Day probably was not what either army expected. Neither Bragg nor Rosecrans planned an attack or a withdrawal. Just as, before the battle, both commanders prepared to assault the enemy's right wing, so now both simply waited to learn what the other would do.

At dawn Confederate skirmishers went forward all along the line, but nothing beyond a prodding action was intended. A Union soldier remembered that a few shots began to be exchanged between the picket lines and then, as the firing increased, the picket line became a skirmish line. "It occurred to him," the Yankee said, "that he preferred fighting in line of battle," because it was not a "pleasant sensation to feel that the bullets which came in your direction are intended specially for your own benefit!"[1] Up and down the line tentative skirmishes took place, sharpshooters harrassed the enemy's pickets, and there were sporadic exchanges of artillery, a few of them rather fiercely contested.

Polk's corps took over the Round Forest which the Rebels had fought so hard to conquer the day before; except for pickets, it had been abandoned during the night to shorten the Union line. Polk then tried to press up against Thomas' troops in the center of the Federal line but could not advance beyond the Round Forest. All he had gained, as Shelby Foote expressed it, were "more blue

---

[1]Freeman, "Battle," 240.

corpses, along with the unwelcome task of digging their graves in order to rid his nostrils of their stench."[2]

Compared to the day preceding, relatively few casualties were being sustained by either army. Perhaps for that very reason when men were struck down, their death seemed all the more vividly horrifying to those who watched. Michael H. Fitch remembered that the Rebels had a battery firing three-inch solid shot down the Nashville Pike. The shots would strike the macadamized surface and ricochet for a hundred or more yards. These ricocheting shots, Fitch said, took two Yankee lives in rather rapid succession. The first shot tore through a soldier's right arm, between the elbow and shoulder. Passing through both arms and his body, the dead man's arms were left hanging by only a slender bit of flesh and muscle. The other Federal, just relieved from the front, was walking to the rear when a shot struck him squarely in the middle of his knapsack, ripping a hole through the sack and his chest. Fitch said the impact lifted the mangled soldier off the ground, slamming him on his face more than twenty feet away from the point where he was hit.[3]

As such gory spectacles erupted here and there, the Confederates were paroling wounded prisoners, gathering up pieces of captured Federal equipment, and the cavalry continued to raid Union trains and ambulances on the Nashville Pike. Yankee soldiers roamed the field looking for fallen comrades, or something to eat. Many Federals, due to the successes of Rebel cavalry operating in their rear, were hungry.

A sergeant of Company K, Twenty-first Wisconsin Infantry, named Mead Holmes, Jr., wrote that "from Thursday until Sunday . . . much of the time we lay in the mud, the rain often pouring upon us. . . . Our rations were out, but a young horse was shot within ten feet of me, and we ate the noble fellow, the colonel, adjutant, and men, all partaking; nor was it bad for a hungry soldier."[4] The grandfather of General William (Billy) Mitchell was fighting in the Union army at Stones River. John L. Mitchell was

[2]Foote, *Civil War*, II, 96.
[3]Fitch, *Echoes*, 109.
[4]Holmes, *Soldier*, 130.

(*Above*): A pyramid of cannon balls on a granite slab is a reminder of the casualties and terror inflicted by artillery as the fierce struggle raged at Stones River. (*Below*): A tranquil scene along Stones River, as it appears today near the Union artillery site and McFadden's Ford.

an intelligent, highly educated, twenty-year-old member of Company I, Twenty-fourth Wisconsin. He remembered that the scenes at Murfreesboro "and its dread surroundings horrified me with war. . . . We suffered from the inclement weather and the almost total lack of provisions. Some of the men ate horses; less aristocratic palates, I was told, took mule. I contented myself with parched corn."[5] And General Rousseau reported that "during much of the time, my men had neither shelter, food nor fire. I procured corn, which they parched and ate, and some ate the horse steaks cut and broiled from the horses upon the battlefield. Day and night, in the cold, wet, and mud, my men suffered severely. . . ."[6]

The most significant tactical occurrence of January 1 was on the east bank of Stones River. While Bragg did not think about occupying the hill east of the river that overlooked McFadden's Ford, the Federals were sending a division across the stream to claim that strategic ground. If Bragg intended to renew the attack he should have taken action, because guns on this elevation would be within easy range of the Union position west of the river. And, if for no other reason than to protect his own army from flanking fire, he needed to control this hill. Unfortunately for the Rebels, it was the Yankees who thought of it first.

Early in the morning, about three o'clock, Colonel Samuel Beatty, who had succeeded to the command of Van Cleve's division when that officer's wound worsened, was ordered by General Crittenden to move the division across Stones River and hold the hill overlooking the ford. By daybreak, Colonel Samuel W. Price's lead brigade was fording the river, a strong skirmish line from the Fifty-first Ohio regiment pushing out in front. Only a few hundred yards beyond the river the skirmishers flushed a Rebel outpost from Pegram's cavalry, drove it back after a brief fight, and moved on to gain the high ground which lay about one-half of a mile away from the river. The Federals were then on the scene of the last major struggle at Stones River.[7]

Price massed his brigade in a double line of battle, lying per-

[5]John L. Mitchell, *In Memoriam: Twenty-Fourth Wisconsin Infantry* (Milwaukee, 1906), 27, 28.
[6]*OR*, 379.
[7]*Ibid.*, 575, 608, 612-14.

pendicular to the river. Sheltered by woods, the Yankees looked southeast over a large field, perhaps one-fourth of a mile across, broken only by corn stalks that remained from last year's crop and a few small buildings on their right. From right to left the front line consisted of the Fifty-first Ohio, whose right flank was anchored on Stones River, the Eighth Kentucky, and the Thirty-fifth Indiana regiments. The second line had the Twenty-first Kentucky on the right and the Ninety-ninth Ohio on the left.[8]

Colonel James P. Fyffe's brigade marched up next, filed into position farther to the northeast of Price and forward into the cornfield. Also deploying in double line of battle, Fyffe had the Forty-fourth Indiana and Thirteenth Ohio in advance, while the Fifty-ninth Ohio and Eighty-sixth Indiana were in reserve. The brigade's eastern or left flank rested "in air" on a country lane; there was a gap, of at least a regimental front, between Fyffe and Price.

Beatty's third brigade, under Colonel Benjamin C. Grider, was placed astride the river, two regiments in a hollow slightly east of the stream, ready to move wherever needed, and the other two on the west bank, in support of the Third Battery, Wisconsin Light Artillery.[9]

Meanwhile, at Bragg's command, the Rebels had reoccupied Wayne's Hill, almost a mile southeast of where Price and Fyffe had just gone into line. It was Colonel Joseph Palmer's Confederate brigade from Breckinridge's division that moved onto the hill at daybreak. Palmer proceeded to send forth several strong combat patrols, with Pegram's troopers in support, that harrassed Beatty's line from about mid-morning throughout the rest of the day.[10]

When the Yankees first spotted these Confederate patrols edging into the far side of the cornfield, as well as a Rebel battery being moved forward from Wayne's Hill, they quickly brought Lieutenant Courtland Livingston's Third Wisconsin Battery and Colonel Grider's two reserve regiments across the river. The artillerists thundered forward, unlimbering four of their guns between the Eighth Kentucky and the Thirty-fifth Indiana, while the other

[8]*Ibid.*
[9]*Ibid.*, 575, 587, 589, 601–2, 604–5.
[10]*Ibid.*, 784, 805.

two were emplaced on the bluff where the Fifty-first Ohio's flank was anchored at the river. Raking the corn field from the flank as well as head-on, the artillery fire soon persuaded the Confederate patrols to retreat, silently fading back into the woods. It was an annoying cat-and-mouse game which the Confederates insisted on playing until dark.[11]

As the duel of nerves at the corn field continued, Colonel Beatty was increasingly concerned about his left flank, fearing the Rebels were merely creating a diversion on his front while massing troops to strike his line on its eastern extremity. His worried reports to Crittenden persuaded the general to send another brigade across Stones River, and Colonel William Grose's command from John M. Palmer's division forded the stream. Before dark, however, Beatty became convinced that the enemy intended nothing more than harassment; thus he returned both the Third Wisconsin Battery and Grose's brigade to the west bank of the river.[12]

Until about midnight all was quiet east of the river. Then a Rebel patrol launched a sharp attack on an outpost of the Thirty-fifth Indiana. As the startling reports and brilliant flashes of a brisk firefight broke the silence of the dark night, Beatty's brigade commanders, fearing a night attack, hurried to prepare their men for action.

It was a false alarm, however; the Confederates again fell back, frayed nerves relaxed, and the Federals, other than those manning the outposts, resumed their sleep. Doubtless the Yankee pickets now kept an unusually alert watch, but the rest of the night passed without the Rebels' reappearing.[13]

Shortly after dawn of January 2, the Third Wisconsin Battery was ordered back across the river, resuming the same position occupied on New Year's Day. Its reappearance triggered the fire of Confederate cannons on Wayne's Hill, but the Union artillerists, seeing that the Rebel shot was highly inaccurate, did not bother to return the fire. As the morning progressed, Colonel Beatty sent forward the Seventy-ninth Indiana regiment, using it to plug the gap between his two brigades that manned the front line. From

[11]*Ibid.*, 575-76, 582, 608, 615.
[12]*Ibid.*, 561, 576.
[13]*Ibid.*, 576, 587, 598, 608, 610.

daybreak until about noon there was very little activity along the Union picket line. Then suddenly the front came alive once more with the familiar sounds of rifled-musketry, and soon the deep-throated artillery voice was added to the fray.[14]

This clash was brought on when General Breckinridge decided to make an estimate of the strength of the Yankee force holding the hill that commanded McFadden's Ford. Placing Lieutenant Colonel John A. Buckner in charge of a strong combat patrol consisting of eight cannon, a battalion from the Eighteenth Tennessee Infantry, plus infantry support from various Confederate outposts, Breckinridge ordered Buckner to feel for the Federal left flank, while he and a group of staff officers reconnoitered the Yankees' right. Tramping through the woods and debouching into the corn field, Buckner's patrol was greeted by the fire of Union skirmishers. While the Rebel infantry quickly deployed, the cannoneers of the Washington Artillery and Bryne's Kentucky Battery hurriedly unlimbered their guns and opened fire with shot and shell, concentrating their barrage on the Third Wisconsin's cannons. The Yankees were both outgunned and exposed to a flanking fire. Colonel Beatty authorized the Wisconsin gunners to withdraw, "to the astonishment of all," according to the report of the Twenty-first Kentucky's commander, who noted bitterly that Price's brigade was seemingly "forgotten, or left there all alone to be sacrificed, in order to draw the enemy on. . . ."[15]

The Rebel batteries now laid down an artillery barrage along the Union line; Buckner's infantry moved out into the corn field and steadily advanced on the Federal line. A Yankee patrol from the Fifty-first Ohio was forced to give ground before the oncoming Confederate line, abandoning several buildings in the field which they had just occupied. Fearing that the buildings would provide cover for Confederate sharpshooters, Lieutenant Colonel Richard W. McClain, commanding the Fifty-first Ohio, launched a vigorous counterattack. The Yankee assault drove the Rebels back across the field; the buildings were soon recovered and set afire.[16]

General Breckinridge, meanwhile, proceeded with his recon-

[14]*Ibid.*, 576, 582, 589-90.
[15]*Ibid.*, 784-85, 803, 805, 613, 615.
[16]*Ibid.*, 615, 805.

naissance. In company with his son Cabell, Theodore O'Hara, and Major James Wilson, Breckinridge rode toward the river, coming upon Polk, Hardee, and Colonel William D. Pickett. They all rode along the river to make a reconnaissance, but shortly Hardee and Polk were summoned back to their own lines by staff officers.

Breckinridge moved forward to Hanson's skirmish line, several hundred yards in advance of the main Confederate position. Warned that it would be dangerous to proceed farther because of Union snipers immediately ahead, Breckinridge ordered that the enemy skirmishers be driven in so that he could see what was behind them. This done, the general soon gained a vantage point from where he could examine the Federal bridgehead. He saw that a sizable Yankee force occupied the crest of a gentle slope which was partially covered with timber. The Federals were in a line almost at a right angle to the front of his own division. The intervening ground lay open for about five hundred yards back from the river. Before he could determine the size of the Union force, a staff officer from Bragg galloped up. The general wanted to see Breckinridge at once. Reluctantly breaking off his reconnaissance, the Kentuckian headed for Stones River and Bragg's headquarters.[17]

While these fitful morning preliminaries, eventually to culminate in a bloody afternoon battle, unfolded on the east bank of the river, a big noisy artillery duel rampaged on the west side. Colonel Charles G. Harker, one of Palmer's brigade commanders, said the action was "the most fearful artillery engagement" that he had experienced, and Brigadier General Milo S. Hascall called the Rebel bombardment "the most terrific fire of shot and shell that we sustained during the entire engagement."[18] It was actually a classic case of sound and fury signifying nothing (if one ignores the relatively small casualty figures) but it was very interesting.

In the early morning hours of January 2 the Rebels had marshaled twenty-two pieces of artillery north of the Cowan house. Masked in a line that stretched for a quarter of a mile, twelve of the guns lay north of the railroad. These were the four-gun bat-

---

[17]*Ibid.*, 785.
[18]*Ibid.*, 504, 471.

teries of Captains T.J. Stanford, W.W. Carnes, and Lieutenant
W.B. Turner. Four guns of Captain W.L. Scott's battery next
rested between the railroad and the Nashville Pike, and the six-
gun battery of Captain Felix H. Robertson was emplaced south of
the pike.

A thousand yards across the way to the northwest was the Yankee front line, manned by Captain Cullen Bradley's Sixth Ohio
Battery, Lieutenant George Estep's Eighth Indiana, and Captain
J.B. Cox's Tenth Indiana, all six-gun batteries. Sometime between
eight and nine o'clock in the morning (the After Action Reports
vary concerning the time) the Confederate artillerists unleashed a
fierce cannonade of solid shot and shell, striking up the railroad
and the Nashville Pike into the surprised Federal gunners. "They
had our range perfectly," reported General Hascall, "so that their
fire was terribly effective from the first."[19]

The Yankees quickly fought back, but Estep's battery could not
maintain its ground. The battery was in an exposed position and
received a very heavy fire as several of the Rebel gunners concentrated on it. Worse yet, the Eighth Indiana's cannon did not have
sufficient range to duel with the Grayclads. Estep had to retire almost at once. Even then, so many of his horses had been killed by
the Rebel bombardment that two of his guns had to be manhan-
dled off the field by a detachment of infantry.[20]

Bradley's battery, emplaced in a better position to the northeast
and having longer-range guns, was at first holding its ground.
Trading shots, blow for blow, with the Confederates, the Sixth
Ohio looked as though it could maintain itself. Then occurred another of those distressing and disheartening blunders that always
seem to happen in the confusion of war. Two hundred and fifty
yards in the rear of Bradley's guns was the Chicago Board of
Trade battery which, without waiting for orders from its Captain
James H. Stokes and apparently mistaking the Federals in their
front for the enemy, opened fire with canister, raking Bradley's

---

[19]*Ibid.*, 455, 471, 476, 479, 504, 521, 581, 722, 732, 742, 751, 756-57. Some of the
Rebel artillery had first fired upon Union infantry attempting to advance from the Round
Forest. Then, after the Yankees retreated, the Confederate gunners turned their attention
to the Federal artillery.
[20]*Ibid.*, 471, 476.

ranks with several rounds. The casualties inflicted, as well as the damage to equipment and morale from this indiscriminate blasting by their fellow Federals to the rear, not to mention the withering barrage from the Rebels, was at last too great. Assailed by both friend and foe, from the front and behind, Bradley's guns pulled out of the line of fire.[21]

The Rebels more than held their own in this fierce duel, also forcing three of the guns in Battery B, First Ohio Light Artillery, to withdraw to a less exposed position. And these Ohio artillerists were some distance behind the Union front line. Furthermore, only one of the five Confederate batteries engaged — Scott's — reported any casualties. But if the Rebel artillery dominated the morning duel on the west bank, the afternoon fight, when the really significant action took place east of the river, would belong to the Union cannoneers.

Shortly after noon, January 2, Breckinridge rode up to Bragg's headquarters along the Nashville Pike, west of the wrecked bridge that had spanned Stones River. The news that Bragg gave the former vice president of the United States was not welcome. Surprised, Breckinridge listened as the commanding general told him that he must attack with his division and take the high ground occupied by the Yankees in his front.

During the night and morning Bragg had sent several cavalry patrols around the Union rear. After initial reports that Rosecrans was withdrawing, Bragg was stunned by later dispatches revealing that the enemy was still present, might be receiving reinforcements, and, worse yet, had occupied the ridge in front of Wayne's Hill. Now, suddenly, Bragg was keenly aware of the threat across the river. Federal artillery implanted on the high ground, he thought, could enfilade Polk's position, while Rebel guns, if on the same eminence, would threaten the left flank of the Yankees. The Confederates must control that ground. Bragg decided to attack. Breckinridge's division, he said, had suffered little in the battle of December 31 and therefore was being given the assignment.[22]

The commanding general of the Confederate army was not fa-

[21]*Ibid.*, 471, 479, 504.
[22]*Ibid.*, 667–68, 784–85. George Brent Diary, Jan. 2, 1862, William P. Palmer Collection of Braxton Bragg Papers, Western Reserve Historical Society, Cleveland, Ohio.

miliar with either the terrain involved or the troop positions. Apparently he had not consulted Hardee, Breckinridge's immediate superior, nor Polk, whose soldiers were supposedly threatened by the Yankee guns. Nor had he summoned Breckinridge for the purpose of soliciting the Kentuckian's opinion, but simply to tell that officer what to do. It seems, in fact, that Bragg probably did not want advice from any of the army's high-ranking officers and particularly not from Breckinridge.[23]

The Kentuckian gave his opinion, nevertheless, protesting at once and strongly that the attack would be suicidal. Fresh from observing the position with his own staff, Breckinridge argued that the high ground west of McFadden's Ford commanded the hill on the east bank. Yankee artillery would rip the Rebel flank as they advanced, and the assault would be disastrous, he said. Bragg, who characteristically bristled whenever his judgment was questioned or even examined, replied with a curt arrogance, "Sir, my information is different. I have given the order to attack the enemy in your front and expect it to be obeyed."[24]

Later, supporters of Breckinridge would say that Bragg resented the manner in which the general had defended the Kentuckians against charges of cowardice and stood up to him about the Asa Lewis execution. They maintained that Bragg chose Breckinridge for the assault in the hope that he would be killed.[25]

Obviously, any further attempt by Breckinridge at discussion or protest was useless. Breckinridge listened as Bragg explained that the attack was to begin less than an hour before sunset, thus giving the Federals no time to recognize or bring up reinforcements before dark. Then the next morning, with his flank secure, Bragg would resume the offensive by sending Polk's troops against the Union center.

Bragg had made some more decisions. Cavalry under Pegram and Wharton had been instructed by Bragg to protect Breckin-

[23]Hughes, *Hardee*, 145. Joseph H. Parks, *General Leonidas Polk, C.S.A.: The Fighting Bishop* (Kingsport, Tenn., 1962), 290. *OR*, 778.

[24]Stevenson, *Battle*, 131. William D. Pickett, "A Reminiscence of Murfreesboro," Nashville *American*, Nov. 10, 1907. *Confederate Veteran*, XXI, 588. Theodore O'Hara to Breckinridge, Jan. 16, 1863, in John C. Breckinridge Papers, New York Historical Society. Horn, *Army*, 207.

[25]Davis, *Breckinridge*, 340-41.

ridge's right flank and cooperate in the attack. Also in support would be Captain Felix Robertson's six-gun battery and two sections under Captain Henry C. Semple. General Polk would be ordered to lay down an artillery barrage at 3:45 P.M. to soften the enemy line in front of Breckinridge. The main attack would begin fifteen minutes later, signaled by a single shot from the center of Bragg's line. Finally, Bragg placed Brigadier General Gideon J. Pillow, whose leadership of Rebel troops, according to one authority, made him immensely valuable to the Federals, in charge of one of Breckinridge's brigades.[26]

Dismayed by his orders, the dejected Breckinridge returned to his command and began making preparations for the attack. He stoically confided in his friend Brigadier General William Preston, formerly assistant adjutant general (chief of staff) to Albert Sidney Johnston, Preston's brother-in-law, who died in his arms at Shiloh, "General Preston, this attack is made against my judgment and by the special orders of General Bragg. Of course we all must try to do our duty and fight the best we can. But if it should result in disaster and I be among the slain, I want you to do justice to my memory and tell the people that I believed this attack to be very unwise and tried to prevent it." According to his biographer, this was the only time during the war that Breckinridge spoke of the possibility of death before a battle.[27]

None of Breckinridge's brigade commanders approved of Bragg's order. In fact, Breckinridge's attitude was mild when compared with one of his brigadiers. Brigadier General Roger W. Hanson wanted to kill Bragg. Clifton Breckinridge later said that Hanson denounced the attack order as "murderous" and was so infuriated because of the division's being ordered to do the impossible that he wanted to go at once to headquarters and shoot Bragg. Breckinridge and Preston talked him out of it. Hanson had only a short time to live. He would die in the assault.[28]

While Breckinridge brooded over his assignment, General Pillow, who had that day arrived in Murfreesboro, came up with

[26]*OR*, 667-68, 785-86. Horn, *Army*, 207. Davis, *Breckinridge*, 341. Connelly, *Autumn*, 63. Connelly, *Army of the Heartland*, 125.

[27]Davis, *Breckinridge*, 342.

[28]*Ibid*.

Bragg's directive to take command of Palmer's hard-fighting brigade, returning that officer to the leadership of the Eighteenth Tennessee, his own regiment.

Born in Williamson County, Tennessee, fifty-six-year-old Gideon J. Pillow was a lawyer who had spent most of his life in the aristocratic plantation atmosphere of Columbia, Tennessee. The greatest single boon to his military career had come from his friend and neighbor, President James K. Polk, who appointed Pillow to a brigadier generalship when the Mexican war began. Although he accomplished nothing of consequence, beyond irritating his fellow officers and activating the wrath of his commander, General Winfield Scott, who accused him of insubordination, Pillow emerged from the war convinced that he was a competent military man and wearing the insignia of a major general—thanks again to the President. When the Civil War began, Pillow, with high connections in Tennessee and the Confederacy, was made a brigadier general in the Confederate army and quickly resumed his old habits, becoming involved in a feud with General Polk. As the Confederates attempted to defend the perimeter along the Kentucky-Tennessee border in late 1861 and early 1862, Pillow's lying, intrigue, inordinate ambition, and incompetence were manifest to any one who took the time to look carefully—which, however, few did. Breckinridge, who had known Pillow before, could not have been pleased by that general's presence, but there was nothing that the Kentuckian could do about it.[29]

There may now have been disagreement between Breckinridge and Captain Felix H. Robertson about the use of the artillery. Robertson's six-gun battery of Napoleons, along with Captain Henry C. Semple's four guns, had been ordered across the river to support Breckinridge's assault. While the Confederate infantry was assembling at their jumping-off places, Robertson and Breckinridge, according to Robertson, argued about the artillery's role in the attack. Robertson claimed Breckinridge thought the infantry and artillery should move forward simultaneously, the guns

[29]*Ibid.* 342. Connelly, *Army of the Heartland*, 46-49, 104-6. Edwin C. Bearss, "The Union Artillery and Breckinridge's Attack," Research Project Number 2, Stones River National Military Park (July 1959), II, 47.

positioned between two lines of infantry, while Robertson maintained that General Bragg only intended the artillery to advance after the infantry had swept the enemy from the crest above McFadden's Ford. The official report filed by Breckinridge mentions no such controversy.

Robertson's record is suspect. He said nothing about a disagreement in his After Action Report, dated January 12, 1863, but only in a second report, dated February 18, 1863—a report that, unlike the first, was highly critical of Breckinridge's conduct of the assault and, still more damaging to Robertson's veracity, was prepared at the special order of General Bragg, to go directly to Bragg. Probably, in later trying to explain the failure of the January 2 assault, Bragg decided to pass the blame to Breckinridge and, having correctly gauged Robertson's less than ideal character, used the young artillery captain to his own advantage. "Reading between the lines," Robertson understood what Bragg really wanted and, ambitious as he was, cast his lot with the army's commanding general, readily obliging Bragg in the political struggle that followed the battle with a report attacking Breckinridge.[30]

The one fact clearly established is that when Breckinridge's advance began, the artillery, both the division's guns under Major Rice E. Graves and the supporting batteries under Robertson's command, did not move forward with the infantry.

Undoubtedly Breckinridge felt that he was being victimized by Bragg's blundering, but even more blundering seemed to be in order—this time Breckinridge himself contributing to it. Bragg had designated Wharton's and Pegram's cavalry to support the Kentuckian's attack. But there is no evidence that Breckinridge made any attempt to communicate with the cavalrymen until it was too late. Sometime between three and three-thirty, when all his dispositions had been made, Breckinridge was questioned by Pillow about establishing communications with the cavalry. When the Kentuckian replied that nothing had been done, Pillow urged that contact be made at once. Only then did Breckinridge send staff officers searching for Wharton and Pegram, but they

---

[30]*OR*, 758-61, 785-87. Davis, *Breckinridge*, 351-52.

could not find them. Apparently Breckinridge was so upset about being ordered to make what he thought would be a disastrous attack that he simply failed to arrange for proper cooperation with the cavalry.[31]

Meanwhile, as the Rebels prepared to make their attack, Union observers were noting the enemy's increased activity east of the river. Up until mid-afternoon of January 2 there were only six Yankee batteries, totaling twenty-four guns, posted on the west bank of Stones River, atop the ridge overlooking McFadden's Ford. Moved into position during the morning of New Year's Day, six cannon of the Seventh Battery, Indiana Light Artillery, were stationed on the right, while two guns of Battery G and three guns of Battery M, First Ohio Light Artillery, were on the left. There was one more gun from the Second Battery, Kentucky Light Artillery. Then on January 2, because of menacing Confederate movement across the river, eight more cannon from Batteries H and M, Fourth U.S. Artillery, were brought up and positioned to the right of the Seventh Indiana's guns, and four guns of Battery F, First Ohio Light Artillery, were emplaced still farther to the right.

Once the Rebel assault was underway, Captain John Mendenhall, chief of Artillery, would succeed in bringing up fifteen more guns from the reserve. These consisted of three guns from Battery B, First Ohio Light Artillery, six guns of the Chicago Board of Trade Battery, and six more from the Eighth Battery, Indiana Light Artillery. Also, the Third Wisconsin Battery, withdrawing to the west bank soon after the attack began, would add another six guns, bringing the total amassed on the commanding ground west of Stones River to forty-five. Besides these guns on the ridge, two six-gun batteries, the Sixth Ohio and the Twenty-sixth Pennsylvania, emplaced near the railroad about a mile southwest of McFadden's Ford, would be able to open an enfilading fire on the left flank of the attacking Confederate column. Altogether, Mendenhall would succeed in marshaling fifty-seven guns with which to pound Breckinridge's charging Rebels. And infantry support fire would be supplied by men from Brigadier General Charles Cruft's brigade and Brigadier General James S. Negley's division.[32]

[31]Connelly, *Autumn*, 64. Davis, *Breckinridge*, 343.
[32]Edwin C. Bearss, "Stones River: The Artillery at 4:45 p.m., January 2, 1863," *Civil*

At the crisis of the Battle of Stones River on the third day of the struggle, the effect of Mendenhall's artillery on Breckinridge's assault, although it has received only modest recognition, was probably the decisive factor.

War Times Illustrated (Feb. 1964), 12, 13. Also see Bearss, "Breckinridge's Attack," I, 17-19; II, 24, 25, 31-35. When his battery opened fire on Breckinridge's troops, Lt. Charles C. Parsons, commanding the Fourth U.S. Light Artillery, employed his four 3-inch rifles, holding his four 12-pounder Napoleons in reserve. Before very long, his cannoneers had exhausted all rifled ammunition in their limbers and somebody had taken away the caissons. Parsons therefore ordered up his Napoleons and sent his rifles to the rear. During the ensuing engagement, one of his Napoleons was dismounted by fire from the Confederate guns. Also see the various reports in the *OR*.

11

"A Terrible Affair"

It was about to happen—on a cold, gloomy, Friday afternoon in January. Beside a river whose name few people outside of Middle Tennessee had ever heard, and close to a town equally obscure, one of the spectacular, breathtaking moments of the entire war was at hand. The determined Confederate brigades that anxiously formed for the assault east of Stones River were not as numerous as those in the famous charge at Gettysburg six months later, or the even larger though little-known Rebel assault twenty miles to the west at Franklin nearly two years afterward, but Breckinridge's colorful Confederates, moving out in impressive alignment across the open field, steadily tramping toward the Union line, possessed a pride and participated in a drama that were not surpassed by any of the war's more massive assaults.

The time was four o'clock. Tense Yankees on the high ground above McFadden's Ford, their weapons tightly clutched in readiness for bloody work, watched silently as five thousand Rebels marched against them. This time there would be no surprise like the morning of the battle's first day. This time the Federals were peering down their gun sights as the Grayclads came on.

But the front-line Union forces, with Price's and Fyffe's brigades lying in double line of battle, were less than two thousand strong. Even counting Grider's reserve brigade and Grose's brigade from Palmer's division, the Yankees did not number four thousand soldiers east of Stones River, while the Confederates, enjoying substantially more than a two-to-one advantage over the

Union infantry in the front line, had another two thousand cavalry at hand. Some of the Federals in the front line, seeing the Rebels move unflinchingly up the rise, must have known that they were significantly outnumbered. The Grayclads had the manpower, if textbooks on military tactics mean anything, to crack the Federal front line.

Breckinridge could see his soldiers in panorama from his position behind the center of his second line, the division in an attack formation about a half-mile in width. The Confederate flags and the regimental colors were up as four brigades, about sixteen regiments, heard the command "Forward, march!" repeated up and down the lines by more than a hundred voices. "The pickets and videttes closed in," recalled Gervis D. Grainger, who was in the front line with the Sixth Kentucky, "and we stepped forward to fight one of the most terrific battles that fell to our lot during the Civil War." Grainger thought that "every soldier seemed to realize that the conflict was before him."[1]

Composing Breckinridge's first battle line was Brigadier General Roger W. Hanson's brigade on the left and Gideon Pillow's brigade on the right. Two hundred yards in the rear was the second line, Colonel Randall L. Gibson's brigade on the left and Brigadier General William Preston's brigade following after Pillow's unit.[2] Breckinridge's brigade commanders, except for Pillow, had all been born in Kentucky; Preston and Gibson were graduates of Harvard and Yale, respectively. Gibson, the youngest, was just past his thirtieth birthday. A lawyer and sugar planter living in Louisiana, he had traveled extensively in Europe and served as United States attaché in Madrid. Fighting at Shiloh as colonel of the Thirteenth Louisiana, he took command of the

---

[1]*Four Years*, 14.

[2]*OR*, 785, 795–97, 807–812, 826. From left to right, Hanson's deployment was the Sixth and Second Kentucky Regiments, the Forty-first Alabama, and the Fourth Kentucky. In Pillow's line of battle the position of only one unit, the Eighteenth Tennessee, can be definitely located. The Tennessee unit anchored the far right of Pillow's battle line. Gibson's brigade, from left to right, consisted of the Sixteenth and Twenty-fifth Louisiana Consolidated and the Thirteenth and Twentieth Louisiana Consolidated. The two Louisiana regiments were supported by the Thirty-second Alabama and a Louisiana battalion of sharpshooters. From left to right, Preston's brigade was deployed as follows: First and Third Florida Consolidated, Fourth Florida, Sixtieth North Carolina, and the Twentieth Tennessee.

brigade when Daniel W. Adams was wounded. He led his regiment at Perryville and went into Stones River with a good combat record.[3]

The oldest of the three Kentuckians, born in 1816, was William Preston. After Harvard law school he practiced until the Mexican war, in which he served as a lieutenant colonel. Elected to the legislature and the U.S. Congress as a Whig, he then joined the Democrats and, like Gibson, served in Spain, as U.S. minister during Buchanan's administration. Preston came home when the secession crisis developed, urged Kentuckians to support the Confederacy, and joined his brother-in-law, General Albert Sidney Johnston, at Bowling Green where he was commissioned a colonel on Breckinridge's staff. After the battle of Shiloh he was promoted to brigadier general.[4]

Thirty-five-year-old Roger W. Hanson was probably the most colorful and adventurous of Breckinridge's brigade leaders. He too fought in the Mexican war. Later he participated in a duel, was wounded, and was left with a shortened leg that gave him, according to the *Dictionary of American Biography*, "a peculiar gait." California gold-rush fever sent him hurrying westward, but failing to make a significant strike, he returned to Kentucky to enter politics. When secession occurred he became a colonel in the state guard, favoring neutrality for Kentucky, only to be swept into the conflict, resenting Union encroachment. Hanson, as a colonel, was on the Confederate right at Fort Donelson where he was captured on February 16, 1862. By October he was back with his regiment, perhaps experiencing his greatest achievement on Morgan's expedition against Hartsville, where he helped capture two thousand Union prisoners on December 7, while losing only sixty-eight of his own men. Six days later Hanson was made a brigadier general.[5]

He was a favorite of Breckinridge. "Look at old Hanson!" Breckinridge exclaimed to his staff as he admiringly watched his fellow Kentuckian directing the charge of his brigade. But then Breckin-

[3]Boatner, *CWD*, 341.
[4]*Ibid.*, 668.
[5]*Ibid.*, 373.

ridge saw Pillow, whose conduct at Fort Donelson had brought a censure from the Confederate secretary of war and the wrath of thousands of Rebel prisoners who thought he had "sold them out." Instead of going forward with his brigade, Pillow had remained in the woods, conveniently located behind a large tree. Only after Breckinridge personally ordered him away did he move out with his brigade.[6]

Most of the Rebels making the assault probably did not share the gloomy forebodings of Breckinridge and his brigadiers. Unaware, for the most part, of what awaited them—the massed Union frontal and enfilading artillery fire from the other side of the river—the Confederates were determined to carry the Yankee position as they swung toward the Federal line with unfaltering step. Weapons loaded and bayonets fixed, they grimly moved at double-quick time toward the Union ridge one thousand yards away. Orders were to fire one volley and then give the Yankees the bayonet. From across the river Polk's artillery was striking into the Union line with shot and shell, but the extreme range separating the smoothbore pieces from their targets limited the bombardment's effectiveness. The Federals waited and endured. The tension mounted. On came the Grayclads: eight hundred yards to the ridge; six hundred yards to the ridge.

Then Breckinridge realized that disaster threatened his right wing. Pegram and Wharton's cavalry were not there and a Yankee brigade was overlapping Pillow's line. Breckinridge was compelled to halt his advance until Major Rice E. Graves could bring up a battery to cover that sector. And when Graves ordered Captain Eldridge Wright's four-gun Tennessee battery to bolster Pillow's attack, Wright had scarcely emerged from the woods in the rear when the lead horse on one of the six-pounder gun teams was shot in the head and killed; the driver could not stop the team, the carriage crashed against the dead horse, breaking the pole and disabling the gun. Wright finally got three of his guns into action, blasting away at the Union line, while Rebel infantry in the second

[6]Pickett, "Reminiscence." Rice E. Graves, Charges and Specifications of charges against Brigadier General Gideon J. Pillow, n.d., in Breckinridge Papers, Chicago Historical Society; cited in Davis, *Breckinridge*, 343.

line were being shaken out farther to the right to help cover that flank. The Federal line, however, still overlapped the attackers.[7]

Another problem was developing on the Rebel left wing. Because of the flow of the river, the ground over which the Confederates were advancing became more narrow, squeezing some of the troops out of line. Reacting quickly, Major James W. Hewitt, commander of the Second Kentucky, immediately formed his regiment into a column of fours, taking it out of the front line and then pushing forward closely behind the Sixth Kentucky. Also, Hanson's and Pillow's front brigades were now overlapping each other in the center, but nothing was done to correct the alignment as the Rebel assault surged forward.[8]

Four hundred yards to the ridge—and the mental stress continued to build. Neither side, except for their cannon, had opened fire. And now the cannon from across the river were hushed lest they kill their own men. The lay of the land enabled Hanson's "Orphan" Brigade, as Breckinridge came to call it, to close to within one hundred and fifty yards of the Yankee right flank that was positioned behind a rail fence, before they were even exposed to small-arms fire. There the Rebels halted, sent a volley of rifled-musketry fire crashing into the bluecoats' ranks, let out a terrible shrill scream ("a most hideous yell," remembered Lieutenant Colonel Richard W. McClain of the Fifty First Ohio), and dashed toward the Federals—bayonets flashing in the cold winter air.[9]

Not until Hanson's men were within sixty yards did the command to "rise and fire" go down the Union line. The cracking report of the Yankee rifled-muskets sounded up and down the line, the charging Grayclads saw the countless little clouds of smoke appearing from hundreds of weapons, and a storm of bullets tore through their ranks. Gervis Grainger was one of the Rebels racing toward the Federal line. "Their guns . . . blazed in our faces," he said. "Comrades were falling on either hand as we advanced at full run into the very jaws of death."[10]

But the Yankee volley did not come close to arresting the Con-

[7]*OR*, 786, 808–9, 823.
[8]*Ibid.*, 833. Bearss, "Breckinridge's Attack," II, 6.
[9]*OR*, 615.
[10]Grainger, *Four Years*, 14.

federate's charge. And there was not time to reload. The Rebels were upon them, mounting their works from end to end. The fighting was desperate, hand-to-hand, and short. Men shot their opponents at point-blank range, clubbed them with rifle butts and pistol handles, or struck them with bayonets. Overwhelmed and demoralized, the Union infantry of the Fifty-first Ohio and the Eighth Kentucky fled to the rear while the Confederates reloaded, poured a deadly fire of musketry into their routed ranks, and screamed in triumph.[11]

Farther to the Rebel right, Pillow's rugged Tennessee brigade had closed to within a hundred yards of the Yankee line before a deafening cheer rose from the ranks of the Thirty-fifth Indiana as the regiment unleashed a withering fire that staggered the Confederate advance. At the same time the Seventy-ninth Indiana, lying farther to the east on the flank of the Thirty-fifth, also opened on the Rebels with a devastating storm of lead. The intense fire and frantic action was described by a Confederate of the Twentieth Tennessee, his regiment having moved into the front line of the Grayclad assault: "The Yankees poured a volley into the Twentieth Regiment that made them . . . waver like a drunken man." He said that a soldier named William Nevins, charging on his left side, was cut down by this first volley as a bullet tore through the man's leg — a wound soon necessitating amputation.[12]

Before the Confederates could recover their poise, the Federals had reloaded and were raking them again with a well-aimed fire. The Rebels went to the ground, the Twentieth Tennessee scrambling forward to a rail fence, from which they opened up a blazing musketry fire against the Yankees. "We had the advantage," reported W.J. McMurray, "and the slaughter was terrible." For several minutes (one participant thought it was ten) the two lines blasted away at each other. Then the Rebels charged. "The regiment did not take time to climb the fence," McMurray recalled, "but caught the fence about the third rail from the bottom, and the fence, line and all went over together."[13]

The Gray line rose, screeching and screaming, dashing forward

[11]*OR*, 615, 827, 833.
[12]McMurray, *Twentieth Tennessee*, 239.
[13]*Ibid.*

Battles and Leaders of the Civil War

Photograph by Rudy E. Sanders

(*Above*): The colorful Confederate General Roger W. Hanson was killed in the Rebel assault east of Stones River on the last day of battle, an assault which Hanson had bitterly denounced as "murderous." (*Below*): Rail fences, widespread over the fields and farms where the battle was fought, sometimes were obstacles in the path of attacking soldiers and sometimes provided partial cover behind which men crouched as they fired at the enemy.

for forty or fifty yards over ground swept by musketry and broke directly into the Yankee position. Already the Thirty-fifth Indiana was falling back, even before it received the full fury of the Rebel onslaught. When Colonel Bernard F. Mullen, commanding the Thirty-fifth, had seen the regiments on his right streaming to the rear and some of the Seventy-ninth soldiers on his left beginning to fade, he quickly dispatched an aide scurrying rearward to bring forward the Ninty-ninth Ohio regiment for reinforcement. The Ohioans refused to come. The determined Mullen repeated his request, only to learn that the Ninty-ninth was no longer present. Apparently the Ohioans thought they could recognize a lost cause when they saw one and had hastily departed from the field. Realizing that his regiment, with no support on its right flank, was doomed to slaughter and capture if it remained where it was, Mullen gave the order to retreat. He issued the order a second time when many of his hard-fighting Hoosiers refused to break contact with the Confederates. Even then, a number did not retire and were left behind, where they were either killed or captured.[14]

The retreat of the Thirty-fifth Indiana left open the right flank of the Seventy-ninth and it too fell back, with the victorious Tennesseans of Pillow's brigade in hot pursuit. Colonel Price's entire Yankee brigade, holding the right wing of the Union position beside the river, had been routed; the disaster was made complete when fleeing front-line soldiers dashed pell-mell through the reserve ranks of the Twenty-first Kentucky and the Ninty-ninth Ohio, throwing them also into confusion. After firing only a few poorly aimed volleys at Hanson's hard-charging, animated Rebel brigade, these Federal regiments had given away, joining the panic-stricken rush to cross Stones River.[15]

There had been one chance to save the Union right wing under Price. If Grider's reserve brigade could have been brought into action earlier, Price's command might have held its ground. But Grider's unit, thinking the Rebels would not attack until the next day, had stacked their weapons and relaxed. The Confederate onslaught took the brigade by surprise. Grabbing their rifled-muskets

[14]OR, 611.
[15]Bearss, "Breckinridge's Attack," II, 13.

and hastily forming into line of battle, Grider's regiments marched to the fight at the order of their division commander, Colonel Beatty. From right to left were the Nineteenth Ohio, Ninth Kentucky, and Eleventh Kentucky regiments. Apparently undaunted by the desperate situation, they moved eagerly toward the battle only to be met by Price's regiments, racing headlong for the rear and running directly through their ranks.

"Nothing could have been more discouraging to my men than the aspect of affairs at that time," reported Lieutenant Colonel George H. Cram, commanding the Ninth Kentucky, "but they never faltered." The colonel continued, "I allowed the retreating mass to pass through my lines, the enemy all the time pouring into us a destructive fire. . . . " When the panic-stricken men of Price's brigade had stormed through, Grider's Federals closed up their ranks as, almost instantly, the surging Rebels tore into them—and were brought to a halt. Grider's regiments fought furiously. The colonel himself was almost ecstatic. "We have them checked," he exuberantly told Beatty. "Give us artillery and we will whip them!"[16]

Indeed the Confederates had collided with a hard-fighting Yankee brigade and were taking heavy losses. So far, Roger Hanson had been lucky. Courageously directing his brigade from an exposed position, he had seen his Kentuckians overwhelm the Federal front line, re-form, and pursue the fleeing enemy toward the ford. One wonders if, in spite of his prophecy of a "murderous" assault, the general may have fleetingly thought that perhaps the attack would succeed after all.

Then it happened; a Yankee bullet struck him; inflicting a mortal wound, and staff officers huddled about him as he lay on the ground. Seeing the commotion, General Breckinridge came up and knelt beside his friend. Hanson's last words were said to have been, "I die in a just cause, having done my duty."[17]

Their general was cut down, but Hanson's infantry were pouring a galling fire into Grider's Yankees; now the Rebels got unexpected help as the capricious fortunes of war turned in their favor. When Hanson's brigade smashed its way over the Yankee front

---

[16]*OR*, 587, 591, 593, 595.
[17]*Confederate Veteran*, XXI, 127.

line, another of its regiments, the Sixth Kentucky, was squeezed out of position as the Second Kentucky had been earlier. Discontent to merely follow in the brigade's rear, Colonel Joseph H. Lewis, commanding the Sixth, led his men by the left flank along the river bank, and a detachment from the Second Kentucky followed right behind. Scrambling along the bank of the river, Lewis' Kentuckians suddenly emerged on the right flank of the Nineteenth Ohio and unleashed a terrible enfilading fire into the surprised Buckeyes. The Rebels were also getting more help on their front line. Colonel Gibson, coming up and quickly evaluating the situation, committed two of his regiments to reinforce Hanson's brigade.

The pressure on the Yankees was mounting rapidly. There was not time to bring up artillery support, Livingston's Third Wisconsin battery having pulled back earlier to the west bank of the river when he saw that Price's front line could not hold. Even then Livingston's third section of guns had almost been captured by Lewis' Confederates, who were advancing along the river bank.

Grider's confidence that he could hold his line if only he had artillery support was quickly destroyed. His right was crumbling. The Rebels were driving all along his front and on his flank. Portions of the Nineteenth Ohio were heading to the rear as Grider heard Major Charles F. Manderson, the Nineteenth's commander, calling out, "We are flanked on our right; . . . fall back and rally at the foot of the hill, if we can." The collapse of the Nineteenth left open the flank of the Ninth Kentucky and, like a row of falling dominoes, Grider's whole line retreated — another Yankee brigade overwhelmed.[18]

Meanwhile, farther to the northeast, the Rebel assault was reaching high tide as calamity struck the Union brigade under Fyffe. When the Confederates launched their attack Colonel Fyffe was back near the ford, talking with Colonel Beatty and General Rosecrans. Their discussion was abruptly terminated as a courier galloped up with news that the enemy was about to advance; Colonel Fyffe mounted and rode to his headquarters. He arrived in time to see the advancing line of Hanson's and Pillow's brigades

[18]OR, 827, 833, 797, 587-88, 595-96.

colliding with the Yankees under Price. Only one of Fyffe's regiments, the Forty-fourth Indiana anchoring his right flank, was close enough to give fire support to Price's line as the heavy masses of Rebel infantry bore down upon it.

Fyffe told his regimental commanders to wheel their units to the right, for he intended to take the Grayclads in their exposed right flank. Unfortunately, he had not reckoned with the oncoming second Southern battle line, composed of Preston and Gibson's brigades, that now moved to the attack. Suddenly Fyffe realized that Price's whole unit had collapsed, his own right flank was thus unsupported, and, worse yet, the Rebels were closer to McFadden's Ford than he was. Fearing his brigade would be cut off, Fyffe ordered a retreat, which soon turned into a shambles. Fyffe himself was thrown from his horse and disabled. At least one of his regiments, the Fifty-ninth Ohio, panicked and ran right through the Twenty-third Kentucky, trampling some of its men who lay behind a rail fence.[19]

It was no more than thirty minutes since Breckinridge had launched his assault and three Yankee brigades were routed. One remained; General Grose's command from Brigadier General John M. Palmer's division was charged with the defense of the left flank of the Union bridgehead. So far, Grose's brigade was untouched except for some of Fyffe's fleeing Yankees rampaging through it. Now Rebel infantry of Preston's brigade swung to the east, determined to crush these Federals whose advance position was held by the Twenty-third Kentucky and the Twenty-fourth Ohio.

Perhaps no Confederate unit deserved more credit for carrying this Yankee line than the Twentieth Tennessee. Passing across an open field, the Tennesseans were swept by a devastating fire. Their colonel, Thomas B. Smith, seeing that no cover was available, yelled to his men to charge! Surging forward with bayonets, the Tennesseans, despite the loss of Smith who was badly wounded, set the example for the rest of the brigade as they drove savagely into the Federals. When the fierce fight was over both Union regiments were routed and the Twentieth Tennessee alone had taken

[19]*Ibid.*, 598–99, 601, 602–6.

about two hundred prisoners. The only Yankees still in fighting trim east of Stones River were Grose's three remaining regiments — and they had fallen back to the vicinity of the Hoover house.[20]

Probably the Federals had enough manpower east of Stones River, if it had been used effectively, to have held their front line. But Grider's reserve brigade never got into action until Price's front line infantry were routed. In Fyffe's front-line brigade, only one regiment supplied any effective flanking fire on the Rebel attacking columns as they drove in against Price. Then when Price was overwhelmed, Fyffe's soldiers found themselves outflanked and, trying to retreat, they panicked and went to pieces. Finally, Grose's brigade, which was supposed to anchor the Union left, was, like Grider's reserve, never in the fight until both of the front-line brigades had gone to the rear, one overwhelmed and the other panicked.

The weight of the Rebel assault, four brigades strong, had gone in against Price's lone brigade, assisted by two regiments, the Seventy-ninth Indiana from Grider's command and the Forty-fourth Indiana from Fyffe's brigade. The Rebel force was concentrated while the Union strength was dispersed, enabling the Confederates to dispose of the Yankee infantry in piecemeal fashion. The Grayclads should not have accomplished as much as they did.

A glorious victory was at hand, or so it must have seemed to the jubilant Southerners, as the Federal line retreated before the advancing Rebels. Some of the Confederates, infantry from the Sixth and Second Kentucky and Gibson's Louisiana brigade, had even charged across the river in pursuit of the fleeing Yankees.

Actually, what seemed the forerunner of victory was a prelude to disaster. As the retreating Federals were pushed back toward the river, they drew the hotly pursuing Rebels down the forward slope and within range of some forty-five cannon massed on the hill west of Stones River. Now the Union artillerists had the chance they had been waiting for, to shoot at the foe without harming their comrades. Unleashing a fierce cannonade, darkening the sky with smoke, and striking across the river into the ranks of the Confederates, the Federal guns dealt destruction up and down the lines.

[20]*Ibid.*, 562, 569, 573, 821–22.

Battles and Leaders of the Civil War

Striking across Stones River at McFadden's Ford with shot, shell, and canister, massed Union cannons tore gaping holes in the Confederate ranks, perhaps decisive in repelling their assault on the Federals east of the river in the late afternoon of January 2, 1863.

It was suddenly, as one writer expressed it, "as if the Rebs had opened the door of hell, and the devil himself was there to greet them."[21] The soggy river bottom over which the Yankees had been driven had become a death trap as the Federal gunners blazed away with deadly effect.

Among the Rebels hit was Spencer Talley of the Twenty-eighth Tennessee. He lay on the ground and felt blood running down his side, but he was not sure if the bullet had lodged in him or passed on through. At last rising and stumbling toward the rear, his attention came to rest on a mutilated body. Something seemed familiar. Then he realized that it was the body of his colonel, P.D. Cunningham. And he stared at the coat he had so recently worn to the courthouse ball. Now it was torn by enemy shot and saturated by the blood of the man who had been kind enough to lend it.[22]

"The great jaws of the trap on the bluff from the opposite side of the river were sprung," wrote L.D. Young of the Orphan Brigade, "and bursting shells that completely drowned the voice of man were plunging and tearing through our columns, ploughing up the earth at our feet in front and behind, everywhere. . . ." Possibly the most shocking occurrence that Young witnessed took place in Company E. "A shell exploded," he said, "right in the middle of the company, almost literally tearing it to pieces. When I recovered from the shock the sight I witnessed was appalling. Some eighteen or twenty men hurled in every direction."[23]

W.J. McMurray wrote that "if a soldier ever saw the lightning and heard the thunder bolts of a tornado, at the same time the heavens opened and the stars of destruction were sweeping everything from the face of the earth; if he was in this battle he saw it."[24]

More than one of the Rebel regiments proudly carried a flag made in part from a piece of Mrs. Breckinridge's wedding dress, a fact that in itself is a commentary on the times and the attitude toward Southern womanhood. The Eighteenth Tennessee possessed such a flag, made by Miss Mat Watkins of Murfreesboro and presented to the regiment shortly before the battle. Three color-

[21]Womack, "River," 10.
[22]*Ibid.*
[23]*Ibid.*
[24]*Ibid.*

bearers had fallen on December 31 and now the carnage was even worse. Six went down on January 2.

Seeing that another color-bearer, George Lowe, was hit, shot through the body, William L. McKay said that he caught the flag staff to prevent it from striking the ground. Almost instantly McKay was shot through the right thigh and he too fell. Captain Nat Gooch then ordered a soldier to pick up the flag and was told to "pick it up yourself!" Gooch did pick it up and was soon wounded severely in the shoulder. Finally, after still another man had been cut down carrying the colors, Logue Nelson of Murfreesboro managed to carry the flag through the rest of the battle.[25]

Frank Battle was carrying the colors of the Twentieth Tennessee. He dropped to the ground and comrades all around thought he was shot. Actually Battle was unharmed and trying to tie together the strands of the colors that had been ripped again and again by enemy bullets. In a moment he arose and went forward with them once more, miraculously, or so it seemed, avoiding injury.[26]

All around the terrible slaughter continued; it must have seemed that nobody would escape. Making the situation more deadly for the Rebels was the rifled-musketry fire from General Crittenden's infantry support, stationed with the artillerists on the west bank. Some of the Southerners were within easy range and many were being picked off by Yankee sharpshooters. Still worse, now that the Rebels had taken the crest of the hill overlooking McFadden's Ford, it was soon clear that the position was dominated by Federal artillery. And Breckinridge did not have all his artillery present anyway. Major Graves quickly set up the division's guns (and Captain Elbridge Wright was killed) but Robertson's and Semple's guns could not be found. Frantically Breckinridge sent staff officers to locate them.

Despite Breckinridge's order that Robertson should move his guns onto the crest as soon as it was taken, the Texan "decided to alter the plan," as he himself expressed it. Robertson never moved his batteries beyond the woods during the attack. It was just as well. The Rebel artillery on the crest, even with Robertson's can-

---

[25]William L. McKay memoirs, Confederate Collection, TSLA. *Confederate Veteran*, XIX, 55, 156.

[26]McMurray, *Twentieth Tennessee*, 240.

non, would still have been outnumbered, outgunned, and occupying a poor position. This additional artillery could not have changed the outcome of the attack.

Also, the Rebel assault had led to disorganization and intermingling of units. In the face of devastating cannon fire and deadly accurate rifled-musketry it became virtually impossible, in some cases, to maintain any semblance of organization.[27]

Despite the insurmountable odds, there were some Confederates who just would not quit. The actions of a color-bearer for the Sixth Kentucky, whose name is lost to history, must have seemed almost mad — as if he were seeking death. After the Rebels had been repulsed and his comrades gone, he lingered on the field as long as there was any infantry left. Then reluctantly going to the rear, halting frequently, facing the enemy, and holding the colors high, he would cry out with a loud voice, "Here's your Sixth Kentucky!"[28]

Another type of emotion overwhelmed Gervis Grainger. He was among the Rebels who had pushed on across the river. Together with a dozen comrades, he held up in expectation that the main Confederate body would soon follow. Grainger took cover behind a large sycamore tree and quickly became involved in an exchange of small-arms fire with Yankee infantry lodged in a cabin farther up the bank of the river. Then the Federal artillery opened with a tremendous roar and a dense cloud of smoke soon enveloped everything, but Grainger continued firing at the Bluecoats in the cabin.

Suddenly he heard a brass band playing to his right, saw a Yankee line five or six columns deep advancing to cross the shoal, and realized that all his comrades were gone. The Confederates were retreating, while the Federals were preparing to counterattack. Grainger said that he fired one shot at the Union color-bearer and then dashed for the river. The bank became a bluff at the water's edge but he leaped as far as possible and dropped into the water, frantically making for the east shore while the Federals sent a hail of bullets crashing after him. Water was spattering all around but

[27]OR, 759, 785, 798, 806, 813, 817, 827. Davis, *Breckinridge*, 345-46. Connelly, *Autumn*, 65.
[28]*Confederate Veteran*, XXIX, 136.

somehow every bullet missed its mark and Grainger scrambled onto the far bank, continuing his mad race for safety as the Union infantry kept firing — and missing.

Several hundred yards from the river he found momentary refuge behind a tree, and he lay down and raised his feet to rest against the trunk while the water ran out of his boots. On his feet again, Grainger continued his dash for the rear through screaming shot and bursting shell. He tried to capture a riderless horse as it ran by, only to witness the grisly spectacle of the horse's head being severed by a cannon shot. Death and destruction were all about. Grainger saw four men carrying a wounded soldier on a litter. Another cannon ball smashed diagonally into the litter, killing one man at each corner and the man whom they were carrying. The two survivors joined Grainger and finally they reached safety in a wooded area beyond the range of the Federal artillery.[29]

Another Confederate who experienced the awful reversal sustained by the attackers said that when the order was given to retreat, "some rushed back precipitately, while others walked away with deliberation, and some even slowly and doggedly, as though they scorned the danger or had become indifferent to life. But they paid toll at every step back over that ground which they had just passed with the shout of victors. In addition to the execution done by the main body of the Federals, who had now become pursuers, they were terribly galled by Grose, who, in the main, had held his ground, and was pouring a destructive enfilade fire into the shattered column."

Continuing his account, Ed. P. Thompson remembered that "near the line where Beatty's division received the charge, the Confederates rallied and re-formed; but the Federals were in too close pursuit, and the new formation was too weak to offer any effectual resistance, so it presently broke. . . . When the Confederate troops had reached the line of rifle pits from which they had first started, and which were still held, in part, by Cobb's battery and the Ninth Kentucky Infantry, they rallied again and the pursuit ceased — the Federals following but little beyond the original line of Beatty."[30]

[29]Grainger, *Four Years*, 14, 15.
[30]Ed Porter Thompson, *History of the Orphan Brigade* (Louisville, 1898), 182.

Battles and Leaders of the Civil War

(*Above*): The Union left advances to counterattack on the evening of January 2, 1863. (*Below*): Peaceful and beautiful, the Stones River National Cemetery seems to be guarded by the great eagle atop an impressive monument to the dead of the Regular Brigade.

When Bragg was informed that Breckinridge's troops were beginning to retreat, he ordered Brigadier General J. Patton Anderson's brigade to cross the river and provide reinforcement. The battle, of course, was all over when Anderson arrived, too late for his infantry to help. Besides, the Federals had mounted a strong counterattack.

With heavy reinforcements at hand and a little daylight remaining, the Yankees acted quickly, although it was apparently an impatient brigade commander who sensed that the time was right and triggered the attack. Generals Crittenden, Negley, Palmer, and Rosecrans looked on from the ridge that bristled with Union artillery. Colonel John F. Miller of Negley's division, without waiting for orders from his general, moved out against the Rebels. Then Colonel Timothy R. Stanley's brigade joined him, ordered forward by Generals Rosecrans and Negley.

Cheering wildly as they surged after the retiring Grayclads, the Yankees now realized that the momentum of battle had changed. Other units joined in, as thousands of Federals splashed across the stream to the east bank. Grider's and Price's shattered commands, anxious to redeem themselves, quickly responded. There were units from Fyffe's brigade, and from the commands of Hazen, Davis, Johnson, Palmer, Morton, and, of course, that part of the infantry from Grose's brigade that had never been broken — all now pursuing the Rebels, forcing their artillery back from the ridge above the ford, finally compelling them to once more take up their original line along Wayne's Hill. Nothing had been changed by the short, bloody fight, the Federals regaining everything they had held before the assault took place.[31]

It was over and it was tragic — tragic because the Confederate brigade commanders and the division commander had known that it would not succeed. If the Federals had not used their manpower so inefficiently the Rebels probably could never have broken the enemy's front line. But having overwhelmed the infantry, the Rebels still confronted the Yankee artillery, which Breckinridge had thought would doom the attack to failure — and it did. The assault was one more example in the long disheartening his-

[31]*OR*, 434, 408, 184-85, 451.

tory of battle commanders' gambling with the lives of thousands, contrary to all reasonable calculations for success. That evening, as the rain poured again, Colonel George W. Brent of Bragg's staff sat in a tent and laconically described the fatal attack in his diary:

The division moved beautifully across an open field to the work. A murderous fire was opened upon them. The enemy had concentrated a large force there and had combined a concentric fire from his artillery upon it. Our troops nevertheless, marched up bravely and drove the enemy from the hill. The left of the division improvidently crossed the river contrary to orders: It was driven back in confusion. In the meantime the enemy in large force assailed the right of the division, and it was compelled to retire. The cavalry on the right were ordered to cooperate, but they were mere spectators. It was a terrible affair. . . .[32]

[32]J. Stoddard Johnson, "Diary," Jan. 2, 1863, Palmer Collection of Bragg Papers, Western Reserve.

12

"Mary Had a Little Lamb"

I never, at any time, saw him more visibly moved," recalled a Rebel officer as he spoke of General Breckinridge's conduct after the awful assault. "He was raging like a wounded lion, as he passed the different commands from right to left; but," the officer continued, "tears broke from his eyes when he beheld the little remnant of his old brigade — his personal friends and fellow countrymen; and a sorrowful exclamation escaped his lips, to find, as he said, his 'poor Orphan Brigade torn to pieces.'"[1]

A young soldier who participated in the British assault on the Somme, July 1, 1916, the blackest day in the history of the British army, when an incredible sixty thousand casualties were suffered, wrote afterward, "From that moment all my religion died. All my teaching and beliefs in God had left me, never to return."[2] Breckinridge's division, taking seventeen hundred casualties out of no more than five thousand engaged, actually had a higher percentage of loss than was sustained by the British on the Somme. One wonders what irreparable psychological damage had been wreaked upon the minds of those Rebels who had survived.

The crushing blow to Breckinridge's assault meant that the Rebel army now had little chance to win the battle, although it took Bragg some time to admit this fact. When the last Confederate soldier had dragged himself from under the range of the Yankee guns, the Battle of Stones River was over, although sporadic

[1]Thompson, *Orphan Brigade*, 183.
[2]Martin Middlebrook, *The First Day on the Somme* (Glasgow, Scotland, 1971), 316.

202

firing would continue through the night and the next morning.

During the night following Breckinridge's charge, Spencer Talley reported to the hospital set up in the courthouse on the Murfreesboro town square. There was not enough room for all the wounded. Makeshift hospitals had been established in schools, churches, hotels, and homes, while in some cases the wounded were simply stretched out in the halls or on porches and sidewalks. As Talley waited for the overworked doctors to examine his wound, the body of Colonel Cunningham was brought in from the battlefield and placed nearby. "When his body was brought to the Hospital my heart was full of sorrow," wrote Talley, "and regardless of my wound I secured a vessel of water and washed his blood stained face, and hands. The coat which I had worn a few nights before to the grand ball and festival was now spotted and saturated with his life's blood. I removed the stains from his coat as best I could with the cold water and a rag, combed his unkempt hair and whiskers as his body laid with many others in the Court House at Murfreesboro."[3]

A still heavier demand than the one they faced after the first two nights of the battle was now placed on the already overtaxed doctors, nurses, and medical supplies. Almost everyone, it seemed, was trying to help. Even Mrs. Breckinridge was in the midst of the wounded, with lint and bandages ministering to the suffering, particularly those of her husband's division. Soldiers remembered her as small and quiet, but in spite of the anxiety and tired look on her face, still pretty as she moved among the wounded and mangled. Especially they recalled her attempting to comfort General Hanson as he lay dying.[4]

An effort was being made to move some of the wounded out of Murfreesboro in order that they might be more properly cared for elsewhere. One young girl, who with her sister was enrolled at a small college in Winchester, Tennessee, wrote that "after the Battle of Murfreesboro some of the wounded soldiers were brought to the College and we could hear their moans from suffering."[5]

---

[3]Womack, "River," 11.

[4]*Confederate Veteran*, I, 325.

[5]Emma Middleton Wells, comp., "Reminiscences of the War Between the States," Historical Collection, Chattanooga Public Library, Chattanooga, Tenn.

Many of the wounded were being transported to Georgia. J.L. Haynes was a railroad engineer who had driven a trainload of ammunition into Murfreesboro on the evening before the battle started. Now he was pulling out of Murfreesboro with a different load. "I left Murfreesboro the day after the battle with a train of wounded men," Haynes recalled. "Two miles east of Stevenson, Alabama, the spikes were pulled out of the track and my train was ditched, killing seven of the wounded. I had many a soldier tell me during the war that he had rather take his chances in [the army] than on [the railroad]," concluded Haynes.[6]

One of the wounded on his way into Georgia via rail was Dr. W.A. Lowe, who had been shot through an eye during the first day of the battle. Although its destination was Atlanta because of the hospitals there, the train stopped at Marietta. No hospitals were in that small town, but several of the wounded, hearing that a number of Nashville refugees were present, slipped off the train. Making their way to the hotel, they sent word that they wanted to see the Nashville ladies. Dr. Lowe was from Shelby County, but he too had left the train at Marietta.

Mrs. Irby Morgan, sister-in-law of General John H. Morgan, happened to be in Marietta at that time, and she left the following account of the wounded soldiers, particularly Dr. Lowe:

I went down to see them. Went from room to room, and found twenty-seven poor fellows — some terribly wounded — shot in the legs and arms, and one had his eye put out. . . . I went in one room and found Dr. Lowe, from Shelby County, shot through the eye, the ball coming out of the back of his neck, and it was strange that it did not kill him. His hair was very long, all bloody, and dried to his face, and all caked with blood around his eye, or the socket, as the eye was gone. I felt sick of heart but went to work with my nurse to assist me. I had warm water brought, and with a soft cloth bathed the bloody hair until I could remove it from the wounded part, got a pair of scissors, and soon made the poor fellow more comfortable by cutting off his long, matted hair, and a more grateful man I never saw.[7]

Dr. Lowe recovered his strength, and notwithstanding this wound that could have disqualified him for active service, re-

[6]*Confederate Veteran*, VI, 255.
[7]Mrs. Irby Morgan, *How It Was: Four Years Among the Rebels* (Nashville, 1892), 34, 35.

turned to the army, serving until the end of the war. Afterward he led a useful life as a physician until his death in 1899. His brother James, though unmarked at Murfreesboro, was later killed at Missionary Ridge.[8]

All around Murfreesboro there were soldiers, Union and Confederate, who felt that they had seen more than enough of war. "We realized then what war really was, as some of those engaged had not before," remembered a Yankee. "Most of us, I suppose, were at one time in our experience as soldiers rather anxious to participate in a battle. Perhaps we were not quite willing that the war should end without our having had that experience. If," he concluded, "the writer had cherished any such feeling, it disappeared after Stones River." Another Federal, Charles Doolittle, would have agreed. Writing to a friend named Mollie, he said, "I have often expressed the desire to be able to witness the terrible strife of a fierce battle, but I can say now that my curiosity is fully satisfied."[9]

Doolittle was helping to attend the wounded, and he stated that "we took just the same care of the rebel wounded that we did of our own men. . . . Many a one of them said we were different from what they had supposed."[10] While the Confederates waited upon by Doolittle may have felt that the Federals were not so bad after all, William McKay formed a quite different opinion.

Badly wounded in the thigh during Breckinridge's assault, McKay experienced a seemingly unending nightmare of pain and anguish. "I remained helpless and partially unconscious until our command retreated," he wrote. "I saw the Yankees coming and attempted to get up but could not. Our men moved up a battery of three guns and planted them just over where I lay. The fire from the guns was nearly hot enough to burn my face, and the Yankee bullets rattled on the gun carriages like hail."[11]

Finally the Confederates, with most of their horses killed, had to leave their guns. As McKay lay between the lines, suddenly

[8]*Confederate Veteran*, VIII, 369.

[9]Charles Doolittle to Mollie, Feb. 6, 1863, Doolittle Papers, Knox College Library, Galesburg, Ill.

[10]*Ibid*.

[11]McKay memoirs, Confederate Collection, TSLA.

shrapnel and concussion from a bursting shell fired by the Rebels broke his left arm and badly bruised his body. For hours he remained in the field while a cold drizzle mixed with sleet came down and Federal soldiers marched by him and over him. "I lay where I fell until about midnight and received *brutal* treatment from some of the Yankees," McKay later recounted. "The commanders of companies would say as they passed me, 'look out men; here is a wounded man' and some of them would step over me carefully while others would give me a kick, call me a damned Rebel, and I was covered with black spots from the bruises."

At last two Federals, searching the battlefield for a friend, took pity, secured an ambulance, and had McKay taken to a Federal hospital. The horror was far from ended however. Overworked attendants, thinking he was too near dead to waste their time, laid him out on the ground. McKay's own words speak for themselves: "I lay all day Saturday in the rain without any attention being paid me. When I would ask for water they would say 'you don't need water. We will take you to the graveyard after a while.'"

McKay then felt fortunate that it was raining. He found he could suck the water out of his rain-soaked coat sleeve. After dark on Sunday night some of the attendants, concluding that he was not going to die after all, picked him up, laying him in a tent out of the rain. During the night two wounded Confederates died in the tent and one of them fell across McKay's legs where his body lay for several hours.

Sunday, at noon, McKay found himself moved to another tent where both Rebel and Federal wounded lay. Not until Monday morning was he given breakfast, his first food since Friday before he was wounded. Next came the surgeons, who decided that his wounded leg must be amputated. McKay rebelled, saying that they could not do it, and then he begged and pleaded with them not to do it, until the chief surgeon put an end to the matter. "If the damned Rebel wants to die let him go," was the conclusion.

The surgeons moved on, amputated the leg of a Florida soldier near by, and the next day he died. The foul air and the sight of suffering and death were all around McKay. Two Yankee wounded were close at hand, one right beside him, and they also died. "So the three men nearest to me died," wrote McKay, "and none of them seened to be wounded as badly as I was."[12]

While McKay lay suffering through the night following Breck-inridge's charge, Gervis Grainger, after his mad dash across the river to escape from the Federals, found that it fell his lot to stand guard. "I had only time to wring the water from my socks and get my blanket, which was dry," remembered Grainger. "Wrapping it about my dripping clothes," he continued, "I went to my post of duty . . . in advance of the picket line. The night was bitter cold. My pants were frozen as far up as the tops of my boots, the warmth of my body only preventing my clothes from freezing."

About two o'clock in the morning, Grainger was relieved from duty and ordered to start moving out on the Manchester Pike. Sunrise found him six or eight miles away from Murfreesboro, where at last a halt was called and the soldiers stopped to eat. "I was thoroughly exhausted," he said, "having fought the battle, stood guard until two o'clock and marched to this place without food, sleep or rest. I was sick through and through. Lying down on a log in the sun for rest, I was taken with a chill which lasted some hours. I was permitted to march at will. Procuring an abandoned horse, I rode all day and stayed in a school house that night. I was taken with pneumonia and was sent to Wartrace by ambulance, thence to Chattanooga. I remembered nothing after reaching the station until, several days later, I regained consciousness and found myself in the hospital."[13]

Grainger's plight would have been readily understood by many of the soldiers, especially those on the picket lines. "A cold sleet fell all last night and our wet clothes are frozen on us," wrote Johnny Green of the Orphan Brigade. "Our suffering is so great that the men have gotten out of the trenches and made fires out of such wood as they can find. . . . In this cold weather standing picket is terrible, wet to the skin and clothes freezing, but we take care to keep our cartridges dry."[14]

The bitter cold weather, being no respecter of persons or

[12]*Ibid.*
[13]Grainger, *Four Years*, 16, 17.
[14]Kirwan, *Johnny Green*, 69.

causes, inflicted suffering indiscriminately on the wounded of both sides. Joseph Teeter of the Thirty-fourth Illinois, shot through the body, had fallen on a cluster of small bushes which concealed and partially held him off the ground. For three days he lay in a semi-conscious state, without any protection from the freezing cold of the nights, as well as the chilling discomfort of the days, until at last help came.[15]

Henry Freeman was walking close to several captured Rebel batteries on the night after Breckinridge's charge, when he felt a hand grabbing at his overcoat. A wounded Confederate lying near one of the guns was begging to be carried back where he would be less likely to be trodden upon. "One of his legs had been mangled by a shell," Freeman said. "He was carefully picked up on a blanket and, as tenderly as possible, carried a little to the rear, and given a drink of water from a canteen. He was exceedingly grateful, and requested, in case he died, that his mother, whom he said lived in Alabama, might be written. . . ."[16]

In the deluge of confusion, anguish, sorrow, pain, and bitterness that swept over the battlefield area, perhaps W.H. Steele, a Union soldier, experienced some of the same emotions that the Rebel McKay was enduring. Along with other wounded men, Steele was loaded into an army wagon and taken into Murfreesboro. Laid down on the upper floor of a brick house, he remained there three days with only a canteen of water and an ear of corn for nourishment. When the Confederates pulled out, Steele was eventually found by his brother who, although sick, had left a hospital in Nashville to look for him. The story was told that when Steele's pants were removed, "they were so stiffened by his blood that they, being placed on the floor in an upright position, remained so as readily as two pieces of stovepipe would have done."[17]

John Gorgas, lucky to still be alive, was more fortunate than Steele. In the picket line of the Thirty-fourth Illinois at the battle's beginning, Gorgas was pulling back to the main body of troops when he was shot in the region of the hip. Still running in spite of the wound, he was hit by another bullet that punctured the left

[15]Payne, *Thirty-Fourth Illinois*, 57.
[16]Freeman, "Battle," 242.
[17]Payne, *Thirty-Fourth Illinois*, 57.

side of his neck, but that too failed to bring him down. Then, partially turning to look behind him, he was struck by yet another shot that smashed his chin and struck him in the shoulder; this time Gorgas went to the ground. Fortunately, however, he was taken by the Confederates to the house of a planter who gave him the best care for the next several months while he recovered.[18]

Also lucky was another wounded Yankee, Arnold Harrington, who was captured but fell into the hands of friends of former days from Texas, who gave him all the care possible under the circumstances.[19]

The accounts of the distress and horrors following the battle seem almost endless as one reads the letters, diaries, and regimental histories that tell the story of that bloody winter in Tennessee. Perhaps those dark days and nights of trouble, suffering, and loss are nowhere better summarized than in Colonel John Beatty's moving account:

I ride over the battlefield. In one place a caisson and five horses are lying, the latter killed in harness, and all fallen together. Nationals and Confederates, young, middle-aged, and old, are scattered over the woods and fields for miles. Poor Wright, of my old company, lay at the barricade in the woods which we stormed on the night of the last day. Many others lay about him. Farther on we find men with their legs shot off; one with brains scooped out with a cannon ball; another with half a face gone; another with entrails protruding; young Winnegard . . . has one foot off and both legs pierced by grape [sic] at the thighs; another boy lies with his hands clasped above his head, indicating that his last words were a prayer. Many Confederate sharpshooters lie behind stumps, rails, and logs, shot in the head. A young boy, dressed in the Confederate uniform, lies with his face turned to the sky and looks as if he might be sleeping. . . . Many wounded horses are limping over the field. One mule . . . had a leg blown off on the first day's battle; next morning it was on the spot where first wounded; at night it was still standing there, not having moved an inch all day, patiently suffering, it knew not why nor for what. How many poor men suffered through the cold nights in the thick woods . . . calling in vain . . . for help, and finally making their last solemn petition to God![20]

[18]*Ibid.*, 56.
[19]*Ibid.*, 57.
[20]Beatty, *Memoirs*, 159, 160.

People react in varied ways to the experience of such carnage. There are those who will laugh and some who will cry. There are men whose attempts to make jokes will reveal a sick humor and others whose stoical expression seems emotionless. And some, if there is opportunity, will get drunk. When it is all over, many will get drunk. Maybe the reason is to celebrate victory—or to forget defeat. More likely, the reason is deeply involved with the simple but all-pervading realization that the awful thing is finally over and, somehow, you have lived through it.

A night or two after the battle, John Beatty recalled coming upon his division commander, General Rousseau, in company with two other generals. "In the evening I met Rousseau, McCook and Crittenden. They had been imbibing freely. Rousseau insisted upon my turning back and going with them to his quarters." Beatty thought that Crittenden, Breckinridge's old friend, was the merriest —and the drunkest—of the party. "On the way he sang," Beatty reported, "in a voice far from melodious, a pastoral ditty with which childhood is familiar: 'Mary had a little lamb, His fleece was white as snow, and everywhere that Mary went, The lamb was sure to go.' Evidently the lion had left the chieftain's heart," concluded Beatty, "and the lamb had entered and taken possession."[21]

Back in Nashville, Confederate longings for a victory at Murfreesboro had been given new hope when the report of the first day of heavy fighting came in, announcing the defeat of Rosecrans' right wing. Men gathered in small groups at their doorsteps to discuss the probabilities; women met in parlors and prepared lint and bandages for the wounded, as faith in the Southern cause seemed to find new strength. All during that eventful New Year's Eve excitement was intense in many a Nashville home. Rebels clustered in the streets the next day with a sense of joy, even as several hundred Confederate prisoners, taken in battle, were marched through the city to the state house. Their passage up the streets was greeted by smiles and the waving of handkerchiefs. But at last the truth came—truth too bitter for immediate belief.

Once more, the bright light of Rebel hope was suddenly snuffed out. It was like Fort Donelson, Shiloh, and Perryville all over

---

[21]*Ibid*, 160.

again. After expectations had soared so high, the letdown seemed the more cruel. Stones River was the death-knell of hope for many a Confederate in Nashville—and in Tennessee. From that day Rebels despaired as never before, increasingly disheartened in their cause and robbed of that simple unquestioning faith that they would ultimately succeed.[22] A few days later when the Confederates had fallen back to Tullahoma, J. Stoddard Johnson recorded a one-sentence understatement, January 7, 1863. He confided to his diary that the battle and movement so far to the rear "has had a bad effect on the troops and the public mind."[23]

"'Stones River!' What a host of memories comes back with the name!" wrote Mrs. L.D. Whitson in her effervescent style as she recalled the battle. "It seems but yesterday since we laid our hands on the cold, dead face of General [James] Rains, who was shot through the heart, killed instantly. . . . It seems but yesterday since the screams of his sister, who refused to be comforted. . . . What must have been the feelings of the . . . young wife . . . environed by Yankees in . . . Nashville, unable to come to him?"[24]

Soon after the battle, while burial details were digging graves and preparing huge trenches into which hundreds of dead would be placed, General Rosecrans was approached by a minister who requested permission to take the body of General Rains back to his home at Nashville for burial. Rosecrans readily consented, but, stung by an intimation that the Confederates of Nashville were intending to make the funeral a Rebel ovation, he addressed the minister in a straightforward and brusque manner: "I wish it to be distinctly understood that there is to be no fuss made over this affair—none at all sir. I won't permit it, sir, in the face of this bleeding army. My own officers are here, dead and unburied, and the bodies of my brave soldiers are yet on the field, among the rocks and cedars. You may have the corpse, sir; but remember distinctly that you can't have an infernal secession 'pow-wow' over it in Nashville!"[25]

It was, of course, highly predictable that Rosecrans, true to his

---

[22]Fitch, *Annals*, 633.
[23]Palmer Collection of the Braxton Bragg Papers, Western Reserve.
[24]Whitson, *Maurice*, 116, 119.
[25]Fitch, *Annals*, 658.

Leading his Confederate brigade in a sweep around the right flank of the Union position, General James E. Rains of Nashville fell from his horse mortally wounded as his command slashed into the Yankee lines.

character, would be at mass on Sunday morning following the battle. "One of the most impressive scenes of the war," thought a Union observer,

was the celebration of high mass by Father Trecy in a rude log cabin upon the battlefield of Stones River, on Sunday morning, the 4th of January, 1863—the day after the retreat of the Rebels from Murfreesboro. It was a beautiful morning—the first after a week of rainstorms. Dead soldiers and horses were still strewn over the fields, and burial parties were engaged at their solemn task. The General in command, his staff and guests, assembled in and around that . . . cabin, while the holy rites were celebrated, and a short address delivered by our chaplain, from the text: "In Ramah was there a voice heard, lamentation, and weeping, and great mourning, Rachel weeping for her children, and would not be comforted, because they are not." (Matthew 2:18.)

"Every heart was touched," concluded the Federal, "and the pent-up feelings of strong men who had striven in those scenes of battle sought relief in tears."[26]

Time had been required for both sides to realize that the battle was over. An unproductive council had been held at Bragg's head-quarters late on the night of January 2. Early on the morning of January 3, probably about two A.M., Bragg was awakened and handed a note written by Cheatham and Withers, with an endorsement from Polk. "We deem it our duty to say to you frankly," declared Cheatham and Withers, "that, in our judgment, this army should be promptly put in retreat." Contending that only three brigades (divisions?) were still reliable for combat, the generals concluded, "We do fear great disaster from the condition of things now existing, and think it should be averted if possible." Polk's statement was, "I greatly fear the consequences of another engagement at this place in the ensuing day. We could now, perhaps, get off with some safety and some credit, if the affair is well managed." Bragg, sitting up in bed, reportedly did little more than glance at the message before telling the courier, Lieutenant W.B. Richmond, "Say to the general we shall maintain our position at every hazard."

After receiving Bragg's reply, Polk sent the note to Hardee say-

[26]*Ibid.*, 329–30.

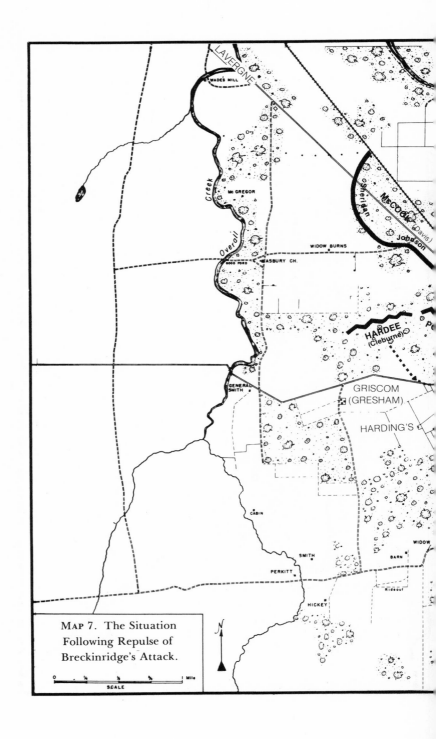

MAP 7. The Situation Following Repulse of Breckinridge's Attack.

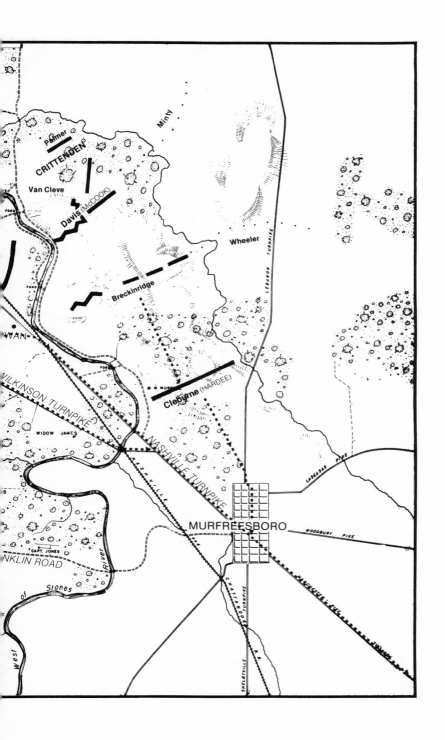

Palmer

CRITTENDEN

Minty

Van Cleve

Davis (McCOOK)

Wheeler

Breckinridge

LEBANON TURNPIKE

WILKINSON TURNPIKE

Cleburne (HARDEE)

WIDOW JAMES

NASHVILLE TURNPIKE

LASCASAS PIKE

MURFREESBORO

WOODBURY PIKE

CAPT. JONES

FRANKLIN ROAD

River

Stones

West

of

SHELBYVILLE TURNPIKE

MANCHESTER PIKE

ing that he thought "the decision of the general unwise, and, am compelled to add, in a high degree." Hardee offered no advice. Nothing could be done until morning anyway. Soon after Bragg arose the next morning the army's situation looked quite different to him.

Rain was falling steadily and the rising river might isolate the two wings of the army. Cavalry reports gave no further hope that the Federals would withdraw. On the contrary, a fresh brigade (Spears') of Union reinforcements had arrived, together with a train of supplies from Nashville. Worst of all, Bragg's staff had been studying the papers captured when McCook's headquarters were overrun, which indicated the strength of that corps at eighteen thousand. Bragg was convinced that Rosecrans must have more men on the field than he had thought, projecting an effective force of nearly seventy thousand Yankees in his front. The Rebel army could muster little more than twenty thousand effectives.

Now Bragg was alarmed. At ten A.M. he sent for Polk and Hardee. There was no disagreement; all three men were convinced that the army must withdraw. Later, when writing his report, Bragg stated, "Common prudence and the safety of my army, upon which even the safety of our cause depended, left no doubt in my mind as to the necessity of my withdrawal from so unequal a contest."

Midnight was approaching when the Rebels retreated on January 3 in a pouring rain. Not even a rearguard action was fought with the Yankees, who were caught off guard by the withdrawal and were perhaps no more anxious for further bloodshed than were the Confederates. At least they made only a halfhearted effort to pursue.

Winchester, fifty miles southeast, was the destination of Bragg himself, where he planned to establish a new line along the Elk River. Polk was ordered to retreat to Shelbyville, twenty-three miles from Murfreesboro, while Hardee would fall back on Tullahoma, thirty-five miles away. But when Polk reported from Shelbyville that the Union army was still at Stones River, Bragg revised his plans. Instructing Hardee to stop at Wartrace, on a line with Polk's troops, Bragg set up headquarters at Tullahoma. Astride the Nashville & Chattanooga Railroad, he began organizing a new defensive position along the Duck River.[27]

Meanwhile, the ordeal of William McKay continued to unfold. Having barely survived and avoided the amputation of his mangled leg, it was not until January 7 or 8 that real hope was kindled when a man named Casper Freas, in company with a Mrs. Clemons, came upon McKay in the Federal hospital at Murfreesboro. The woman was in search of her husband (he was never found), whose two brothers had both been killed on the last day of the battle. Surprised to find McKay, who had been reported dead by a soldier claiming to have actually examined the corpse, Mr. Freas took an immediate interest in him. Procuring a surgeon's certificate which testified that McKay was mortally wounded, Freas secured a pass to take him to his own home. After a harsh cursing from the provost marshal who issued his parole, McKay found himself loaded into a wagon. The one friend he had made among the Federal surgeons packed in a pair of blankets, a bottle of whiskey, and some tea, coffee, and sugar — but the blankets and whiskey disappeared as soon as the surgeon was out of sight, swiped by the Yankee guards.

At last McKay's wagon completed the ten-mile trip to the home of Freas. "I could not understand," McKay wrote, "why he would burden himself with a wounded man." Eventually, he realized. Freas was a Union sympathizer, merely using McKay for his own interests, as he hoped to prevent the Confederates, who would know that he was caring for a wounded Rebel, from harming his property. In the meantime, Freas was planning a quick departure to Indiana. "The night he left," remembered McKay, "proved to be the most horrible of all my trials."

Freas and his family exited the house about midnight, placing McKay in the care of a big black man who promised to look after him through the night. As soon as the family had gone McKay said that the black began bringing in fence rails to make a fire by putting one end on the fire and the other out on the floor. "I

[27]OR, 682, 683, 691–92, 700–701. Connelly, *Autumn*, 66, 67. Parks, *Polk*, 291–93. Hughes, *Hardee*, 145–47. Davis, *Breckinridge*, 348.

begged him to desist," wrote McKay, "but he would not obey me." Instead he kept bringing in rails, saying he was going to make a *good* fire—and then go home!

Indeed McKay soon had a tremendous fire but, unable to move, spent part of the night in terror, fully expecting that the house would catch fire and he would be burned to death. Finally the fire died down, and then the severe cold set in, leaving McKay badly chilled and despondent when a neighbor happened to find him the next day. It would be summer before McKay, nursed by a Confederate family, eventually regained enough strength to struggle about on a pair of crutches.[28]

Perhaps McKay was a fitting symbol of Bragg's mangled and broken army as it retreated from Murfreesboro. Weary, hungry, and ragged, the soldiers straggled along the road for miles. The story was told that a wild-looking Texan, spotting a miserable, broken-down mule, seized it and improvised a halter and stirrups from stray pieces of rope. Bareheaded and barefooted, the unwashed, unshaven Texan wore a rusty-looking hunting shirt and sat grotesquely perched astride the mule, smoking a corncob pipe. General Bragg and his staff rode up, attracted by the man's unusual appearance. "Who are you?" inquired Bragg. "Nobody" was the answer. "Where did you come from?" was the next question as the general pressed the conversation. "Nowhere" replied the Texan. "Where are you going?" said Bragg. "I don't know," the unkempt man answered. "Then where do you belong?" Bragg insisted. "Don't belong anywhere," snapped the Texan.

Then came the climax. Exasperated, the general asked, "Don't you belong to Bragg's army?" "Bragg's army! Bragg's army!" exclaimed the Texan. "Why, he's got no army! One half of it he shot in Kentucky, and the other half has been whipped to death at Murfreesboro!" The general turned and rode away.[29]

---

[28]McKay memoirs, Confederate Collection, TSLA.
[29]Fitch, *Annals*, 653.

13

"I Can Never Forget"

In Thomas Hardy's play *The Dynasts*, the following statement appears: "My argument is that war makes rattling good history; but peace is poor reading. So I back Bonaparte for the reason that he will give pleasure to posterity" (Pt. I, Act III, scene v). Much may justly be written against the horror and tragedy of war, but the fact remains that the study of war grips the imagination of innumerable people. Probably the reason is partly as James Jones straightforwardly expressed his cynical opinion in writing about World War II. "There had to be something, somewhere, in all of us that loved it," he said.[1]

Regardless of whether or not one accepts what might be termed a "war-lover" philosophy, a major reason for the perennial interest in war is found in the intriguing realm of analysis: Why were certain decisions made or not made? If some event had developed differently, would it have changed the final decision of battle? Did the outcome hinge upon a strong personality — or perhaps a weak personality? Considering such factors as terrain, weather, and time, what tactical possibilities might have yielded greater success than those employed? These are the kind of questions that bring freshness, vitality, and fascination to the study of war.

At Stones River on December 31 the Rebels were so close to victory that one wonders how the Union army could have escaped disaster if Carter Stevenson's seventy-five-hundred-man division

---

[1]James Jones, *World War II* (New York, 1977), 32.

had been present. Jefferson Davis' decision to detach and order the unit to Mississippi to reinforce John Pemberton may have cost the Confederacy a victory on the first day of the battle. The president's action is hard to understand. His insistence that any Yankee threat to Bragg or Pemberton could be met by shifting reinforcements from one army to the other was impractical. Any defense of Davis' decision is difficult, considering that the distance involved was great, that the Union army under U.S. Grant and the Tennessee River were between the Rebel forces, and that therefore a railroad trip all the way south to Mobile before turning northwest for the journey's last leg would be required.

Joe Johnston's advice that Pemberton be reinforced from the trans-Mississippi region was more reasonable. That area was not as vital as the territories defended by Bragg and Pemberton and the Federals had not committed as much strength to threaten the trans-Mississippi. After a quick visit to Murfreesboro, Davis relied too much on his judgment that Rosecrans' army was not about to attack Bragg. Perhaps the president, attempting to hold every inch of territory whether he had sufficient forces for the task or not, was incapable of facing the realities of logistics. And maybe Davis did not fully appreciate the value of defending the railroad from Nashville through Chattanooga to Atlanta in order to prevent its use as a major supply line for an invading Union army attempting to drive into the southeastern Confederacy.

Davis' decision was unwise, and the presence of seventy-five hundred more Rebel troops on the first day at Stones River might have changed the outcome, but only, of course, if Bragg had used the division judiciously. He did not employ the reinforcements under John Breckinridge effectively. In fact, after launching the initial attack, Bragg's influence for the rest of the engagement was more negative than positive. His actions do not encourage faith that he would have used Stevenson's decision, had it been present, to the best advantage.

Specifically, it is reasonable to suggest that Breckinridge's brigades might have been used to reinforce William J. Hardee, rejuvenating the initial Rebel drive against the Federal right and occupying the Nashville Pike in McCook's sector. After the surprise and momentum of the early morning attack it is doubtful that the Yankees could have withstood another devastating assault on that weakened flank. Hardee was probably correct when he wrote that if a fresh division could have replaced Pat Cleburne's exhausted troops, the rout of the enemy's right flank would have been complete and the battle decided. Yet the Rebels squandered their opportunity.

Bragg said that when Breckinridge's brigades crossed the river it was too late to send them to reinforce Hardee. On this point Bragg was probably correct, but the important factor is that a reserve to reinforce Hardee should have been provided earlier. Bragg was hesitant and uncertain in the decisive morning hours of December 31, when he could have committed Breckinridge's troops as reinforcements for Hardee. If it were too late to bolster Hardee's attack—as Bragg claimed—when Breckinridge finally crossed Stones River, the basic reason was that Bragg himself had wasted too much time in deciding to bring those soldiers across the river.

Equally bad were the piecemeal manner in which Breckinridge's units were thrown against the Union salient at the Round Forest and the excessively long intervals between attacks that allowed the defenders too much time to prepare for the reception of the next assault. Still another possibility for employing Breckinridge's division was to send it across the river, farther to the north, striking the left flank of the Union line. This tactic would have taken a minimum of marching and could well have caught the Federals by surprise, when they were off balance following the early morning assault on the right side of their line. Also, such a move had much to commend it from the standpoint of strategic terrain. It would have assured the protection of the Rebel right, taking away the high ground, both east and west of the river, from which the Union eventually threatened the Confederate northern flank.

Bragg was also on shaky ground in concluding after the first day's fight that Rosecrans would withdraw and apparently making no plans either for the possibility of a continuing struggle on the morrow, or a pursuit of the enemy if indeed the Yankees did retreat.

Very important action took place on January 1, although it did not involve a major assault by either army. The Union sent a division to the east bank of Stones River to occupy the hill that overlooked McFadden's Ford. If the Rebels intended either to renew the attack or merely to maintain their position and protect their northern flank, they needed to control that strategic terrain upon which artillery could be marshaled. Bragg did not seem concerned about the position until the Federals had already taken command of it. Then, on January 2, the Rebel commander blundered again. He ordered Breckinridge's division to drive the Yankees off the high ground east of the river.

Evidence indicates that Bragg was not familiar with either the terrain or the troop positions. Without asking Breckinridge, Hardee, or Polk for their opinions, he instructed Breckinridge to make the attack. Breckinridge gave his opinion anyway. It was highly unfavorable. Bragg seemed angry that his judgment was questioned and simply reiterated his orders for the attack.

The frontal assault, across almost a thousand yards of relatively open terrain where the attackers would be swept by flanking fire from across the river as they neared the enemy line and subjected to a more concentrated cannonade if they carried the hill, was unwise. But it was typical of what Bragg had done at Shiloh in trying to reduce the Hornets' Nest. At Stones River he remained wedded to the tactics of the Mexican war which, before the advent of the rifled-musket, had yielded satisfactory results. Now they were more apt to be climaxed by a slaughter, such as that depicted by a young Alabama soldier who described how his regiment made three desperate charges at Stones River in spite of his comrades' falling by the score.[2]

The Yankee occupation of the hill was a real danger to the Confederates, but Bragg should have been familiar enough with the terrain — after all, he had been in the Stones River area for several weeks — to appreciate its significance earlier than the Federals. Having failed in this and allowed them to occupy it, he should have hit their left flank on the hill, thus both reducing the normal casualties expected from a frontal assault and taking away the effectiveness of Union artillery on the west bank, which could not then have fired without inflicting casualties indiscriminately on both sides. It was also imperative that something be done to neu-

[2]Charles T. Jones, Jr., "Five Confederates: The Sons of Bolling Hall in the Civil War," *Alabama Historical Quarterly* 24 (1962), 167.

tralize the Yankee artillery on the west bank of the river if Breckinridge were to successfully lead a frontal assault and hold the hill once taken. But, unfortunately for the Rebels, Bragg again demonstrated a lack of imagination and a stubborn disposition.

With the exception of the devastating opening flank attack on the morning of December 31, Bragg fought the battle of Stones River badly. Having developed neither an efficient intelligence system nor an adequate staff to access information and make plans, he had been both surprised by the Federal advance and, for the better part of three days, uncertain of the direction from which the enemy was approaching. In selecting Murfreesboro as a point of concentration, Bragg had chosen a position that could be easily flanked and necessitated spreading his army over too wide an area. The position where he chose to fight, along the banks of Stones River, was not particularly suited for either defensive or offensive warfare. Bragg failed to entrench his army, proving that he had missed the most obvious lessons of Shiloh and Perryville: that defenders in a strong position usually suffered significantly fewer losses than attackers.

Oblivious to the technological changes that made prewar assault tactics into a formula for self-destruction, decisively strengthening the advantages of defensive combat, Bragg again showed a disastrous penchant for rash frontal attacks. He did not demonstrate ability, in any sense, to modify his tactics to meet a new situation on the battlefield. In fact, he seemed almost paralyzed, making virtually no decision of consequence after sending some of Breckinridge's troops against the Round Forest in mid-afternoon of December 31 until about noon of January 2. Perhaps Bragg lost his nerve under the strain of combat, as some have suggested; maybe, as seems more likely, his mind was simply too narrow and lacking in imaginative power.

What of his Union opponent? Overall, Rosecrans appears to better advantage than Bragg, but in fighting strictly on the defensive, he had fewer chances to make mistakes. Possibly there are still chinks in his armor. For example, his is the responsibility for an apparently hazy attack plan, particularly as it involved Alexander McD. McCook. In his official report and elsewhere, Rosecrans speaks of calling a meeting of all corps commanders at his headquarters where the battle plan was fully explained. This seems a bit grandiose. In reality the meeting was almost embarrassingly informal.

Thomas Crittenden, fatigued and having already talked with Rosecrans in the afternoon, was excused from any evening consultations. George Thomas apparently came early, received instructions, and left. David Stanley and McCook appeared afterward and heard explanations of the proposed attack about nine o'clock or later. Even more damning of Rosecrans' planning is that McCook subsequently denied that he had been called to headquarters, contending that he went out of a sense of duty—and his instructions to Jefferson C. Davis on the night of December 30 seem to support the truth of this assertion. McCook said he learned the details of Rosecrans' attack plan only when he later read them in a newspaper. Particularly, McCook may never have understood exactly what part his attack was to have in the total picture of Federal operations on December 31.

It should also be noted that Horatio Van Cleve and Thomas Wood, who were to lead the Union assault from their left flank position, did not receive directions to cross the river until after dawn on the thirty-first of December. Admittedly, there is not as much evidence upon which to base a conclusion as the historian would desire, but that which is available suggests the likelihood that Rosecrans' attack plan may have been somewhat carelessly and loosely conveyed to his subordinates. This in turn indicates a possibility that the plan might not have been clearly formulated in Rosecrans' own mind.

What was Rosecrans' intention anyway? Was he merely trying to drive the Rebels back on their line of communications? He was not marshaling troops in a fashion, or giving instructions that would indicate a prime goal either to get in the Rebel rear or cut the Confederates off from their railroad communications. On this score Bragg's performance compares favorably with Rosecrans'. It is clear that the Rebel commander intended to cut the Union communications to Nashville, but precisely what Rosecrans intended and how he intended to do it are rather murky.[3]

[3]Williams, *Lincoln Finds a General*, IV, 264-65. *OR*, 188-200, 574-75; Part 2, 275, 381-82, 383. Cist, *Army*, 130-31.

Another interesting question is whether or not Rosecrans might have launched a counterattack on December 31. To have continued with his original attack plan, thus placing a river between the two segments of his forces when he was already under assault, would have been too risky, and surely he was correct in canceling his own attack. But could he have counterattacked the Rebel left? As the Confederates' assault force advanced northward their left flank was badly exposed.

Rosecrans probably made the correct decision in not counterattacking — if he thought about it. His right wing was being driven furiously. The immediate task for the commander was to shore it up and insure the protection of the railroad and the pike for supplies and reinforcements from Nashville. In fact, the situation was so bad that if Sheridan's division of McCook's corps had not made such a determined resistance, Rosecrans' army well might have been beaten. Sheridan's men conducted a fighting retreat, then warded off resolute Confederate assaults, particularly in the cedars and limestone outcroppings just north of the Wilkinson Pike. The Rebels wheeled up their guns to within two hundred yards of Sheridan's position, but attack after attack still failed, with heavy losses on both sides. When he eventually abandoned that blood-soaked area, Sheridan's delaying action had given Rosecrans time to form a new line along the Nashville Pike.

Considering the many evidences of panic on the Union right and the fact that much of McCook's corps had retreated for nearly three miles, Rosecrans wisely employed Crittenden's troops, the only ones available that might have been used in a counterattack, in forming a defensive line that could stem the Rebel onslaught. The Union simply could not afford the luxury of an attempted counterattack. In this situation it was too much of a gamble. It is very doubtful, because of the additional and tougher problems inherently associated with an attack, plus the frenzied atmosphere of those early morning hours of the battle, that a Federal force adequate in size, discipline, and morale could have been organized and placed in position to launch an assault. If Rosecrans had tried it and failed, his counterattacking force would have been cut off from the rest of the army and Bragg could then have employed superior numbers against either segment of the Federal army.

Rosecrans reported the battle to Washington as a Federal victory. The enemy had fallen back, but the Union general had not destroyed the Rebel army or gained any really important territory. Actually, the battle at Stones River was a victory in only a narrow sense, but, considering overall conditions, politically and diplomatically as well as militarily, Rosecrans' victory pronouncement was welcome news to President Lincoln. After Fredericksburg and Chickasaw Bayou, the President needed some good military news and so did the country. "God bless you and all with you," Lincoln telegraphed Rosecrans on January 5, 1863. Stones River raised popular morale and strengthened the government at home and abroad. Lincoln was deeply grateful to Rosecrans.[4]

While the public estimate of Rosecrans rose in the aftermath of Stones River, Bragg's image reached a new low. Criticism had been heavy following Perryville, but the attacks were even more severe when the truth was learned about Murfreesboro. The general's dispatches on the night of December 31 had encouraged people to anticipate a great victory. Later many felt that they had been cheated or misled and their bitter sentiments were focused upon Bragg. Newspaper editorials were aggressive and highly critical.[5]

The Chattanooga *Daily Rebel*, stating that the army disliked Bragg, had no confidence in him, and that the retreat from Murfreesboro was made against the advice of his generals with whom he had no rapport anyway, was particularly irritating to Bragg.[6] Reading the newspaper editorial aloud to his staff on January 10, the general inquired if it were true that he no longer enjoyed the army's confidence? If so, he would resign his command, he said. Bragg also wrote a letter to all corps and division commanders requesting them to verify in writing that they had advised a retreat from Murfreesboro. Actually, he sent two versions, the first also asking for an opinion about the army's confidence in him.

Bragg did not receive the support for which he had hoped. But neither did he resign. The opinion of his staff was that it would be advisable for him to ask to be relieved. As for the circular letter to

---

[4]*OR*, 184–85. Williams, *Lincoln and His Generals*, 208.
[5]Richmond *Examiner*, Feb. 25, 1863. Augusta *Daily Chronicle*, Jan. 6, 1863. Mobile *Register* cited in Connelly, *Autumn*, 73.
[6]Jan. 6, 1863.

corps and division leaders, Cheatham and Polk assured the general that they had advised a retreat, but both Hardee and Breckinridge disclaimed any part in the decision to withdraw. As to the army's having confidence in the commander, Hardee, Breckinridge, and Cleburne, plus the brigade commanders under the last two, all replied negatively. Bragg, they said, did not have the army's confidence. Hardee phrased the matter bluntly: "Frankness compels me to say that the General officers whose judgment you have invoked are unanimous in their opinion that a change in the command of the army is necessary. In this opinion I concur."[7]

While Polk did not respond to Bragg on the question of the army's confidence in its commander, he and Hardee had both asked President Davis to place Joe Johnston in command. It is equally clear that Cheatham had no warm feeling for Bragg, having said, soon after Stones River, that he would not serve under Bragg again.

The relationship between Cheatham and Bragg soon became worse. Various reports that Cheatham was drunk on the first day of the battle at Murfreesboro caused Bragg to order Polk to censure that general in writing. This Polk did, but in his official report of the battle he also commended Cheatham for his leadership of his command at Stones River.

Bragg was angry and, in his report of the battle, blamed Cleburne's heavy casualties of December 31 on Cheatham, contending that the Tennessean had failed to attack promptly. Cheatham considered resigning from the army, but his friends persuaded him to stay on. That relations between Bragg and Cheatham were strained is an understatement.

Bragg was also blaming McCown for delaying the morning attack on the first day of the battle. He did not like McCown and why he placed that general in such an important position for the attack is a puzzle. For his part, McCown was unwisely open in making criticisms of Bragg. At last Bragg ordered him arrested, and a court-martial found McCown guilty of defying army regulations, but not of delay on December 31. McCown was suspended from command for six months.

[7]Hardee to Bragg, Jan. 12, 1863, Hardee Papers, Alabama State Department of Archives and History, Montgomery.

Bragg's longest and bitterest struggle was with John Breckinridge. Feelings were so intense that some of Breckinridge's subordinates, thinking Bragg had selected the Kentuckian as a scapegoat for his own failures, urged him to resign from the army and challenge Bragg to a duel. Fortunately, the fight was confined to paper. Bragg charged that Breckinridge was late in coming to reinforce Polk on the first day of the battle and had failed to align his troops properly or to use his cavalry effectively on the last day. He implied that such failures could have cost a Rebel victory. Bragg was also obtaining statements from artillery Captain Felix Robertson (whom he had to coax into sending in a second report containing criticisms of Breckinridge), staff member George Brent, and General Gideon Pillow to support his criticisms of Breckinridge.

The Kentuckian was equally busy, requesting to see Bragg's report of the battle (which the general refused to allow, having sent his own critical report to Richmond even before he received Breckinridge's report), marshaling statements from his staff members to refute Bragg's charges, and calling for a court of inquiry. The clash seemed to promise interminable difficulties, but ultimately Breckinridge was transferred to Mississippi and tempers at last cooled down—although the bitter feelings between the two men were never healed.

Clearly, the Rebel high command, in the aftermath of Stones River, reeked with dissension. And, in fact, Davis finally ordered Joe Johnston to replace Bragg. Johnston seemed extraordinarily concerned that he would be criticized for having sought, perhaps even intrigued, to gain the position. He also seemed sympathetic with Bragg because of the serious illness which his wife was then undergoing. Besides, Johnston's old wound, suffered in the Fair Oaks engagement, was pairing him severely. Johnston reported to the president that he was physically unfit for field duty and that Bragg's presence with the army was therefore required.[8]

Thus Bragg remained in command, and the Army of Tennessee continued to be plagued with discord. Unfortunately for the Rebels, Bragg would command through two more battles, at Chickamauga and Chattanooga. The Union army at Murfreesboro rested

[8]Connelly, *Autumn*, 74–86, gives an excellent and well-supported discussion of the infighting between Bragg and his generals.

(*Left*): After the battle most of the dead were buried on the field. When the National Cemetery was established in 1865, located where some of the heaviest fighting occurred, the government disinterred the Union dead and reburied them there. Of more than 6,100 Union burials, 2,562 were not identified. The picture above is a typical tombstone marking the grave of a fallen soldier. (*Right*): On a gently rising slope beneath scattered trees in the midst of the 20-acre Stones River National Cemetery stands a memorial cannon barrel inscribed with the number of Union soldiers buried in the cemetery. Of the 6,886 graves 6,139 are Union Civil War dead, their bodies collected within a radius of approximately 90 miles from Murfreesboro.

astride the railroad to Chattanooga, thirty miles farther southeast than it had been on Christmas Day, 1862. Probably few people in either army were aware that in London Ambassador Charles Francis Adams was effectively using this battle to support his contention that the United States of America was going to win the war.

Stones River had cost more than twenty-four thousand casualties and most soldiers wondered what, if anything, had been accomplished by the sacrifice. Both sides awaited the renewal of the dance of death, knowing that the war would go on almost as if the massive carnage in the little town southeast of Nashville had never occurred.

On February 17, 1863, an unknown private in the Union army at Murfreesboro scribbled some poetic musings which he entitled "Only A Private." One stanza was particularly appropriate:

> Ah, perhaps we have hardened our hearts
> Until death no impression imparts,
> Nor the sorrow and anguish of friends;
> He was "only a private;" — 'tis sad
> That his valor such slight notice had;
> Now his body with common earth blends.[9]

Many a soldier, lonely and despondent, doubtless felt that the death of an ordinary man in the ranks made little or no impression, that his sacrifice was soon forgotten.

But there were civilians and soldiers who would never cease to remember, people for whom the scenes of horror and anguish always remained present and vivid. The bloody aspects of war were forcibly impressed on them as the trainloads of wounded and maimed surviors of the battle came pouring into the Union base at Nashville, or the Confederate cities of Chattanooga and Atlanta, during those sad January days following the struggle at Murfreesboro. Into many a town or village struggled the wounded in groups of two or three — or alone. Churches, schools, public buildings, and private homes served to care for the wounded, both Federal and Confederate, while improvised cemeteries were rapidly filled.

Perhaps the greatest significance of the Battle of Stones River,

[9]Fitch, *Annals*, 679.

in the perspective of history, was not that the Union had advanced another few miles to the southeast, or inflicted nearly twelve thousand casualties,[10] or compelled the Rebels to retreat, but simply that the Federal army had prevented a Confederate victory at a time when the Union cause could hardly stand another defeat and Rebel morale, especially in the Western theater, so desperately needed both the psychological and material boost of a great triumph. The Confederate Army of Tennessee would not attack again and, in the summer of 1863, would be flanked and forced back all the way into north Georgia. In his inimitable style, even allowing for a bit of exaggeration, Lincoln probably best expressed the significance of Stones River in a letter to Rosecrans on August 31, 1863:

"I can never forget," the president said, "whilst I remember anything, that about the end of last year and beginning of this, you gave us a hard-earned victory, which, had there been a defeat instead, the nation could scarcely have lived over."[11]

[10]Livermore, *Numbers and Losses*, 97.
[11]Roy P. Basler, ed., *The Collected Works of Abraham Lincoln*, 8 vols. (New Brunswick, N.J., 1953), VI, 424.

Organization of the
UNION ARMY

At the Battle of Stones River,
December 31, 1862–January 2, 1863

Reprinted from: *War of the Rebellion: A Compilation of the
Official Records of the Union and Confederate Armies*

ARMY OF THE CUMBERLAND
Maj. Gen. William S. Rosecrans, Commanding

Artillery.
Col. James Barnett.

Provost Guard.
10th Ohio Infantry Lieut. Col. Joseph W. Burke.

GENERAL ESCORT.
Anderson Troop, Pennsylvania Cavalry, Lieut. Thomas S. Maple.

Right Wing.
Maj. Gen. Alexander McD. McCook.

FIRST DIVISION.
Brig. Gen. Jefferson C. Davis.

Escort.

36th Illinois Cavalry, Company B, Capt. Samuel B. Sherer.
2d Kentucky Cavalry, Company G: Capt. Miller R. McCulloch.
Lieut. Harvey S. Park.

First Brigade.

Col. P. Sidney Post.
59th Illinois, Capt. Hendrick E. Paine.
74th Illinois, Col. Jason Marsh.
75th Illinois, Lieut. Col. John E. Bennett.
22d Indiana, Col. Michael Gooding.

Second Brigade.

Col. William P. Carlin.
21st Illinois: Col. J.W.S. Alexander.
Lieut. Col. Warren E. McMackin.
38th Illinois, Lieut. Col. Daniel H. Gilmer.
101st Ohio: Col. Leander Stem.
Lieut. Col. Moses F. Wooster.
Maj. Isaac M. Kirby.
Capt. Bedan B. McDonald.
15th Wisconsin, Col. Hans C. Heg.

Third Brigade.

Col. William E. Woodruff.
25th Illinois: Maj. Richard H. Nodine.
Col. Thomas D. Williams.
Capt. Wesford Taggart.
35th Illinois, Lieut. Col. William P. Chandler.
81st Indiana, Lieut. Col. John Timberlake.

Artillery. [a]

3d Minnesota Battery, Capt. William A. Hotchkiss.
5th Wisconsin Battery: Capt. Oscar F. Pinney.
Lieut. Charles B. Humphrey.
8th Wisconsin Battery: Capt. Stephen J. Carpenter.
Sergt. Obadiah German.
Lieut. Henry E. Stiles.

---

[a]The Second Minnesota was attached to the Second Brigade, Fifth Wisconsin to the First Brigade, and Eighth Wisconsin to the Third Brigade.

SECOND DIVISION.
Brig. Gen. Richard W. Johnson.

First Brigade.

Brig. Gen. August Willich (c)
Col. William Wallace.
Col. William H. Gibson.
89th Illinois, Lieut. Col. Charles T. Hotchkiss.
32d Indiana, Lieut. Col. Frank Erdelmeyer.
39th Indiana, Lieut. Col. Fielder A. Jones.
15th Ohio: Col. William Wallace.
Capt. A.R.Z. Dawson.
Col. William Wallace.
49th Ohio: Col. William H. Gibson.
Lieut. Col. Levi Drake.
Capt. Samuel F. Gray.

Second Brigade.

Brig. Gen. Edward N. Kirk (mw)
Col. Joseph B. Dodge.
34th Illinois: Lieut. Col. Hiram W. Bristol.
Maj. Alexander P. Dysart.
79th Illinois: Col. Sheridan P. Read.
Maj. Allen Buckner.
29th Indiana: Lieut. Col. David M. Dunn.
Maj. Joseph P. Collins.
30th Indiana: Col. Joseph B. Dodge.
Lieut. Col. Orrin D. Hurd.
77th Pennsylvania: Lieut. Col. Peter B. Housum.
Capt. Thomas E. Rose.

Third Brigade.

Col. Philemon P. Baldwin.
6th Indiana, Lieut. Col. Hagerman Tripp.
5th Kentucky, Lieut. Col. William W. Berry.
1st Ohio, Maj. Joab A. Stafford.
93d Ohio, Col. Charles Anderson.

Artillery.[a]

5th Indiana Battery, Capt. Peter Simonson.

1st Ohio, Battery A, Lieut. Edmund B. Belding.

1st Ohio, Battery E, Capt. Warren P. Edgarton.

Cavalry.

3d Indiana, Companies G, H, I, and K, Maj. Robert Klein.

THIRD DIVISION
Brig. Gen. Philip H. Sheridan.

Escort.

2d Kentucky Cavalry, Company L, Lieut. Joseph T. Forman.

First Brigade.

Brig. Gen. Joshua W. Sill (k)

Col. Nicholas Greusel.

36th Illinois: Col. Nicholas Greusel.

Maj. Silas Miller.

Capt. Porter C. Olson.

88th Illinois, Col. Francis T. Sherman.

21st Michigan, Lieut. Col. William B. McCreery.

24th Wisconsin, Maj. Elisha C. Hibbard.

Second Brigade.

Col. Frederick Schaefer (k)

Lieut. Col. Bernard Laiboldt.

44th Illinois, Capt. Wallace W. Barrett.

73d Illinois, Maj. William A. Presson.

2d Missouri: Lieut. Col. Bernard Laiboldt.

Maj. Francis Ehrler.

15th Missouri, Lieut. Col. John Weber.

Third Brigade.[b]

Col. George W. Roberts (k)

---

[a]The Fifth Indiana was attached to the Third Brigade, Battery A to the First Brigade, and Battery E to the Second Brigade.

[b]Formerly First Brigade, Thirteenth Division.

Third Brigade (Cont.)

Col. Luther P. Bradley.

22d Illinois: Lieut. Col. Francis Swanwick.

Capt. Samuel Johnson.

27th Illinois: Col. Fazilo A. Harrington.

Maj. William A. Schmitt.

42d Illinois, Lieut. Col. Nathan H. Walworth.

51st Illinois: Col. Luther P. Bradley.

Capt. Henry F. Wescott.

Artillery.[b]

Capt. Henry Hescock.

1st Illinois, Battery C, Capt. Charles Houghtaling.

4th Indiana Battery, Capt. Asahel K. Bush.

1st Missouri, Battery G, Capt. Henry Hescock.

Center.

Maj. Gen. George H. Thomas.

PROVOST GUARD.

9th Michigan, Infantry Col. John G. Parkhurst.

FIRST DIVISION

Maj. Gen. Lovell H. Rousseau.

First Brigade.

Col. Benjamin F. Scribner.

38th Indiana, Lieut. Col. Daniel F. Griffin.

2d Ohio: Lieut. Col. John Kell.

Maj. Anson G. McCook.

33d Ohio, Capt. Ephraim J. Ellis.

94th Ohio: Col. Joseph W. Frizell.

Lieut. Col. Stephen A. Bassford.

10th Wisconsin, Col. Alfred R. Chapin.

Second Brigade.

Col. John Beatty.

---

[b]The Fifth Indiana was attached to the Third Brigade, Battery A to the First Brigade, and Battery E to the Second Brigade.

Second Brigade (Cont.)
42d Indiana, Lieut. Col. James M. Shanklin.
88th Indiana: Col. George Humphrey.
Lieut. Col. Cyrus E. Briant.
15th Kentucky: Col. James B. Forman.
Lieut. Col. Joseph R. Snider.
3d Ohio, Lieut. Col. Orris A. Lawson.

Third Brigade.
Col. John C. Starkweather.
24th Illinois, Col. Geza Mihalotzy.
79th Pennsylvania, Col. Henry A. Hambright.
1st Wisconsin, Lieut. Col. George B. Bingham.
21st Wisconsin, Lieut. Col. Harrison C. Hobart.

Fourth Brigade.
Lieut. Col. Oliver L. Shepherd.
15th United States, 1st Battalion: Maj. John H. King.
Capt. Jesse Fulmer.
16th United States, 1st Battalion, and Company B,
2nd Battalion: Maj. Adam J. Slemmer.
Capt. R.E.A. Crofton.
18th United States, 1st Battalion, and Companies A and D,
3rd Battalion, Maj. James N. Caldwell.
18th United States, 2d Battalion, and Companies B, C, E, and F,
3d Battalion, Maj. Frederick Townsend.
19th United States, 1st Battalion: Maj. Stephen D. Carpenter.
Capt. James B. Mulligan.

Artillery.[a]
Capt. Cyrus O. Loomis.
Kentucky, Battery A, Capt. David C. Stone.
1st Michigan, Battery A, Lieut. George W. Van Pelt.
5th United States, Company H., Lieut. Francis L. Guenther.

Cavalry.
2d Kentucky (six companies), Maj. Thomas P. Nicholas.

---

[a]Battery A, Kentucky, was attached to the Third Brigade; Battery A, First Michigan, to the Second Brigade; and Battery H, Fifth United States, to the Fourth Brigade.

SECOND DIVISION.

Brig. Gen. James S. Negley.

First Brigade.

Brig. Gen. James G. Spears.
1st Tennessee, Col. Robert K. Byrd.
2d Tennessee, Lieut. Col. James M. Melton.
3d Tennessee, Col. Leonidas C. Houk.
5th Tennessee, Col. James T. Shelley.
6th Tennessee, Col. Joseph A. Cooper.

Second Brigade.

Col. Timothy R. Stanley.
19th Illinois: Col. Joseph R. Scott.
           Lieut. Col. Alexander W. Raffen.
11th Michigan, Col. William L. Stoughton.
18th Ohio, Lieut. Col. Josiah Given.
69th Ohio: Col. William B. Cassilly.
           Maj. Eli J. Hickcox.
           Capt. David Putnam.
           Capt. Joseph H. Brigham.
           Lieut. Col. George F. Elliott.

Third Brigade.

Col. John F. Miller.
37th Indiana: Col. James S. Hull.
           Lieut. Col. William D. Ward.
21st Ohio, Lieut. Col. James M. Neibling.
74th Ohio, Col. Granville Moody.
78th Pennsylvania, Col. William Sirwell.

Artillery.

Kentucky, Battery B, Lieut. Alban A. Ellsworth.
1st Ohio, Battery G, Lieut. Alexander Marshall.
1st Ohio, Battery M,[a] Capt. Frederick Schultz.

---

[a]Attached to Second Brigade.

THIRD DIVISION.[b]
Brig. Gen. Speed S. Fry.

Escort.
2d Kentucky Cavalry, Company B, Captain Henry E. Collins.

First Brigade.
Col. Moses B. Walker.
82d Indiana, Col. Morton C. Hunter.
12th Kentucky, Col. William A. Hoskins.
17th Ohio, Col. John M. Connell.
31st Ohio, Lieut. Col. Frederick W. Lister.
38th Ohio, Col. Edward H. Phelps.

Second Brigade.
Col. John M. Harlan.
10th Indiana, Col. William B. Carroll.
74th Indiana, Col. Charles W. Chapman.
4th Kentucky, Col. John T. Croxton.
10th Kentucky, Lieut. Col. William H. Hays.
14th Ohio, Col. George P. Este.

Third Brigade.
Brig. Gen. James B. Steedman.
87th Indiana, Col. Kline G. Shryock.
2d Minnesota, Col. James George.
9th Ohio, Col. Gustave Kammerling.
35th Ohio, Col. Ferdinand Van Derveer.

Artillery.
1st Michigan, Battery D, Capt. Josiah W. Church.
1st Ohio, Battery C, Capt. Daniel K. Southwick.
4th United States, Company I, Lieut. Frank G. Smith.

FOURTH DIVISION.
Brig. Gen. Robert B. Mitchell.

---

[b]The First Brigade (except the Twelfth Kentucky) and Church's battery were the only troops of this division engaged in the battle of Stone's River. All commanders are given as they stood December 31, 1862. The First Brigade (Walker's) reached the field from La Vergne at 10 A.M., Dec. 31.

First Brigade. [a]

Brig. Gen. James D. Morgan.
10th Illinois, Lieut. Col. McLain F. Wood.
16th Illinois, Lieut. Col. James B. Cahill.
60th Illinois, Col. Silas C. Toler. [b]
10th Michigan, Lieut. Col. C.J. Dickerson. [b]
14th Michigan: Lieut. Col. Myndert W. Quackenbush. [c]
Lieut. Col. Milton L. Phillips.

Second Brigade.

Col. Daniel McCook.
85th Illinois, Col. Robert S. Moore. [c]
86th Illinois, Lieut. Col. David W. Magee.
125th Illinois, Col. Oscar F. Harmon.
52d Ohio, Lieut. Col. D.D.T. Cowen. [b]

Cavalry.

2d Indiana, Company A, Capt. John G. Kessler.
5th Kentucky, Maj. John Q. Owsley.
3d Tennessee, Col. William C. Pickens. [d]

Artillery.

2d Illinois, Battery I, Capt. Charles M. Barnett.
10th Wisconsin Battery, Capt. Yates V. Beebe. [e]

Unattached Infantry.

8th Kansas (five companies), Col. John A. Martin.
1st Middle (10th) Tennessee, Col. Alvan C. Gillem.

Artillery Reserve.

11th Indiana Battery, Capt. Arnold Sutermeister.
12th Indiana Battery, Lieut. James A. Dunwoody.
1st Michigan, Battery E, Capt. John J. Ely.

---

[a]Formerly Second Brigade, Thirteenth Division.

[b]Eight companies Sixtieth Illinois, two companies Tenth Michigan, and five companies Fifty-second Ohio, detached under command of Col. Daniel McCook, and engaged in skirmish at Cox's Hill, January 3.

[c]Detached under command of Brig. Gen. J.G. Spears, January 2 and 3 and, with the First Brigade, Second Division, center, participated in the battle of Stone's River, January 3.

[d]Detachments with General Spears and Colonel McCook, January 2 and 3.

[e]Two sections with General Spears, January 2–5.

FIFTH DIVISION.[a]
Brig. Gen. Joseph H. Reynolds.

First Brigade.
Col. Albert S. Hall.
80th Illinois, Col. Thomas G. Allen.
123d Illinois, Col. James Monroe.
101st Indiana, Col. William Garver.
105th Ohio, Lieut. Col. William R. Tolles.

Second Brigade.
Col. Abram O. Miller.
98th Illinois, Col. John J. Funkhouser.
17th Indiana, Col. John T. Wilder.
72d Indiana, Maj. Henry M. Carr.
75th Indiana, Col. Milton S. Robinson.

Artillery.
18th Indiana Battery, Capt. Eli Lilly.
19th Indiana Battery, Capt. Samuel J. Harris.

Left Wing.
Maj. Gen. Thomas L. Crittenden.

FIRST DIVISION.
Brig. Gen. Thomas J. Wood (w)
Brig. Gen. Milo S. Hascall.

First Brigade.
Brig. Gen. Milo S. Hascall.
Col. George P. Buell.
100th Illinois, Col. Frederick A. Bartleson.
58th Indiana: Col. George P. Buell.
Lieut. Col. James T. Embree.
3d Kentucky: Col. Samuel McKee.
Maj. Daniel R. Collier.
26th Ohio, Capt. William H. Squires.

---

[a]Not engaged at Stone's River. Commanders given as they stood December 31, 1862.

Second Brigade.

Col. George D. Wagner.

15th Indiana, Lieut. Col. Gustavus A. Wood.

40th Indiana: Col. John W. Blake.

Lieut. Col. Elias Neff.

Maj. Henry Leaming.

57th Indiana: Col. Cyrus C. Hines.

Lieut. Col. George W. Lennard.

Capt. John S. McGraw.

97th Ohio, Col. John Q. Lane.

Third Brigade.

Col. Charles G. Harker.

51st Indiana, Col. Abel D. Streight.

73d Indiana, Col. Gilbert Hathaway.

13th Michigan, Col. Michael Shoemaker.

64th Ohio, Lieut. Col. Alexander McIlvain.

65th Ohio: Lieut. Col. Alexander Cassil.

Maj. Horatio N. Whitbeck.

Artillery. [a]

Maj. Seymour Race.

8th Indiana Battery, Lieut. George Estep.

10th Indiana Battery, Capt. Jerome B. Cox.

6th Ohio Battery, Capt. Cullen Bradley.

SECOND DIVISION.

Brig. Gen. John M. Palmer.

First Brigade.

Brig. Gen. Charles Cruft.

31st Indiana, Col. John Osborn.

1st Kentucky, Col. David A. Enyart.

2d Kentucky, Col. Thomas D. Sedgewick.

90th Ohio, Col. Isaac N. Ross.

Second Brigade.

Col. William B. Hazen.

---

[a]The Eighth Battery was attached to the First Brigade, the Tenth Battery to Second Brigade, and the Sixth Battery to the Third Brigade.

Second Brigade (Cont.)

110th Illinois, Col. Thomas S. Casey.

9th Indiana, Col. William H. Blake.

6th Kentucky, Col. Walter C. Whitaker.

41st Ohio, Lieut. Col. Aquila Wiley.

Third Brigade.

Col. William Grose.

84th Illinois, Col. Louis H. Waters.

36th Indiana: Maj. Isaac Kinley.

Capt. Pyrrhus Woodward.

23d Kentucky, Maj. Thomas H. Hamrick.

6th Ohio, Col. Nicholas L. Anderson.

24th Ohio: Col. Frederick C. Jones.

Maj. Henry Terry.

Capt. Enoch Weller.

Capt. A.T.M. Cockerill.

Artillery.

Capt. William E. Standart.

1st Ohio, Battery B, Capt. William E. Standart.

1st Ohio, Battery F: Capt. Daniel T. Cockerill.

Lieut. Norval Osburn.

4th United States, Companies H and M, Lieut. Charles C. Parsons.

THIRD DIVISION.

Brig. Gen. Horatio P. Van Cleve (w)

Col. Samuel Beatty.

First Brigade.

Col. Samuel Beatty.

Col. Benjamin C. Grider.

79th Indiana, Col. Frederick Knefler.

9th Kentucky: Col. Benjamin C. Grider.

Lieut. Col. George H. Cram.

11th Kentucky, Maj. Erasmus L. Mottley.

19th Ohio, Maj. Charles F. Manderson.

Second Brigade.

Col. James P. Fyffe.

Second Brigade (Cont.)
44th Indiana: Col. William C. Williams.
Lieut. Col. Simeon C. Aldrich.
86th Indiana, Lieut. Col. George F. Dick.
13th Ohio: Col. Joseph G. Hawkins.
Maj. Dwight Jarvis, Jr.
59th Ohio, Lieut. Col. William Howard.

Third Brigade.
Col. Samuel W. Price.
35th Indiana, Col. Bernard F. Mullen.
8th Kentucky: Lieut. Col. Reuben May.
Maj. Green B. Broaddus.
21st Kentucky, Lieut. Col. James E. Evans.
51st Ohio, Lieut. Col. Richard W. McClain.
99th Ohio: Col. Peter T. Swaine.
Lieut. Col. John E. Cummins.

Artillery.
Capt. George R. Swallow.
7th Indiana Battery, Capt. George R. Swallow.
Pennsylvania, Battery B (26th), Lieut. Alanson J. Stevens.
3d Wisconsin Battery, Lieut. Cortland Livingston.

Cavalry.
Brig. Gen. David S. Stanley.

CAVALRY DIVISION.
Col. John Kennett.

First Brigade.
Col. Robert H.G. Minty.
2d Indiana, Company M, Capt. J.A.S. Mitchell.
3d Kentucky, Col. Eli H. Murray.
4th Michigan, Lieut. Col. William H. Dickinson.
7th Pennsylvania, Maj. John E. Wynkoop.

Second Brigade.
Col. Lewis Zahm.

Second Brigade (Cont.)
1st Ohio: Col. Minor Milliken.
Maj. James Laughlin.
3d Ohio, Lieut. Col. Douglas A. Murray.
4th Ohio, Maj. John L. Pugh.

Artillery.
1st Ohio, Battery D (section), Lieut. Nathaniel M. Newell.

Reserve Cavalry. [a]
15th Pennsylvania: Maj. Adolph G. Rosengarten.
Maj. Frank B. Ward.
Capt. Alfred Vezin.
1st Middle Tennessee (5th), Col. William B. Stokes.
2d Tennessee, Col. Daniel M. Ray.

Unattached.
4th U.S. Cavalry, Capt. Elmer Otis.

MISCELLANEOUS.
Pioneer Brigade.
Capt. James St. C. Morton.
1st Battalion, Capt. Lyman Bridges.
2d Battalion, Capt. Calvin Hood.
3d Battalion, Capt. Robert Clements.
Illinois Light Artillery, Stokes' Battery, Capt. James H. Stokes.

Engineers and Mechanics.
1st Michigan, Col. William P. Innes.

Post of Gallatin, Tenn. [b]
Brig. Gen. Eleazer A. Paine.

Ward's Brigade.
Brig. Gen. William T. Ward.
102d Illinois, Lieut. Col. Frank C. Smith.

---

[a]Under the immediate command of General Stanley, Chief of Cavalry.
[b]Not engaged at Stone's River. Commanders given as they stood December 31, 1862.

Ward's Brigade (Cont.)

100th Illinois, Lieut. Col. Henry F. Vallette.
70th Indiana, Col. Benjamin Harrison.
79th Ohio, Col. Henry G. Kennett.
Indiana Light Artillery, 13th Battery, Capt. Benjamin S. Nicklin.

Cavalry.

1st Kentucky, Col. Frank Wolford.
7th Kentucky, Lieut. Col. John K. Faulkner.
11th Kentucky, Lieut. Col. William E. Riley.

Organization of the
CONFEDERATE ARMY

At the Battle of Stones River,
December 31, 1862–January 2, 1863

Reprinted from: *War of the Rebellion: A Compilation of the Official Records of the Union and Confederate Armies*

ARMY OF TENNESSEE
Gen. Braxton Bragg, Commanding

Polk's Corps.
Lieut. Gen. Leonidas Polk.

FIRST DIVISION.
Maj. Gen. Ben Franklin Cheatham.

First Brigade.
Brig. Gen. Daniel S. Donelson.
8th Tennessee: Col. W.L. Moore.
Lieut. Col. J.H. Anderson.
16th Tennessee, Col. John H. Savage.
38th Tennessee, Col. John C. Carter.
51st Tennessee, Col. John Chester.
84th Tennessee, Col. S.S. Stanton.
Carnes' (Tennessee) battery, Lieut. L.G. Marshall.

Second Brigade
Brig. Gen. Alexander P. Stewart.
4th Tennessee,⎱ Col. O.F. Strahl.
5th Tennessee,⎰
19th Tennessee, Col. F.M. Walker.
24th Tennessee: Col. H.L.W. Bratton.
Maj. S.E. Shannon.
31st Tennessee,⎱ Col. E.E. Tansil.
33d Tennessee,⎰
Mississippi Battery, Capt. T.J. Stanford.

Third Brigade.
Brig. Gen. George Maney.
1st Tennessee,⎱ Col. H.R. Feild.
27th Tennessee,⎰
4th Tennessee (Provisional Army), Col. J.A. McMurry.
6th Tennessee,⎱ Col. C.S. Hurt.
9th Tennessee,⎰ Maj. J.L. Harris.
Tennessee Sharpshooters, Capt. Frank Maney.
Smith's (Mississippi) battery, Lieut. William B. Turner.

Fourth (Preston Smith's) Brigade.
Col. A.J. Vaughan, Jr.
12th Tennessee, Maj. J.N. Wyatt.
13th Tennessee: Lieut. Col. W.E. Morgan.
Capt. R.F. Lanier.
29th Tennessee, Maj. J.B. Johnson.
47th Tennessee, Capt. W.M. Watkins.
154th Tennessee, Lieut. Col. M. Magevney, Jr.
9th Texas, Col. W.H. Young.
Allin's (Tennessee) Sharpshooters: Lieut. J.R.J. Creighton.
Lieut. T.F. Pattison.
Tennessee Battery, Capt. W.L. Scott.

SECOND DIVISION.
Maj. Gen. Jones M. Withers.

First (Deas') Brigade.
Col. J.Q. Loomis (w)
Col. J.G. Coltart.

First (Deas') Brigade (Cont.)

19th Alabama.

22d Alabama.

25th Alabama.

26th Alabama.

39th Alabama.

17th Alabama Battalion Sharpshooters, Capt. B.C. Yancey

1st Louisiana (Regulars), Lieut. Col. F.H. Farrar, Jr.

Robertson's battery, Capt. F.H. Robertson.

Second Brigade.

Brig. Gen. James R. Chalmers (w)

Col. T.W. White.

7th Mississippi.

9th Mississippi, Col. T.W. White.

10th Mississippi.

41st Mississippi.

9th Mississippi Battalion Sharpshooters, Capt. O.F. West.

Blythe's (Mississippi) regiment.

Garrity's (Alabama) battery.

Third (Walthall's) Brigade.

Brig. Gen. J. Patton Anderson.

45th Alabama, Col. James G. Gilchrist.

24th Mississippi, Lieut. Col. R.P. McKelvaine.

27th Mississippi: Col. T.M. Jones.

Lieut. Col. J.L. Autry.

Capt. E.R. Neilson.

29th Mississippi: Col. W.F. Brantly.

Lieut. Col. J.B. Morgan.

30th Mississippi, Lieut. Col. J.I. Scales.

39th North Carolina,[a] Capt. A.W. Bell.

Missouri Battery, Capt. O.W. Barret.

Fourth (Anderson's) Brigade.

Col. A.M. Manigault.

24th Alabama.

28th Alabama.

---

[a]Joined brigade December 31; transferred, January 2, to Manigault's brigade.

Fourth (Anderson's) Brigade (Cont.)
34th Alabama.
10th South Carolina,⎫ Col. A.J. Lythgoe.
19th South Carolina,⎭
Alabama Battery, Capt. D.D. Waters.

Hardee's Corps.
Lieut. Gen. William J. Hardee.

FIRST DIVISION.
Maj. Gen. John C. Breckinridge.

First Brigade.
Brig. Gen. Daniel W. Adams (w)
Col. Randall L. Gibson.
32d Alabama: Lieut. Col. Henry Maury.
              Col. Alexander McKinstry.
13th Lousisiana,⎫ Col. R.L. Gibson
20th Louisiana,⎭ Maj. Charles Guillet.
16th Louisiana,⎫ Col. S.W. Fisk.
25th Louisiana,⎭ Maj. F.C. Zacharie.
14th Louisiana Battalion, Maj. J.E. Austin.
Washington Artillery (5th Battery), Lieut. W.C.D. Vaught.

Second Brigade.
Col. J.B. Palmer.
Brig. Gen. Gideon J. Pillow.
18th Tennessee: Col. J.B. Palmer.
                Lieut. Col. W.R. Butler.
26th Tennessee, Col. John M. Lillard.
28th Tennessee, Col. P.D. Cunningham.
32d Tennessee, Col. Ed. C. Cook.
45th Tennessee, Col. A. Searcy.
Moses' (Georgia) battery, Lieut. R.W. Anderson.

Third Brigade.
Brig. Gen. William Preston.
1st Florida,⎫ Col. William Miller.
3rd Florida,⎭

Third Brigade (Cont.)
4th Florida, Col. William L.L. Bowen.
60th North Carolina, Col. J.A. McDowell.
20th Tennessee: Col. T.B. Smith.
              Lieut. Col. F.M. Lavender.
              Maj. F. Claybrooke.
Tennessee Battery: Capt. E.E. Wright.
              Lieut. J.W. Mebane.

Fourth Brigade.
Brig. Gen. R.W. Hanson (mw)
Col. R.P. Trabue.
41st Alabama: Col. H. Talbird.
              Lieut. Col. M.L. Stansel.
2d Kentucky, Maj. James W. Hewitt.
4th Kentucky: Col. R.P. Trabue.
              Capt. T.W. Thompson.
6th Kentucky, Col. Joseph H. Lewis.
9th Kentucky, Col. T.H. Hunt.
Kentucky Battery, Capt. R. Cobb.

Jackson's Brigade[a]
Brig. Gen. John K. Jackson.
5th Georgia: Col. W.T. Black.
              Maj. C.P. Daniel.
2d Georgia Battalion Sharpshooters, Maj. J.J. Cox.
5th Mississippi, Lieut. Col. W.L. Sykes.
8th Mississippi: Col. J.C. Wilkinson.
              Lieut. Col. A. McNeill.
Pritchard's (Georgia) battery.
Lumsden's (Alabama) battery, Lieut. H.H. Cribbs.

SECOND DIVISION.
Maj. Gen. P.R. Cleburne.

First Brigade.
Brig. Gen. L.E. Polk.
1st Arkansas, Col. John W. Colquitt.

---

[a]Temporarily assigned to Breckinridge's division.

First Brigade (Cont.)
13th Arkansas.
15th Arkansas.
5th Confederate, Col. J.A. Smith.
2d Tennessee, Col. W.D. Robison.
5th Tennessee, Col. B.J. Hill.
Helena (Ark.) Artillery, Lieut. T.J. Key.

Second Brigade.
Brig. Gen. St. John R. Liddell.
2d Arkansas, Col. D.C. Govan.
5th Arkansas, Lieut. Col. John E. Murray.
6th Arkansas, { Col. S.G. Smith.
7th Arkansas, { Lieut. Col. F.J. Cameron.
{ Maj. W.F. Douglass.
8th Arkansas: Col. John H. Kelly
Lieut. Col. G.F. Baucum.
Warren Light Artillery (Miss.), Lieut. H. Shannon.

Third Brigade.
Brig. Gen. Bushrod R. Johnson.
17th Tennessee: Col. A.S. Marks.
Lieut. Col. W.W. Floyd.
23d Tennessee, Lieut. Col. R.H. Keeble.
25th Tennessee: Col. J.M. Hughs.
Lieut. Col. Samuel Davis.
37th Tennessee: Col. M. White.
Maj. J.T. McReynolds.
Capt. C.G. Jarnagin.
44th Tennessee, Col. John S. Fulton.
Jefferson Flying Artillery (Miss.), Capt. Putnam Darden.

Fourth Brigade.
Brig. Gen. S.A.M. Wood.
16th Alabama, Col. W.B. Wood.
33d Alabama, Col. Samuel Adams.
3d Confederate, Maj. J.F. Cameron.
45th Mississippi, Lieut. Col. R. Charlton.
15th Mississippi Battalion Sharpshooters, Capt. A.T. Hawkins.
Alabama Battery, Capt. Henry C. Semple.

McCOWN'S DIVISION[a]
Maj. Gen. J.P. McCown.

First Brigade.[b]
Brig. Gen. M.D. Ector.
10th Texas Cavalry, Col. M.F. Locke.
11th Texas Cavalry: Col. J.C. Burks.
Lieut. Col. J.M. Bounds.
14th Texas Cavalry, Col. J.L. Camp.
15th Texas Cavalry, Col. J.A. Andrews.
Texas Battery, Capt. J.P. Douglas.

Second Brigade.
Brig. Gen. James E. Rains (k)
Col. R.B. Vance.
3d Georgia Battalion, Lieut. Col. M.A. Stovall.
9th Georgia Battalion, Maj. Joseph T. Smith.
29th North Carolina, Col. R.B. Vance.
11th Tennessee: Col. G.W. Gordon.
Lieut. Col. William Thedford.
Eufaula (Ala.) Light Artillery, Lieut. W.A. McDuffie.

Third Brigade.
Brig. Gen. Evander McNair (j)
Col. R.W. Harper.
1st Arkansas Mounted Rifles.[c] Col. R.W. Harper.
Maj. L.M. Ramsaur.
2d Arkansas Mounted Rifles,[c] Lieut. Col. J.A. Williamson.
4th Arkansas, Col. H.G. Bunn.
30th Arkansas: Maj. J.J. Franklin.
Capt. W.A. Cotter.
4th Arkansas Battalion, Maj. J.A. Ross.
Arkansas Battery, Capt. J.T. Humphreys.

CAVALRY.[d]
Brig. Gen. Joseph Wheeler.

---

[a]Of Smith's corps, serving with Hardee.
[b]The regiments of this brigade serving as infantry.
[c]Serving as infantry.
[d]Forrest's and Morgan's commands on detached service.

Wheeler's Brigade.
Brig. Gen. Joseph Wheeler.
1st Alabama, Col. W.W. Allen.
3d Alabama: Maj. F.Y. Gaines.
Capt. T.H. Mauldin.
51st Alabama: Col. John T. Morgan.
Lieut. Col. J.D. Webb.
8th Confederate, Col. W.B. Wade.
1st Tennessee, Col. James E. Carter.
— Tennessee Battalion, DeWitt C. Douglass.
— Tennessee Battalion, Maj. D.W. Holman.
Arkansas Battery, Capt. J.H. Wiggins.

Buford's Brigade.
Brig. Gen. A. Buford.
3d Kentucky, Col. J.R. Butler.
5th Kentucky, Col. D.H. Smith.
6th Kentucky, Col. J.W. Grigsby.

Pegram's Brigade.[a]
Brig. Gen. John Pegram.
1st Georgia.
1st Louisiana.

Wharton's Brigade.
Brig. Gen. John A. Wharton.
14th Alabama Battalion, Lieut. Col. James C. Malone.
1st Confederate, Col. John T. Cox.
3d Confederate, Lieut. Col. William N. Estes.
2d Georgia: Lieut. Col. J.E. Dunlop.
Maj. F.M. Ison.
3d Georgia (detachment), Maj. R. Thompson.
2d Tennessee, Col. H.M. Ashby.
4th Tennessee, Col. Baxter Smith.
— Tennessee Battalion, Maj. John R. Davis.
8th Texas, Col. Thomas Harrison.
Murray's (Tennessee) regiment, Maj. W.S. Bledsoe.
Escort company, Capt. Paul F. Anderson.

[a]Probably incomplete.

Wharton's Brigade. (Cont.)

McCown's escort company, Capt. L.T. Hardy.

White's (Tennessee) battery, Capt. B.F. White, Jr.

ARTILLERY.[b]

Baxter's (Tennessee) battery.

Byrne's (Kentucky) battery.

Gibson's (Georgia) battery.

[b]Byrne's battery mentioned in Breckenridge's report. The others do not appear to have been engaged in the campaign. Baxter's battery reported as at Shelbyville, December 31, and Gibson's was ordered, December 1, 1862, to Chattanooga, Tenn., to be fitted for the field.

BIBLIOGRAPHY

PRIMARY MATERIALS

Records

War of the Rebellion: A Compilation of the Official Records of the Union and Confederate Armies. 129 vols. Washington, D.C., 1880–1901.

Collected Works, Memoirs, Diaries, Reminiscences

Basler, Roy P., ed. *The Collected Works of Abraham Lincoln.* 8 vols. New Brunswick, N.J., 1953.

Beatty, John. *Memoirs of a Volunteer, 1861–1863.* New York, 1946.

Bickham, William D. *Rosecrans' Campaign with the Fourteenth Army Corps, or the Army of the Cumberland: A Narrative of Personal Observations with Official Reports of the Battle of Stone River.* Cincinnati, 1863.

Billings, John D. *Hardtack and Coffee or the Unwritten Story of Army Life.* Boston, 1887.

Blegin, Theodore C., ed. *The Civil War Letters of Colonel Hans Christian Heg.* N.p., Minn., 1936.

Buell, Clarence, and Robert Johnson, eds. *Battles and Leaders of the Civil War.* 4 vols. New York, 1887–88.

Chestnut, Mary B. *A Diary from Dixie*, ed. Ben Ames Williams. Boston, 1905.

Confederate Veteran. 40 vols. Nashville, 1893–1932.

Fisher, Horace Cecil. *A Staff Officer's Story: The Personal Experiences of Colonel Horace Newton Fisher in the Civil War.* Boston, 1960.

Fitch, John. *Annals of the Army of the Cumberland*. Philadelphia, 1864.

Fitch, Michael. *Echoes of the Civil War As I Hear Them*. New York, 1905.

Freeman, Henry V. "Some Battle Recollections of Stone's River." *Military Order of the Loyal Legion of the United States, Illinois Commandery*. Vol. 3, 1895.

Grainger, Gervis D. *Four Years with the Boys in Gray*. Franklin, Ky., 1902.

Hascall, Milo S. "Personal Recollections and Experiences Concerning the Battle of Stone River." *Military Order of the Loyal Legion of the United States, Illinois Commandery*. Goshen, Ind., 1889.

Hazen, General William B. *A Narrative of Military Service*. Boston, 1885.

Holmes, Mead, Jr. *A Soldier of the Cumberland*. Boston, 1864.

Johnson, Stoddard. "Diary." Braxton Bragg Papers, William P. Palmer Collection, Western Reserve Historical Society, Cleveland, Ohio.

Jones, Katharine M., ed. *Heroines of Dixie*. New York, 1955.

Jordan, General Thomas, and J.P. Pryor. *The Campaigns of Lieutenant–General N.B. Forrest, and of Forrest's Cavalry*. Ohio, 1973.

Kendall, Henry M. "The Battle of Stone River." *Military Order of the Loyal Legion of the United States, Commandery of the District of Columbia*. Washington, D.C., 1903.

Kniffin, G.C. "An Interview with Abraham Lincoln." *Military Order of the Loyal Legion of the United States, Commandery of the District of Columbia*. Washington, D.C., 1903.

Lindsley, John B., ed. *The Military Annals of Confederate Tennessee*. Nashville, 1886.

Mitchell, John L. *In Memoriam: Twenty-Fourth Wisconsin Infantry*. Milwaukee, 1906.

Morgan, Mrs. Irby. *How It Was: Four Years Among the Rebels*. Nashville, 1892.

Palmer, John M. *Personal Recollections of John M. Palmer: The Story of an Earnest Life*. Cincinnati, 1901.

Parkhurst, John G. "Recollections of Stone's River," *Military Order of the Loyal Legion of the United States, Michigan Commandery*. Detroit, 1890.

Pickett, William D. "A Reminiscence of Murfreesboro." Nashville, *American*, Nov. 1907.

Robertson, John. *Michigan in the War*. Lansing, Mich., 1882.

Sheridan, Philip H. *Personal Memoirs*. 2 vols. New York, 1888.

Sherwood, Isaac R. *Memories of the War*. Toledo, Ohio, 1923.

Smith, Frank H. "'The Duck River Rifles,' The Twenty Fourth Tennessee Infantry," in Jill K. Garrett and Marise P. Lightfoot, eds., *The Civil War in Maury County, Tennessee*. Columbia, Tenn., 1966.

Smith, Robert. "Confederate Diary." Transcribed by Jill K. Garrett. Columbia, Tennessee, 1975.

Stevenson, Alexander F. *The Battle of Stone's River*. Boston, 1884.

Thruston, Gates P. *Personal Recollections of the Battle in the Rear at Stone's River, Tennessee*. Nashville, n.d.

Van Horn, Thomas B. *The Life of Major General George H. Thomas*. New York, 1882.

Whitson, Mrs. L.D. *Gilbert St. Maurice*. Louisville, 1875.

Womack, J.J. *The Civil War Diary of Captain J.J. Womack, Company E., Sixteenth Tennessee Volunteers*. McMinnville, Tenn., 1961.

Woodard, J.H. "General A. McD. McCook at Stone River." *Military Order of the Loyal Legion of the United States, Los Angeles Commandery*. Los Angeles, 1892.

Wyeth, John A. *Life of General Nathan Bedford Forrest*. Dayton, Ohio, 1975.

Yaryan, John Lee. "Stone River." *Military Order of the Loyal Legion of the United States, Indiana Commandery*. Indianapolis, 1898.

Unit Histories

Bennett, Charles W. *Historical Sketches of the Ninth Michigan Infantry (General Thomas' Headquarters Guard)*. Coldwater, Mich., 1913.

Bennett, L.G., and William M. Haigh. *History of the Thirty-Sixth Regiment Illinois Volunteers, During the War of the Rebellion*. Aurora, Ill., 1876.

Briant, C.C. *History of the Sixth Regiment Indiana Volunteer Infantry*. Indianapolis, 1891.

Cope, Alexis. *Fifteenth Ohio Infantry*. Columbus, 1916.

Crary, A.M. *Seventy-Fifth Illinois Infantry*. Herrington, Kansas, 1915.

Duke, Basil W. *Morgan's Cavalry*. New York, 1906.

Fleharty, S.R. *Our Regiment: A History of the 102nd Illinois Infantry Volunteers*. Chicago, 1865.

Gibson, J.T. *History of the Seventy-Eighth Pennsylvania Infantry*. Pittsburgh, 1905.

Hannaford, E. *The Story of a Regiment: A History of the Campaigns and Associations in the Field of the Sixth Regiment Ohio Volunteer Infantry*. Cincinnati, 1868.

Harden, H.O. *Ninetieth Ohio Infantry*. Stoutsville, Ohio, 1902.

Hartpence, William R. *History of the Fifty-first Indiana Veteran Volunteer Infantry*. Cincinnati, 1894.

Haynie, J. Henry. *The Nineteenth Illinois*. Chicago, 1912.

Hight, John J., and Gilbert R. Stormont. *Fifty-Eighth Indiana Infantry*. Princeton, Ind., 1895.

Kirwan, A.D., ed. *Johnny Green of the Orphan Brigade: The Journal of a Confederate Soldier*. Lexington, 1956.

Lathrop, David. *The History of the Fifty-Ninth Regiment Illinois Volunteers*. Indianapolis, 1865.

McMurray, W.J. *History of the Twentieth Tennessee Regiment of Volunteer Infantry, C.S.A*. Nashville, 1904.

Newlin, W.H. *A History of the Seventy-Third Regiment of Illinois Infantry Volunteers*. n.p.: published by authority of the Regimental Reunion Association of Survivors of the 73rd Illinois Infantry Volunteers, 1890.

Owens, Ira S. *Seventy-Fourth Ohio Infantry*. Yellow Springs, Ohio, 1872.

Payne, Edwin W. *History of the Thirty-Fourth Regiment of Illinois Volunteer Infantry*. Clinton, Iowa, 1903.

Thompson, Ed Porter. *History of the Orphan Brigade*. Louisville, 1898.

Watkins, Samuel R. *"Co. Aytch," Maury Grays, First Tennessee Regiment*. Jackson, Tenn., 1952.

Worsham, W.J. *The Old Nineteenth Tennessee Regiment, C.S.A.: June 1861–April, 1865*. Knoxville, 1902.

Manuscripts

Braxton Bragg Papers. William P. Palmer Collection, Western Reserve Historical Society, Cleveland, Ohio.

John C. Breckinridge Papers. New York Historical Society.

Joseph Cumming Papers. Southern Historical Collection, Univ. of North Carolina, Chapel Hill.

Charles Doolittle Papers. Knox College Library, Galesburg, Ill.

James A. Hall Papers. Alabama State Department of Archives and History, Montgomery.

James A. Hall Papers. Walter K. Hoover Collection, Smyrna, Tenn.

William J. Hardee Papers. Alabama State Department of Archives and History, Montgomery.

William Ogburn Papers. Held by Susan Knight, Nashville.

John M. Palmer Papers. Illinois State Historical Library, Springfield.

T.B. Roy Papers. Alabama State Department of Archives and History.

Tennessee State Library and Archives, Nashville.
  Confederate Collection
      M.M. Clack, letter about him from son Tommie Clack
      Ruth White Cook Confederate scrapbook
      John E. Gold narrative
      William L. McKay memoirs
      W.E. Yeatman memoirs

Edwin Huddleston. "Nashville: Its Personality and Progress," pamphlet in the Nagy Collection on Nashville Public Schools, Tennessee State Library and Archives.

Emma Middleton Wells, comp. "Reminiscences of the War Between the States." Public Library Historical Collection, Chattanooga, Tenn.

Newspapers

Chattanooga *Daily Rebel*
Columbia, Tennessee, *Herald*
Murfreesboro *Daily Rebel Banner*
Nashville *American*
Nashville *Dispatch*
New Orleans *Delta*
Richmond *Examiner*
Washington *Evening Star*

SECONDARY MATERIALS

Books and Papers

Ambrose, Stephen E. *Halleck: Lincoln's Chief of Staff.* Baton Rouge, 1962.

Bearss, Edwin C. "The Battle of Hartsville and Morgan's Second Kentucky Raid." Research Project No. 4, Stones River National Military Park, Jan. 1960.

————. "The Rebels Concentrate at Stones River." Research Project No. 5, Stones River National Military Park, March 1960.

————. "The Union Artillery and Breckinridge's Attack." Research Project No. 2, Stones River National Military Park, July 1959.

Boatner, Mark M., III. *The Civil War Dictionary*. New York, 1959.

Catton, Bruce. *The American Heritage Short History of the Civil War*. New York, 1960.

————. *Never Call Retreat*. New York, 1965.

————. *This Hallowed Ground*. New York, 1956.

Cist, Henry M. *The Army of the Cumberland*. New York, 1882.

Connelly, Thomas L. *Army of the Heartland*. Baton Rouge, 1967.

————. *Autumn of Glory: The Army of Tennessee, 1862–1865*. Baton Rouge, 1971.

Coppee, Henry. *Great Commanders, General Thomas*. New York, 1895.

Cruden, Robert. *The War That Never Ended: The American Civil War*. Englewood Cliffs, N.J., 1973.

Davis, William C. *Breckinridge: Statesman, Soldier, Symbol*. Baton Rouge, 1974.

DeBerry, John H. "Confederate Tennessee." Ph.d. diss., Univ. of Kentucky, 1967.

Dyer, John P. *From Shiloh to San Juan: The Life of "Fighting Joe" Wheeler*. Baton Rouge, 1961.

Folmsbee, Stanley J., Robert E. Corlew, and Enoch L. Mitchell. *Tennessee, A Short History*. Knoxville, 1969.

Foote, Shelby. *The Civil War: A Narrative*. 3 vols. New York, 1958–1975.

Harper's Encyclopedia of U.S. History. New York, 1902.

Harrison, Lowell H. *The Civil War in Kentucky*. Lexington, 1975.

Henderson, C.C. *The Story of Murfreesboro*. Murfreesboro, Tenn., 1929.

Henry, Robert Selph. *"First With the Most" Forrest*. Indianapolis, 1944.

————. *The Story of the Confederacy*. Indianapolis, 1931.

Hesseltine, William B., and David L. Smiley. *The South in American History*. Englewood Cliffs, N.J., 1960.

Hoover, Walter K. *A History of the Town of Smyrna, Tennessee*. Nashville, 1968.

Horn, Stanley F. *The Army of Tennessee: A Military History*. New York, 1941.

_____, ed. *Tennessee's War, 1861–1865*. Nashville: Tennessee Civil War Centennial Commission, 1965.

Hughes, Nathaniel Cheairs. *General William J. Hardee: Old Reliable*. Baton Rouge, 1965.

Johnson, Allen, and Dumas Malone, eds. *Dictionary of American Biography*. 21 vols. New York, 1928–37.

Jones, Archer. *Confederate Strategy from Shiloh to Vicksburg*. Baton Rouge, 1961.

Lamers, William M. *The Edge of Glory: A Biography of General William S. Rosecrans, U.S.A.* New York, 1961.

Lindsey, David. *Americans in Conflict: The Civil War and Reconstruction*. Boston, 1974.

Livermore, Thomas L. *Numbers and Losses in the Civil War in America, 1861–1865*. New York, 1969.

Long, E.B., and Barbara Long. *The Civil War Day by Day*. New York, 1971.

McDonough, James Lee. *Schofield: Union General in the Civil War and Reconstruction*. Tallahassee, 1972.

_____. *Shiloh—in Hell Before Night*. Knoxville, 1977.

McKinney, Francis F. *Education in Violence*. Detroit, 1961.

McRaven, Henry. *Nashville: Athens of the South*. Chapel Hill, 1949.

McWhiney, Grady. *Braxton Bragg and Confederate Defeat: Field Command*. Vol. I. New York, 1969.

Middlebrook, Martin. *The First Day on the Somme*. Glasgow, Scotland, 1971.

Nevins, Allan. *The War for the Union*. 4 vols. New York, 1960.

O'Connor, Richard. *Sheridan the Inevitable*. Indianapolis, 1953.

_____. *Thomas: Rock of Chickamauga*. New York, 1948.

Parks, Joseph H. *General Leonidas Polk, C.S.A.: The Fighting Bishop*. Kingsport, 1962.

Piatt, Donn. *General George H. Thomas: A Critical Biography*. Cincinnati, 1893.

Potter, David M. *Division and the Stresses of Reunion: 1845–1876*. Glenview, Ill. 1973.

Ridley, Bromfield L. *Battles and Sketches of the Army of Tennessee*. Mexico, Mo. 1906.

Smith, W.D. "The Battle of Stones River Tennessee, December 31, 1862-January 2, 1863." Washington, D.C., 1932.

Thomas, Emory. *The American War and Peace: 1860-1877*. Englewood Cliffs, N.J., 1973.

Thomas, Wilbur. *General George H. Thomas: The Indomitable Warrior*. New York, 1964.

Vance, Wilson J. *Stone's River: The Turning Point of the Civil War*. New York, 1914.

Van Horne, Thomas B. *The Life of Major General George H. Thomas*. New York, 1882.

Warner, Ezra, Jr. *Generals in Blue: Lives of the Union Commanders*. Baton Rouge, 1964.

Watson, MacMillan S. "Nashville During the Civil War." M.A. thesis, Vanderbilt Univ., 1926.

Williams, Kenneth P. *Lincoln Finds A General: A Military Study of the Civil War.* 5 vols. New York, 1949-59.

Williams, T. Harry. *Lincoln and His Generals*. New York, 1952.

Articles

Avery, Mrs. Roy C. "The Second Presbyterian Church of Nashville During the Civil War." *Tennessee Historical Quarterly*, December 1952.

Bryan, Charles F., Jr. "'I Mean to Have them All': Forrest's Murfreesboro Raid." *Civil War Times Illustrated*, January, 1974.

Connelly, Thomas L. "Robert E. Lee and the Western Confederacy: A Criticism of Lee's Strategic Ability." *Civil War History*, June 1969.

Bearss, Edwin C. "Cavalry Operations in the Battle of Stones River," *Tennessee Historical Quarterly*, June 1960.

————. "Stones River: The Artillery at 4:45 p.m., January 2, 1863." *Civil War Times Illustrated*, February 1964.

Davis, Louise. "Box Seat on the Civil War." *The Tennessean Magazine*, March and April 1979.

Hannaford, Eben. "It Seemed Hard to Die of Suffocation." *Civil War Times Illustrated*, June, 1967.

Horn, Stanley F. "The Battle of Perryville." *Civil War Times Illustrated*, February 1966.

————. "The Battle of Stones River." *Civil War Times Illustrated*, February 1964.

_____. "Dr. John Rolfe Hudson and the Confederate Underground in Nashville." *Tennessee Historical Quarterly*, March 1963.

_____. "Nashville During the Civil War." *Tennessee Historical Quarterly*, March 1945.

Jones, Charles T., Jr. "Five Confederates: The Sons of Bolling Hall in the Civil War." *Alabama Historical Quarterly* 24 (1962).

Kaser, David. "Nashville's Women of Pleasure in 1860." *Tennessee Historical Quarterly*, December 1964.

Mitchell, Enoch L., ed. "Letters of a Confederate Surgeon in the Army of Tennessee to his Wife." *Tennessee Historical Quarterly*, March 1946.

McWhiney, Grady. "Braxton Bragg." *Civil War Times Illustrated*, April 1972.

_____. "Braxton Bragg at Shiloh." *Tennessee Historical Quarterly*, March 1962.

Underwood, Betsy Swint. "War Seen Through a Teen-ager's Eyes." *Tennessee Historical Quarterly*, June 1961.

Womack, Robert. "The River Ran Red with Men's Blood." *Accent* (magazine of the Murfreesboro *Daily News Journal*), December 26, 1976.

_____. "Stone's River National Military Park." *Tennessee Historical Quarterly*, December 1962.

INDEX

About the Book

On December 31, 1862, some 10,000 Confederate soldiers streamed out of the dim light of early morning to stun the Federals who were still breakfasting in their camp. Nine months earlier the Confederates had charged the Yankees in a similarly devastating surprise attack at dawn, starting the Battle of Shiloh. By the time this new battle ended, it would resemble Shiloh in other ways — it would rival that struggle's shocking casualty toll of 24,000, and it would become a major defeat for the South. By any Civil War standard, Stones River was a monumental, bloody, and dramatic battle. Yet, until now, it has had no modern, documented history. Arguing that the battle was one of the significant engagements in the war, James Lee McDonough, Justin Potter Distinguished Professor of History at David Lipscomb College, here devotes to Stones River the attention it has long deserved.

Stones River was typeset through the Compugraphic photo composition unit in eleven-point Baskerville with two-point line spacing. The display is also Baskerville from the photo composer. The book was designed by Bob Nance, composed by Metricomp, Inc., printed offset by Thomson-Shore, Inc., and bound by John H. Dekker & Sons. The paper on which the book is printed bears the watermark of S. D. Warren.

THE UNIVERSITY OF TENNESSEE PRESS : KNOXVILLE